W0036044

ADVANCE PRAISE

Piece of War: Narratives of Resilience and Hope by Meha Dixit (PhD) is a masterpiece of real-life experiences of ordinary people living (and who have lived) in some of the world's most vile conflict zones in the world such as in Afghanistan, Indo-Pakistan border, Kashmir Valley, Lebanon and Sierra Leone. It is an extraordinary piece of poignant writing, weaving together the real-life experiences of ordinary people in three different regions of high-intensity armed conflict in South Asia, West Africa and West Asia. This book not only weaves together the narratives of horror and trauma of the selected civil wars, but more importantly, it weaves together the narratives of resilience, coping, and hope of the very same people. It is the latter that is the distinctive feature of this masterpiece. The breadth of coverage and the depth of personal feelings of the extraordinary people living in varied and various war zones woven in simple language make it an essential and exceptional reading for ordinary living minds in addition to academics and researchers.

Muttukrishna Sarvananthan, *Senior Lecturer in Economics, University of Jaffna, Sri Lanka, and the Founder and Principal Researcher, Point Pedro Institute of Development*

Piece of War is a powerful account of the lives of people across conflict zones weaved together by the author Meha Dixit. The author superbly captures a range of emotions while seeing the world through the eyes of those caught up amidst war and conflict. Meha Dixit has gone where few dare to tread and brought out stories of war and conflict, of hope, of resilience, and the yearning of the human spirit. A must read for anyone who wants to understand conflict, its impact on people and finding the pieces which can build peace.

Sidharth Pandey, *News and Investigations Editor, GoNews*

Dr Meha Dixit's *Piece of War: Narratives of Resilience and Hope* is a seminal contribution to conflict zone literature, leveraging her first-hand experience of the lives and longings of violence-ravaged populations across continents to unearth the indefatigable nature of the human spirit. It is a silver linings playbook distilled from the fog of war.

Abdus Salam, *Senior Deputy Editor/News Editor,*
The Hindu, *Delhi*

This important book advances our understanding of war in four significant ways. First, the research concern here is firmly upon the consequences of war rather than the causes and conduct of war. Second, the focus is upon how war affects individuals and communities rather than interstate relations, geopolitics or regional power dynamics. Third, the author explicitly privileges narrative over theory and fieldwork over conceptualization, which distinguishes this book from earlier studies of war in International Relations. Fourth, the book is driven by an understated yet persistent normative concern for the predicament of the weak in awful conflict situations. Meha Dixit's war stories, emerging as they do from a decade of fieldwork in a wide range of conflict and 'post-conflict' locales across South and Southeast Asia, the

Middle East and West Africa, ring true. They will hopefully trigger some alarm bells.

Varun Sahni, *DPhil (Oxon),*
Vice-Chancellor, Goa University

Meha Dixit's book provides a nuanced perspective on conflict resolution. It examines significant questions of the politics of war and the relevance of peace. Thus, it is an engrossing read.

Dr Bijayalaxmi Nanda, *Acting Principal,*
Miranda House, University of Delhi

PIECE OF WAR

Narratives of Resilience and Hope

PIECE
OF
WAR

Narratives
of Resilience
and Hope

MEHA DIXIT

Los Angeles | London | New Delhi
Singapore | Washington DC | Melbourne

First published in 2020 by

SAGE Publications India Pvt Ltd
B1/I-1 Mohan Cooperative Industrial Area
Mathura Road, New Delhi 110 044, India
www.sagepub.in

SAGE Publications Inc
2455 Teller Road
Thousand Oaks, California 91320, USA

SAGE Publications Ltd
1 Oliver's Yard, 55 City Road
London EC1Y 1SP, United Kingdom

SAGE Publications Asia-Pacific Pte Ltd
18 Cross Street #10-10/11/12
China Square Central
Singapore 048423

Published by Vivek Mehra for SAGE Publications India Pvt. Ltd. Typeset in 11/14.5 pt Sabon by Fidus Design Pvt. Ltd, Chandigarh.

Library of Congress Control Number: 2020943968

ISBN: 978-93-5388-506-9 (PB)

SAGE Team: Namarita Kathait, Parul Prasad, Ankit Verma and Kanika Mathur

For my mother Nutan for bearing with my eccentricities and reckless adventures during the course of field research for this book.

Thank you for choosing a SAGE product!
If you have any comment, observation or feedback,
I would like to personally hear from you.

Please write to me at **contactceo@sagepub.in**

Vivek Mehra, Managing Director and CEO, SAGE India.

Bulk Sales

SAGE India offers special discounts
for purchase of books in bulk.
We also make available special imprints
and excerpts from our books on demand.

For orders and enquiries, write to us at

Marketing Department
SAGE Publications India Pvt Ltd
B1/I-1, Mohan Cooperative Industrial Area
Mathura Road, Post Bag 7
New Delhi 110044, India

E-mail us at **marketing@sagepub.in**

Subscribe to our mailing list
Write to **marketing@sagepub.in**

This book is also available as an e-book.

CONTENTS

Foreword by Savita Hande ix

Preface xiii

Acknowledgements xvii

List of Abbreviations xxiii

Chapter 1:   Introduction 1

Chapter 2:   Interpreting War 13

Chapter 3:   Normalizing Militarized Violence 47

Chapter 4:   Footprints and Aftermath throughout Generations 87

Chapter 5:   Children of War 125

Chapter 6:   Gendered Violence 173

Chapter 7:   Resilience, Coping and Hope 213

About the Author 253

FOREWORD

We live in an increasingly complex world that is far more interconnected and interlinked than any time before. One may state that the conventional wars are on a decline in general since the Second World War, if one counts the numbers of these wars and the proliferation. However, world is witnessing far more complex conflicts with increasing expansion and scope of non-state armed groups globally and more so since after the post-cold war era. In 2005, the United Nations and other humanitarian organizations were operating in 5 high-threat areas; now we count that number to 45. Advent of new technologies, use of information as a weapon, climate change and changing geopolitical shifts including a challenge to multilateralism are creating a backdrop for these modern times wars. As I write this forward, world is in the middle of 2020, dealing with another complex thick layer of crisis, a global pandemic, that is raising currently more questions than answers. Experts in all fields are speculating on how this pandemic will impact international relations and how economic and social changes would impact the world in a new decade.

I am reading *Piece of War: Narratives of Resilience and Hope* by Ms Meha Dixit amidst this tumultuous global context that I face every day of my work in the United Nations since the last two decades. 'Finding hope amidst turmoil may well be akin to spotting a fresh leaf on a barren tree or a sudden rain in blazing sun.' This sentence from the concluding page of *Piece of War* makes thus a deep impact and resonates with me.

Meha weaves a mosaic through narratives of common people who find themselves in the middle of modern-day wars. The canvas is broad. It runs from a west African small country of Sierra Leone, lush green beautiful place darned with sandy white Atlantic beaches and also defamed for a 1990s war based on blood diamonds, to Kashmir and Afghanistan, the locations that would raise immediately heightened emotions in Indian minds. This canvas also takes us to Lebanon, Syria, Rohingya refugee camp in Bangladesh and so many other conflict zones. Simple people in those places start speaking through Meha with us. Their lives, their broken hopes due to violence, suppression, fear, years of militarization flow one page after another. Meha sets their stories with no effort while elaborating complex theories of peace and conflict, sociology, psychology along with well-researched strategic references from several UN reports, International Humanitarian Law, and the UN specialized agencies.

For someone like me who had the opportunity to work in many of these countries during my job in the United Nations during last 18 years, these narratives sounded like my alter ego speaking with me. While reading the chapters such as 'Children of War' and 'Gender and War', I was flooded with memories. That group of happy Palestinian children playing in Gaza amidst Israeli attacks, those painfully vacant expressions of girls and women I came across in camps in Sierra Leone and South Sudan and that ancient resilient look of Syrian shop owner seating in middle of rich spices in old Damascus, while explosions were ongoing 2 Kilometres away. They speak so much to me. I am confident they would also speak with all the readers touching their own context.

The eternal argument whether war is a glory, or a tragedy, has indeed brought the humanity to finally look in the mirror after 20th century's catastrophic world wars and compelled us to build organisations such as the United Nations. However, the post-Cold War era and 21st century have brought another challenge of a changing picture of the war. This war is run in homes, in the schools, in worshipping places and in the hospitals. Where the human mind and body is supposed to be nurtured and healed, it could get bombed and maimed. This is another grotesque face of the war! This war has led to unfathomable pains of the women in psychic wards in Afghanistan, about whom Meha speaks in her book. This war is also disturbing those special children in Srinagar where Meha has worked.

The journey in this canvas that Meha brings forth is not for the faint-hearted. Her travels have taken her to remote villages and dangerous camps in Lebanon and Afghanistan. The narratives of Kashmiri youth are heart-wrenching. They raise basic questions about human rights. The haunting memories of war in Lebanon decades back still lurk in the minds of then impacted children. Meha's travels, however, also have taken her to rich cultural heritage that makes young educated women in Herat, western Afghanistan, who proudly create art and find solace in creative pursuits. There is resilience and hope in middle of prolonged painful ongoing saga in these conflict zones that I have always experienced and agree with deeply.

While this book constantly jumps from one continent to another, one conflict-torn country to another, back and forth, based on a decade-long research and field visits, it does it maintaining a smooth flow. It travails from macro theories to micro day-to-day trials and tribulations of common people trapped in these wars that they never asked for. All narratives come with a humility, simplicity, as spoken by the narrators and that is where they would touch the hearts of a reader. This is an excellent anthology and each narrative may deserve a book, a story, a movie. Yet it is very real!

The book ends on a positive note, identifying the resilience and hope amidst these destructions, as it should be. I have seen it every day in my work. In smiles of those children in the Middle East and in hopes of young women in Afghanistan. On the ancient face of that shopkeeper in Damascus, in the walk of Sierra Leonean woman in Freetown and in orphanage in Juba, in South Sudan. These images have imprinted on me permanently. I connect and find same witness in Meha's compilation of narratives.

This is an authentic work of resilience, based on arduous research, interlinking the challenging journeys in conflict zones by a hopeful heart of the author that has met with many beautiful people in these war-torn places. The book through these narratives, however, also raises serious questions on the future of these global trends. I would recommend this book for anyone who wants to have these dialogues with the common people, caught in difficult times and spaces, where they took birth. A thought-provoking mosaic, a result of travels to dangerous places where few dare to visit, complimented with excellent research.

Savita Hande
Principal Security Adviser
United Nations, Afghanistan

PREFACE

This book is a culmination of over-a-decade-long field research in conflict and 'post-conflict' zones such as Afghanistan, Afghanistan–Pakistan border (Torkham–Landi Kotal), Lebanon including the Lebanon–Syria border, Sierra Leone, Kashmir Valley, India's Maoist-affected regions of Chhattisgarh and Odisha, and Indo-Pakistan border in Jammu and Kashmir (J&K) along the International Border (IB) and Line of Control (LoC). It brings together the experiences of individuals in conflict zones across different continents, particularly in Asia, Africa and Middle East.

Although I had been researching on the impact of war on people prior to my visit to Sierra Leone in 2011, interactions with the locals who had either lived through the Sierra Leone war (1990–2002) or those who had participated in it made me want to explore war through the eyes of people. Thereafter, I travelled to the Maoist areas in Chhattisgarh and Odisha and subsequently spent a lot of time in Kashmir, which brought me face to face with the suffering of people living in these regions.

My field visit to the remote villages along the Indo-Pakistan border made me delve deeper into the human aspect of war and conflict. In August 2015, I travelled to the Indo-Pakistan border in J&K (six border villages in Poonch and Jammu districts) along the IB and LoC at the height of border tensions between India and Pakistan.

In August 2015, the Balakot sector in Poonch along the LoC had been at the centre of the border tensions between India and Pakistan, where within two days (15 and 16 August) six civilians including a woman and a 10-year-old boy lost their lives. On 16 August, I took a local bus from Jammu to the Balakot sector. The jarring bus horn, now and then, disrupted the quiet charm of my journey to Poonch. As I reached Balakot, I was greeted with the din of shelling and firing from across the border. Next, I saw some local women, with their heads lowered, returning from the burials of those who lost their lives on 15 and 16 August in Balakot. The entire experience brought me in close touch with the uncertainty of life at the border and consequent anxieties of the border population.

Around the same time, as I watched the images on television of the human cost of war in Yemen and frequent shelling in civilian areas of Najran in Saudi Arabia that borders Yemen, it was hard to believe that it was the same peaceful city where I had spent my early childhood years. This made me further explore the human dimension of war.

My field trip to Afghanistan (Kabul, Kapisa, Parwan, Nangarhar and Herat provinces) in December 2016 and December–January 2017–2018 added another dimension to pain, suffering and everyday 'anxieties' of the people living in conflict zones. These were everyday activities or even pleasures of a 'normal' life—going to work, attending school or university and eating at a cafe. After I returned to India from Afghanistan in 2016, during a phone conversation with Mona, a researcher from Afghanistan, I mentioned about my intention to write a book on everyday life in conflict zones. She asked me if she could suggest something. I was, of course, extremely curious to listen to what she had to say and requested her to go on.

'Most accounts (articles, books, media) which cover conflict zones describe the horrors, suffering and tragedies in these regions,' she said, 'People in Afghanistan also attend schools, universities, go to cafes and enjoy with friends and families.' 'Can you talk about all this in your book?' she asked. Mona reinforced my resolve to travel to other conflict zones including Lebanon–Syria border and visit the Bangladesh–Myanmar border and Rohingya refugee camps in Bangladesh's Cox's Bazar and tell stories of people living in the conflict zones— how they survive, adapt, build resilience and even construct hope in the times of the deepest despair.

During my interactions with those who either have lived through war or continue to live amid it, I gathered that each one carries a 'piece' of war. Since they mostly seem to carry war in parts, large or small, there is a possibility of resilience, coping and even finding hope.

Based on the consent of these people, while some of the real names have been retained, others have been kept confidential to protect their identity.

ACKNOWLEDGEMENTS

While the idea of this book germinated in 2017, the field research began over a decade ago. During the course of the research, I have come across innumerable people in conflict and 'post-conflict' zones who have inspired and deeply moved me. Then there were those who motivated me to write and tell stories of individuals who either live or have lived through an armed conflict including the ones who have had personal encounter with war or conflict-induced violence. I am deeply indebted to all of them, without whom this book would not have seen the light of day.

First, I will begin by thanking all those across South Asia, Middle East and Africa who have been kind enough to spare their time by sharing personal stories of grief, pain, trauma, and even survival, resilience and hope. In Sierra Leone, I owe a debt of gratitude to all the ex-child soldiers, journalists, activists and people I interviewed. One of the ex-child soldiers (name kept confidential) who later turned into an Okada driver (motorbike taxi) tirelessly helped me get around different locations in Freetown for inter-views even during odd hours. I am also extremely grate-ful to Robert McNamara, John Samura, and organizations such as Fambul Tok, UNICEF, UN Women and other non-governmental organizations (NGOs) in Sierra Leone for providing me support in my research work. John Samura was extremely kind to invite me to his place for a delectable meal of fish in peanut curry and other savoury local dishes cooked by his beautiful wife who belongs to the Democratic Republic of the Congo.

In Odisha, I am extremely thankful to Sharanya for hosting me. In Jharkhand, Odisha and Chhattisgarh, I express my gratitude to all the activists, lawyers, journalists, government and police officials for sharing their insight on the Maoist insurgency in the region. Besides, I am deeply indebted to all the tribals in Odisha and Chhattisgarh, who despite their adversities exuded such warmth and fed me scrumptious meals during my visit to their villages. I wish to extend my gratitude to a local family (name kept confidential) for hosting me at their hut for seven days in a Maoist-affected village of Malkangiri in Odisha.

Along the India–Pakistan border (LoC and IB), I am deeply grateful to the residents of the border villages for sharing their personal stories of fear, anxiety and survival and for their warmth and kindness that they extended towards me. I would also like to express my gratitude to Aditya Mishra for facilitating the field trip, to Dinesh who accompanied me to some of the villages and to the local journalists for their support. In Pakistan, I wish to thank Raja Atif Hayat for sharing his views on war as a construct and the situation in his country.

In Afghanistan, I am extremely thankful to Ahmad Fareed Wadan, Shapoor Khalili, Farhad Khalili and the entire family for hosting me. My special thanks to Ahmad's mother for cooking amazing local food for me. During my second trip to Afghanistan, Ahmad tirelessly accompanied me to several places including Herat and Nangarhar in the country. Further, I would like to acknowledge the support offered by Mona, Jovitta Thomas, Hamidullah, Dr Mohammad Haqmal, Zia Ahmadi,

Shafiqullah Shafaq, Nazir Rahguzar, Asiya and Ahmadullah Ahmadi in Afghanistan. I wish to thank the doctors (names kept confidential) who agreed to accompany me to the Afghanistan–Pakistan (Landi Kotal–Torkham) border despite the risks it entailed. I am also immensely grateful to all the Afghans who shared their remarkable experiences of living amid frequent suicide bombings and armed attacks.

In Lebanon and along the Lebanon–Syria border, I would like to acknowledge the support offered by Firas, Shabah Baalbek, Laila Hamdan, Maher and his family, Zico, Ziad and Badri. I also sincerely thank several others who shared with me their experiences of the war in Lebanon. Throughout my stay in Lebanon, Firas was always there for anything I required. Besides providing me immense support in my research, I thank him and his parents for inviting me to their home in the breathtaking Chouf district and offering amazing local food and, of course, the local drink with star anise. Amid the heaviness of my research, Firas helped in lightening the mood by hanging out with me at the cafes and restaurants serving Lebanese cuisine.

Shabah Baalbek had been an amazing support throughout my trip to Beirut and Tripoli. I cannot thank him enough for tirelessly translating the interviews with the Syrian refugees. Leila, whom I met serendipitously at Hamra Street in Beirut, instantly radiated warmth and kindness. I thank her for sharing her experiences of growing up amid the war in Lebanon. Further, I am grateful to UNHCR Lebanon for its assistance in my fieldwork and to all the Syrian refugees at Masna border crossing, Tripoli and Beirut in Lebanon who shared with me their incredible stories of resilience and hope. In Bangladesh, I am immensely grateful to N. Gnanasambandan and Md Abu Bakr for their support in my research on the Rohingya issue.

Besides, I wish to extend my gratitude to all the Rohingya refugees I met in Ukhia and Teknaf along the Bangladesh–Myanmar border who shared their heart-rending experiences of the arduous journeys from the Rakhine state in Myanmar to Bangladesh.

In J&K, while the list is endless which includes the locals, government and police officials and security personnel, some of the people I wish to specially thank are Ayaan Khan and his family, Imran and his family, Ahmad Farooq Wani and his family, Aquib Souba and his family, Saima Rashid and her family, Aiman Khan, Mufti Islah, Majidji, Touseef Raina, Khurram Qadir Wani, Pawan Sharma, Asif Hussain, Peerzada Ashiq, Danish Ismail, Syed Zubair, Sameer Yasir, Umer Mehraj, Sanjay Tickoo, Rishab Chaku, Junaid, Azaan, Hadi, Wasifa, Shobhu di, Ranbir, Ariba, Arjumand Makhdoomi, Muzamil Maqbool, Masrat, Ufair, Rameez, Bilal, Mir Nazir and Qayoom. Spending considerable time in the Kashmir Valley since 2010, I have had the opportunity of interacting with scores of locals in nine districts of the valley. They are among the most generous people I have met. Since my first trip to Kashmir in 2010, some families in Kashmir have hosted me and many have invited me for delightful meals often comprising of Wazwan. I am deeply indebted to the people of Kashmir who live in one of the most heavily militarized regions in the world, subjected to draconian laws and extremely harsh and brutal restrictions, particularly for months after the abrogation of Article 370.

I also wish to extend my gratitude to Professor Siddharth Mallavarapu, my PhD supervisor, Professor Varun Sahni and Professor Siddique Wahid. Professor Mallavarapu has been an amazing guide, who, even after the completion of my PhD, has always encouraged me to pursue field research in conflict zones, alongside an important advice—'Don't be too adventurous.' Throughout the research on this book, that spanned almost a decade, my family and friends have been extremely supportive. I wish to specially thank Abhishek Joshi, Arunima Sahu, Bharghavi Nagaraju, Ujwala Prabha and Sumita. I am deeply thankful to my mother Nutan, sister Neha, brother Samarth, my grandparents, Shashi nani, Ashhar Farooqui and aunt Kafia Farooqi for always being there.

LIST OF ABBREVIATIONS

AFRC	Armed Forces Revolutionary Council
AFSPA	Armed Forces Special Powers Act
APA	American Psychological Association
ARSA	Arakan Rohingya Salvation Army
CCW	Crowd control weapons
CDF	Civil Defence Forces
CRPF	Central Reserve Police Forces
DDR	Disarmament, demobilization and reintegration
IB	International Border
IOM	International Organization for Migration
ISIS	Islamic State of Iraq and Syria
J&K	Jammu and Kashmir
LoC	Line of Control
MSF	Médecins Sans Frontières
NGO	Non-governmental organization
PTSD	Post-traumatic stress disorder
RUF	Revolutionary United Front
SMHS	Shri Maharaja Hari Singh
STF	The Special Task Force
UN	United Nations
UNAMA	United Nations Assistance Mission in Afghanistan
UNHCR	United Nations High Commissioner for Refugees
UNICEF	United Nations Children's Fund
UNOCHA	United Nations Office for the Coordination of Humanitarian Affairs
WFP	World Food Programme

CHAPTER 1

INTRODUCTION

As seen through the eyes of one of the characters in Mia Couto's *Sleepwalking Land* (Terra Sonâmbula), which is set during the wanton and devastating war in Mozambique:

> War is a snake that bites us with our own teeth. Its poison flowed through all the rivers of our soul. We no longer ventured outside during the day, and at night we no longer dreamed. Dreams are the eyes of life and we were blind.[1]

Sleepwalking Land, through its dreamlike narrative, traces the suffering of Mozambique's war (1977–1992). Couto describes how the war had dehumanized the landscape and 'contaminated the whole country'. While straddling the real and the surreal, the book captures the essence of the impact that a war has on the ordinary lives. For many individuals living in conflict regions, war, if not a snake as seen by a character in *Sleepwalking Land*, may well be akin to a monster leaping to devour all it can, that is, living beings, non-living beings, entire villages and cities and even remnants of 'normal' life.

Throughout history, war was considered a normal part of human existence. Historically, war and warriors were

---

[1] Mia Couto, *Sleepwalking Land*, trans. David Brookshaw (London: Serpent's Tail/Profile Books; Translation Year–2006/Portuguese 1992).

frequently glorified. It was only after the First World War, and particularly after the Second World War, which caused immense destruction to civilian life, that war seemed to have lost its splendour. Yet, despite the destruction it causes, even today the glimpses of its romanticization can be seen in military and political circles, media as well as everyday life. Besides, toys such as guns, spears and other weapons are often inspired by war or military life.

Regardless of how war was seen throughout the human history or how it is currently viewed in the academic circles or policy-making debates across the globe, this book attempts to view war through the eyes of people who experience it. Individuals and communities who inhabit the conflict zones are fundamental to this book. While it defines war or armed conflict through different legal, political, military and sociological perspectives, the primary focus is how those living in conflict zones view war. A number of people I spoke to in conflict or 'post-conflict' settings in Africa, Middle East and South Asia told me that they view war in different ways such as 'war as destruction', 'war as terror' and 'war as a game'.

In the following chapters, this would be illustrated through real-life stories of people I met across different conflict zones. Interestingly, for some individuals, war or being in the line of fire can be an enormously thrilling experience. As Shapoor Khalili,[2] a translator to the US troops in Kabul, Afghanistan, who was based in Kabul when I met him in January 2018, said, 'I tremendously enjoy being on the frontline. Before being shifted to Kabul, I was working in some of the worst conflict-affected provinces in Afghanistan.' 'I preferred being on the frontline in those provinces than being in Kabul which is relatively peaceful,' he enthusiastically explained.

---

[2] Name changed.

However, most individuals, particularly civilians, I spoke with in different conflict zones said that living in these regions can be quite an excruciating experience. Yet, most of them also mentioned that they were 'used to war or conflict' or accustomed to it and have no choice other than try to continue with their 'normal' lives.

Referring to the brutal and deadly war in Mozambique (1977–1992), Carolyn Nordstrom in 'War on the Frontlines' notes,

> For the vast majority of Mozambicans, war is about existing in a world suddenly divested of lights. It is about a type of violence that spills out across the country and into the daily lives of people to undermine the world as they know it. A violence that, in severing people from their traditions and their futures, severs them from their lives. It hits at the heart of perception and existence. And that is, of course, the goal of terror warfare: to cripple political will by attempting to cripple all will, all sense.[3]

It may well be pointed out here that intensity and frequency of violence may vary in different conflict zones, depending on the type of conflict (open conflict, low intensity conflict, etc.). Then there are those conflicts which began as extremely violent or were open conflicts but slowly transformed into prolonged low-intensity conflicts. Besides, a number of prolonged conflicts may experience intervals of relative 'peace' followed by bouts of violence or vice versa.

Therefore, the effect on everyday life may vary considering the nature of conflict/war, the intensity and frequency of violence,

---

[3] Carolyn Nordstrom, 'War on the Frontlines', in *Fieldwork under Fire*, eds. Carolyn Nordstrom and Antonius C. G. M. Robben (Berkeley, CA: University of California Press, 1995).

and the level of militarization. Further, in many cases, even though a particular country may be grappling with war, intense fighting may be confined to certain areas, provinces or districts. For instance, during my visits to Afghanistan in 2016 and 2017–2018, Kabul, the capital, witnessed frequent suicide attacks and is often viewed as the city of suicide bombings. Moreover, Helmand and Nangarhar provinces were seen as the most dangerous places to travel to due to intense and frequent fighting and heavy Taliban presence in parts of both the provinces. At that time, the Islamic State also had a strong presence in Nangarhar, and a number of districts in this province have witnessed frequent brutalities by this armed oufit against the local population.

In most conflict zones today, particularly low-intensity or prolonged conflicts where the intensity of violence frequently fluctuates or may have reduced from the time the war began, people often seem to live in a twilight zone, as their lives may straddle chaos and everyday 'normal' and even despair and hope. The book focuses precisely on this kind of everyday existence in conflict zones across different parts of the globe and how people living in these regions make sense of war or conflict.

Next, the book describes everyday life of people in conflict zones in the context of militarization through real-life stories from places such as Kashmir, Indo-Pakistan border, Bangladesh–Myanmar border and Lebanon–Syria border. It also aims to show how sights and sounds of militarized violence, which are reflected through frequent firing, shelling or attacks and bombings, may affect the psyche of common people living in militarized regions. The book argues that militarization of everyday life and militarized violence are visible in different forms, but slowly both may become normalized.

It further discusses the response of people to militarization and everyday violence.

The book further discusses the overall impact of war on ordinary lives. It focuses on the physical and psychosocial impact of militarized violence and conflict on people. Psychosocial repercussions of the conflict are explored through the concepts of trauma and war stress. The book also delves delve into the dominant emotions in conflict zones such as fear and anxiety. These are illustrated through the life at the India–Pakistan border (Line of Control [LoC] and International Border [IB] in Jammu and Kashmir [J&K]), and fears and anxieties of an 'impending' war in Lebanon based on my interactions with people along LoC and IB and Lebanon, respectively.

Next, the book explores the issue of children and youth in war. While outlining a historical perspective of young people in war, it attempts to understand the impact of militarized violence on children and youth. It also draws attention to those who grow up amid conflict or experience some of the worst forms of militarized violence, particularly in the case of intractable conflicts. For instance, in the case of Kashmir, since the militancy began in 1990, those born thereafter or even few years before the militancy have grown up amid heavy militarization of the valley.

As Ahmad Wani, a local shopkeeper in Noorpora, Pulwama district of Kashmir, told me when I met him in August 2019, '*Jabse aankhe kholi hain, tabse military hi dekhi hai* (Since birth we have just seen the military (security forces).'[4] Similarly, Ajaz, a policeman who originally belongs to the

---

[4] Name changed. Indian security forces include the army and the paramilitary forces such as the Central Reserve Police Force (CRPF) and the Border Security Force (BSF).

old town Baramulla, told me, 'Since I was born, I have just seen the military, shutdowns and curfews.' 'Although I have not had any personal experience with the forces, but when I was in 4th or 5th standard, I remember being scared of them because of their weapons and uniform,' he said dejectedly.[5]

The book further explores the issue of gender and war or militarized violence, highlighting how patriarchal attitudes and values are entrenched in the concept of war. While giving a historical perspective of women in war, it discusses the impact of war and militarization on women and girls in contemporary times. It further analyses how females as a group or category experience war or conflict differently from men.

While armed conflict or militarized violence causes immense suffering and may induce stress or war trauma among the people, it is pertinent to ask if conflict devours hope for the individuals and communities who continue to live in the conflict zones. Well, not always. Yet, it does seem to fluctuate or ebb and flow depending on the intensity and frequency of violence, direct personal encounters, as well as environmental factors.

Hope is one of the most significant ingredients for healing and recovery. As Walsh notes, 'In times of deepest despair, hope is most essential for recovery. Hope fuels energies and investment to rebuild lives, revise dreams, renew attachments and create positive legacies to pass on to future generations.'[6] In fact, some individuals in conflict zones told me that since death and violence are ubiquitous in these regions, they have come to value life even more.

---

[5] Name changed.
[6] Froma Walsh, 'Traumatic Loss and Major Disasters: Strengthening Family and Community Resilience', *Family Process* 46, no. 2 (2007): 207–227.

In the context of life in war zones, Stephen C. Lubkemann says that wartime conditions are presumed to reduce people to acting on the basis of what are frequently described as 'more fundamental' and, by implication, culturally and socially undifferentiated needs. In fact, in the throes of war, he continues, people are often assumed to have no motivations but bare survival.[7] However, there is a life beyond violence and everyday anxieties in conflict zones, which is often glossed over. Conflict zones mostly evoke images of violence, suffering and pain, which are frequently bombarded in the media rather than how people survive, cope or construct hope in such situations.

Lubkemann rightly notes that much as a film trailer may represent a drama by tying together only a film's most vivid moments, representations of war that focus merely on 'acute violence may easily sensationalize and distort the analysis of war-time experience, misconstruing the basis of most warscape agency and behavior'.[8] Therefore, it is imperative to focus on how individuals and communities make sense of and cope with suffering and uncertainty of life, and construct hope for the future. The book explores these concepts of resilience, coping and hope. It further attempts to show how people in conflict zones, regardless of their suffering and adversities, continue with their everyday life. It does so by narrating real-life stories of survival, resilience and hope in these regions.

Finally, the book aims to illustrate the significance of positive coping and healing. It shows, through case stories and real-life examples, how people in these regions cope using different

[7] Stephen C. Lubkemann, *Culture in Chaos: An Anthropology of the Social Condition in War* (Berkeley, CA: The University of Chicago Press, 2008).
[8] Ibid.

means and mechanisms such as art, poetry, music, sports, humour, socializing, praying and even practising 'normalcy'.

SHARED EXPERIENCES AND EMOTIONS

In reference to war and conflict, Carolyn Nordstrom writes,

'what happens to individuals in World War II Europe, in Bosnia, in Mozambique, or in the Amazon Basin' is essentially different and 'these experiences are ultimately incommensurable, incomparable, unique'. She rightly continues that there is something unique about being Bosnian, Mozambican or of the Amazon region; however, 'there is as well a shared experience of coeval political violence.'[9]

During my interactions with the people of Afghanistan, most of whom lived under the Taliban rule, they shared similar experiences of shared suffering. These experiences were, in some ways, different from life during the conflict in Sierra Leone, Kashmir, along the India–Pakistan border, Maoist insurgency in Nepal, and Maoist or Naxal areas in India. This reflects specific sociocultural, political and economic contexts of the region, which makes the experience unique as noted by Nordstrom.

Yet there are certain overarching experiences of political violence, destruction of life and banality of death, which are universal to all conflict zones. Therefore, while certain communities or even most people in a country may have shared experiences of war, different from other communities in the

[9] Carolyn Nordstrom, *A Different Kind of War Story* (Philadelphia, PA: University of Pennsylvania Press, 1997).

same country or other war-torn countries, violence and suffering cut across all conflict zones across the globe.

UNIQUELY INDIVIDUAL REALITY

Referring to the war in Mozambique, Carolyn Nordstrom further notes that it is not sufficient to say that women, men, children, refugees, farmers, soldiers, politicians, 'the wounded and the dying all "lived" the war differently'. She continues, clearly a woman who has been shot by soldiers feels the war differently from a man who has seen his village burned. But in truth violence and truth necessary to withstand it successfully are ultimately, and intensely, personal. I will not experience being shot or tortured the same way you or anyone else would. My history, my personality, my circumstances, my physical and social environment of family, friends and enemies make it a uniquely individual reality.[10]

It is the unique as well as shared experiences of the individuals living in conflict zones that this book attempts to capture. The intention is to capture shared experiences of people across different war or conflict zones alongside the experiences that are deeply personal. As Mehraj, an 11th-standard Kashmiri student who is originally from Sopore, referring to the conflict in Kashmir told me, 'Yahan jitne log hain utni hi kahaniyaan hai' (There are as many stories in Kashmir as are the number of individuals here).[11]

To sum it up, at the heart of this book are the following questions.

INTRODUCTION

---

[10] Ibid.
[11] Name changed.

How do individuals and communities experience everyday life in conflict zones? How do they 'adapt' to a conflict situation and construct hope for the future? How do they continue to go about their everyday activities amid violence and even carry on with celebrations, unless these are affected by the conflict, heavy militarization, curfews and shutdowns? To offer a recent example, in early August 2019, the Government of India curtailed the Amarnath pilgrimage in the Kashmir Valley and asked all the tourists to leave the valley citing a terrorist threat from across the border. It sent more security companies to the valley. Few days later, it revoked the autonomy of Kashmir, and imposed strict restrictions in J&K, Kashmir in particular.

'Curfew-like' restrictions were imposed in the valley with some relaxation from time to time. Phone lines were nonfunctional and Internet services were snapped. The Indian government announced the closure of offices and educational institutions. The streets of Lal Chowk and other parts of Srinagar almost wore a deserted look with only a few vehicles and people seen outside. Security forces and policemen outnumbered the civilians on the streets.

Around this time, one evening as I walked towards the footbridge connecting Rajbagh with Lal Chowk in Srinagar, I noticed barricades and concertina. The area was saturated by policemen and security forces. I asked one of the policemen if I could cross the bridge. After asking a few questions, he agreed. I stood at the edge of the bridge, and through the barbed wires gazed at the saffron-hued sky bending towards the Jhelum river; it appeared to be caged. It was reminiscent of how most people in the valley frequently feel.

As I began to cross the bridge, two local women asked the security forces to let them cross to the other side. They looked at me and stopped. 'Where are you from?' one of them asked. I told her about myself. Thereafter, she pointed at the packets of bridal clothes they were carrying which they managed to buy with great difficulty. 'There is a wedding in our family, but now with most shops closed, the curfew and the restrictions, how are we going to celebrate and continue to have the ceremony?' she lamented as her eyes welled up with anguish.

Besides, on 12 August, the day of Eid, due to government curfew, four major mosques in Srinagar—Sonwar, Eidgah, Hazratbal Shrine and Jama Masjid—were closed. Throughout the day, barring few hours in the evening, there were strict restrictions in Srinagar. Everyone I met in Kashmir after this big festival said that they did not celebrate Eid this time. Most families told me that Eid is visible through children; however, this Eid, their children had to stay confined to their homes. They could not even buy new clothes. Many families also told me that they were unable to sacrifice sheep due to strict restrictions, which would have hindered the distribution of meat to their relatives. Some families who belonged to a middle-income or low-income group said that they did not sacrifice sheep since they were unable to earn enough during Eid due to harsh restrictions imposed by the Indian State.

Therefore, massive deployment of troops, curfews and shutdowns in conflict zones may hinder everyday life and festivities, even if the people themselves want to practice 'normalcy' to cope and carry on with celebrations.

CHAPTER 2

INTERPRETING WAR

War, a single word, is capable of conjuring up different images in one's mind—horror, violence, terror, death, devastation and destruction, and even thrill and excitement. While war or conflict theorists define the term technically from various standpoints—historical, legal, military and sociological—ordinary people who live in conflict or war zones frequently define the term through their personal and human experiences.

Since ancient times, military strategists, theorists and thinkers have put forward different definitions of war and described the kind of entities that are involved and what would qualify as the beginning and the end of war. While this chapter briefly defines war through different legal, political, military and sociological perspectives, it is primarily concerned with how those living in war or conflict zones view war. It tries to present the ordinary or human understanding of war and conflict. As Daniel Rothbart, Karina V. Korosteline and Mohammed D. Cherkaoui note, 'In the tumult of contemporary warfare, many civilians find themselves overwhelmed, either directly by the presence of firepower or indirectly through the deprivation of vital needs.'[1]

---

[1] Daniel Rothbart, Karina V. Korosteline, and Mohammed D. Cherkaoui, 'The Place and Plight of Civilians in Modern War', in *Civilians and Modern War: Armed Conflict and the Ideology of Violence*, eds. Daniel Rothbart, Karina Valentinovna Korostelina, and Mohammed D. Cherkaoui (Abingdon: Routledge, 2012).

Therefore, it is pertinent to understand war through the eyes of the people who experience it.

DEFINING WAR

Quincy Wright states,

> In the broadest sense war is a violent contact of distinct but similar entities. In this sense a collision of stars, a fight between a lion and a tiger, a battle between two primitive tribes, and hostilities between two modern nations would all be war. This broad definition has been elaborated for professional purposes by lawyers, diplomats and soldiers and for scientific discussion by sociologists and psychologists.[2]

Historically, one of the most popular definitions of war was offered by the Roman politician and lawyer Cicero (106–43 BC) who defined war as a contending by force. Sociologists have recognized the same popular conception with the qualification that violent contention cannot be referred to as war unless it entails 'actual conflict and constitutes a socially recognized form or custom within the society where it occurs'. From the sociological perspective, war is, hence, 'a socially recognized form of inter-group conflict involving violence'.[3] Hugo Groitus (1583–1645), a Dutch jurist, referring to Cicero's definition states that war is not just a contest but a condition, by which he implies 'a legal condition'.[4] Carl von Clausewitz, one of the most important military theorists, in his work

---

[2] Louise Leonard Wright, *Quincy Wright: A Study of War* (Chicago, IL: University of Chicago Press, 1983), 5.
[3] Ibid.
[4] John A Vasquez, *The War Puzzle Revisited* (Cambridge: Cambridge University Press, 2009).

On War (1832), identifies war as 'a political instrument, a continuation of political activity by other means' (politics being defined in the same work, as the 'trustee' and 'representative of all the interests of the community').[5]

Martin van Creveld, one of the world's most prominent military historians and strategic theorists, notes that throughout history, war has had two key meanings. The Clausewitzian meaning which dictates American thinking views 'war as organized violence to achieve political ends'. This divorces war from normative or ethical structures. Clausewitz devoted scant attention to the question if 'war in general or a specific war was legal or ethical'.[6] The second meaning, which has been used since the Roman empire, sees war as a legal condition, defining the acceptable limits of organized violence.[7]

Several definitions of war have been put forward by different theorists; however, till date, the issue of what constitutes war remains quite complex and tricky. One common academic definition of war comes from the Correlates of War project, which gathers scientific data on wars. 'It defines war as a conflict in which there are 1,000 battlefield deaths.'[8] This project was initiated in 1963 by J. David Singer. Joined by historian Melvin Small, the project commenced its work 'by assembling a more accurate data set on the incidence and extent of inter-state and extra-systemic war in the post-Napoleonic period'. Singer and Small together published

---

[5] Carl von Clausewitz, *On War*, ed. and trans. Michael Howard and Peter Paret (Princeton, NJ: Princeton, 1976), 87, 606–607.
[6] Steven Metz and Phillip R. Cuccia, *Defining War for the Twenty-first Century* (Carlisle, PA: Strategic Studies Institute, 2011).
[7] Ibid.
[8] Nikolas Gvosdev and Andrew Stigler, 'Defining War in an Ill-defined World' (28 June 2011), http://www.nytimes.com/2011/06/29/opinion/29iht-edgvosdev29.html

The Wages of War in 1972 which established a standard definition of war.[9]

WAR: GLORY OR TRAGEDY?

Much has been written about war in literature, poetry and other disciplines. The Mahabharata and the Ramayana, popular sacred books of Hinduism, are among the oldest martial epics that deal with warfare. While the struggle or battle between the Pandavas (five heroic brothers) and Kauravas (Pandava's 100 cousins) is central to Mahabharata, it goes beyond the literal battle by delving into the struggles within a human mind. The epic, which is believed to have been written by Veda Vyasa, is essentially concerned with *dharma* (right action or conduct) and explores the moral and ethical dilemmas confronting human beings.

Valmiki's Ramayana describes the life of Rama, the prince of Ayodhya, who due to his conniving stepmother is exiled to the forest along with his wife Sita. They are both joined by Rama's faithful brother Laxman. During their stay in the forest, Sita is abducted by the demon Ravana, which leads Rama to set out in pursuit of her with the help of a vast army of monkeys led by Sugriva (the monkey king) and Hanuman (the mighty son of the wind god). Finally, the warrior hero Rama is able to defeat Ravana and rescue Sita, returning triumphant to his kingdom and initiating a golden age of justice and righteousness and restoring the rule of *dharma*.

Both Ramayana and Mahabharata deal with the descriptions of wars, deeds of kings and heroes and practical philosophy while also delving into the concepts of virtue, ethics and

---

[9] The Correlates of War Project, http://www.correlatesofwar.org/history

moral values.[10] While Ramayana and Mahabharata rejoice the valour of their various characters during the battles, in a sense glorifying them, the epics essentially focus on justice and righteousness or right conduct during war. L. R. Penna observes that Mahabharat and Ramayana are significant for humanitarian law (laws of war) since the references to the 'precepts of war, the means of warfare, and the treatment of combatants and non-combatants' are quite similar to the modern concepts articulated in the Geneva Conventions and their Additional Protocols.[11]

While Homer's *Iliad*, written in the mid-8th century BCE, is a classic example that reflects the tragedy of war, it also deals with the glory of war. Through its depiction of the Trojan War, *Iliad* explores themes such as martial prowess, heroism, splendour, fame, honour, virtue, loyalty, rage, revenge, jealousy, mourning, losses, devastation, disorder and suffering caused by war. These themes are considered through a large number of characters that are attributed with different traits. For instance, Achilles's (the hero of the Trojan War) rage drives the central plot of *Iliad*. The theme of heroism runs through the epic, which is depicted through Achilles and a large majority of the characters. Abhorrence of war, due to the devastation it causes, is reflected in the attitude of Zeus (the ruler of the gods of Mount Olympos) towards his son Aries (the god of war). Aries is reproached by Zeus as the most detested of all the gods. As Zeus remarks, 'To me you are most hateful of all gods who hold Olympos.'[12]

---

[10] Shri Prakash Singh, 'Concept of Rajdharma in Adi-Kavya: Ramayana and Mahabharata', *Indian Journal of Public Administration* 61, no. 1 (2015): 132–138.
[11] L. R. Penna, 'Written and Customary Provisions Relating to the Conduct of Hostilities and Treatment of Victims of Armed Conflicts in Ancient India', *International Review of the Red Cross Archive*, 1989. Geneva Conventions and their Additional Protocols form the cornerstone of International Humanitarian Law.
[12] *Iliad*, book 5, line 889.

Further, Euripides's *The Trojan Women* (415 BC) has frequently been viewed as one of the most powerful tragedies that portray the horrors, folly and vanity of war. C. A. E. Luschnig says that *The Trojan Women* has long been considered 'one of the greatest pieces of anti-war propaganda ever written'.[13]

However, it was not until the end of the First World War that the term 'war poetry' was employed to describe poetry, which did not rejoice the martial virtues but one that was written by those who had endured battle and described in often brutal terms what it was like to participate in war.[14] During the First World War, millions of people, both combatants and civilians, were brutally injured or lost their lives. The immense destruction this war caused was unprecedented compared to the previous wars.

John H. Johnston in *English Poetry of the First World War* notes, if the epic celebrated primitive combat as heroic and an assessment of individual worth, the key tendency of contemporary war poetry has been to de-glorify modern war, to strip it of its erroneously romantic and adventurous aspects, to underscore its futility, and to represent it as reprehensible and degrading. While the war poetry of the First World War essentially includes the male poets, Catherine Reilly in her bibliography of First World War poetry has identified more than 500 females who wrote on the subject of war. The verse of the women war poets expresses a wide range of human emotions—revulsion, pity, horror, hate, disgust, anger, togetherness, isolation, compassion and love.[15]

---

[13] C. A. E. Luschnig, 'Euripides' "Trojan Women": All Is Vanity', *The Classical World* 65, no. 1 (September 1971): 8–12.
[14] Vernon Scannel, *Not without Glory: Poets of the Second World War* (Abingdon: RoutledgeFalmer, 2013).
[15] John H. Johnston, *English Poetry of the First World War* (Princeton, NJ: Princeton University Press, 2015).

Referring to women's war poetry, Nosheen Khan in *Women's Poetry of the First World War* asserts that a war poetry that does not include the range and depth of female response cannot claim to express the 'truth' of war since it disregards the response of those who, at huge cost, 'produce the primal munition of war-men-with which their destinies are inextricably linked'.[16]

Like the First World War, poets during the Second World War and the subsequent wars across different continents including Asia, Africa and Latin America have decried the vanity and futility of war highlighting the destruction it causes.

Further, artists have described the tragedy of war through songs, paintings and other forms of art. One of the most striking examples of painting is 'Guernica' by Pablo Picasso which was painted as an immediate response to the Nazi's bombing of Guernica during the Spanish Civil War (1936–1939). Guernica reflects the horrors of war and the suffering it causes to the people. However, historically painters have also glorified war. For instance, the European wars in the second half of the 17th century inspired the development of a new form of military painting. It combined the exaltation of military commanders with a distanced and, on the face of it, realistic portrayal of military actions. In Paris, Adam-François van der Meulen, a Flemish painter, developed a form that presented a view of military action exuding tranquillity, led by the king himself overseeing the operation. It aimed at contributing to an image of the French king Louis XIV as the bringer of peace, prosperity and order. Initially emerging in France, Dutch and at a later phase British, painters were

---

[16] Nosheen Khan, *Women's Poetry of the First World War* (Lexington, KY: The University Press of Kentucky, 1988).

engaged in the development, adoption, application and extension of this particular form.[17]

This phenomenon of glorifying princes and kings as heroic warriors in art was not confined to Europe. For instance, the palaces and historical museums across India are replete with portraits of kings, princes and even queens and princesses in their military attire displaying deadly weapons, and paintings of 'glorious' historical battle scenes seemingly rejoicing the valour of the warriors.

Further, many poets and philosophers have been criticized for romanticizing war. Several thinkers believe that Homer celebrated war, which they feel is evident from his depiction of it. Hegel has also been accused of glorifying war. Hans Kohn notes, 'It was the Hegelian glorification of war' which influenced, at least indirectly, the writings and speeches of many German philosophers and writers during the First World War.[18] However, John Plamenatz refutes the claim that Hegel glorified war. Similarly, Constant Smith argues, Hegel, if reasonably interpreted, is not exalting war but merely offering 'a practical description and critical estimate of it as a historical condition'. Smith asserts, 'Hegel is describing, he is not prescribing.'[19]

Whether or not these writers and thinkers romanticized war, historically war was frequently associated with glory and heroic sacrifice. It was essentially after the First World War and particularly after the Second World War, which caused

---

[17] Donald Haks, 'Military Painting in Flux. Flemish, French, Dutch, and British Pictures Glorifying Kings, c. 1700', *Journal of Low Countries Studies* 35, no. 2 (2011): 162–176.
[18] Constance I. Smith, 'Hegel on War', *Journal of the History of Ideas* 26, no. 2 (April–June 1965): 282–285.
[19] Ibid.

widespread damage to civilian lives, that war came to be seen as abhorrent and an aberration. Andrew Bacevich observes the old 20th century aesthetic of war or armed conflict as barbarism, brutality, unsightliness and absolute waste arose from the First World War, as portrayed by writers such as Ernest Hemingway, Erich Maria Remarque and Robert Graves. Subsequent wars such as the Second World War, Korean War and Vietnam War reinforced that aesthetic, in the Vietnam's case with films like *Platoon, Apocalypse Now* and *Full Metal Jacket.*[20]

In earlier times, war was not considered an aberration, but a part of human existence. However, a popular belief circulated towards the end of the century that the establishment of a permanent international court would be a significant step towards a world free of war. 'The 1899 Peace Conference was a point of inflection, a turn in the river, in the effort to move beyond ad hoc international arbitration to adjudication by a permanent international court' as a means to prevent war and preserve international peace and security, observes David D. Caron. The 1899 Peace Conference was not an isolated event and, in fact, the first in a series of such conferences (the second Hague Conference was held in 1907 and the third, scheduled for 1915, was cancelled as a result of the First World War). The legacy of the process commenced in 1899 may be viewed 'most broadly as the continuing refinement of international organization for the maintenance of peace and security'.[21]

---

[20] Andrew J. Bacevich, 'The Normalization of War' (2005), http://cf.linnbenton.edu/artcom/social_science/clarkd/upload/The%20Norma=lization%20of%20War,%20Bacevich.pdf
[21] David D. Caron, 'War and International Adjudication: Reflections on the 1899 Peace Conference', *American Journal of International Law*, 94, no. 1 (2000): 4–30.

In the aftermath of the First World War, the League of Nations was established to put an end to war. Although the League was deemed a failure, it paved the way for the establishment of United Nations (UN) for dealing with humanitarian and human rights issues. One of the key objectives of the UN is to maintain international peace and security. However, despite the emergence of the post-World War view which considers war undesirable and abhorrent, the concept of war continues to be romanticized in military and political circles, media as well as everyday life.

WARS OF THE PAST, PRESENT AND FUTURE

Since the emergence of the modern nation state in the 17th century, war has been regarded as the 'armed conflict between sovereign political entities, that is, between nation states'.[22] However, since the end of the Cold War burgeoning non-traditional conflicts involving non-state actors have fuelled a debate among scholars as to whether the nature of war has undergone change. Concepts such as 'new' and 'hybrid' war have emerged, implying that there is a significant distinction 'between the wars of the past and those of the present and future'.[23]

Mary Kaldor, in her book *New and Old Wars*, argues that it is beyond doubt that the consequences of the end of the Cold War which include the accessibility of surplus weapons, the discrediting of socialist ideologies, the breakup of totalitarian empires and the withdrawal of superpower support to client regimes contributed significantly to the New Wars.

---

[22] Michael Hardt and Antonio Negri, *Multitude: War and Democracy in the Age of Empire* (London: Penguin, 2005).
[23] Metz and Cuccia, *Defining War*.

She continues, the New Wars can be distinguished from the previous wars in terms of their objectives, the methods of warfare and the means of their financial sustenance. The goals of the New Wars concern identity politics as opposed to the geopolitical or ideological goals of previous wars.[24]

She mentions that the conflicts of the post-Cold War era are no longer characterized by state armies but mainly non-state actors such as paramilitary units, local warlords, mercenary groups and criminal gangs who are challenging the authority of the state. She further argues that another feature of the New wars is the emergence of New war economy which is sustained by illegal trade in weapons and drugs, resources such as oil or diamonds with the non-state actors seeking to maintain economic interests.[25] In the Old Wars, Kaldor argues, states are used to finance wars either through taxation or outside patrons.

Graca Machel, former first lady of Mozambique, was chosen by the UN to conduct the first study on children and conflict. The Machel Report which was approved in 1996 by the UN General Assembly makes a distinction between the 'rule-bound' traditional warfare (including national liberation struggles) and the patterns of warfare seen in post-colonial states. The report argues that modern wars involve the 'abandonment of all standards' and have a special 'sense of dislocation and chaos'.[26]

Graca Machel states in the report that war today does not match the traditional notion of two opposed armies 'or even

[24] Mary Kaldor, *New and Old Wars* (Oxford: Blackwell Publishers, 1999).
[25] Mary Kaldor, *New and Old Wars* (Cambridge: Polity Press, 2006).
[26] Graca Machel, 'Promotion and Protection of the Rights of Children: Impact of Armed Conflict on Children, UN Document, A/51/306 (1996).

of an internal conflict pitting an armed opposition force against the established government', in which each side usually follows the 'rules of the game', 'respecting the basic inviolability of civilian non-combatants and the special protection due to the young'.[27]

According to some analysts, the concept of war itself is archaic. They believe that militaries and defence establishments must undertake comprehensive 'retooling or transformation to adjust to contemporary war'. Traditionalists, however, emphasize continuity. They assert that while the character of war has undergone change (as it often does), its fundamental nature persists.[28] In this book, I would use the words 'war' and 'conflict' interchangeably and would define armed conflict broadly as armed combat between political communities (as defined by Keith F. Otterbein).[29]

A number of conflicts today such as Afghanistan, Kashmir, Palestine and Syria have become prolonged and protracted due to their intractability. Further, throughout Africa 'prolonged or chronologically resurgent armed conflict' has served as the main backdrop for the social existence of entire generations since the 1960s or 1970s, observes Stephen Lubkemann.[30] For the people of such regions, war has not been an 'event' that suspends 'normal' social processes, but has rather become 'the normal—in the sense of "expected"— context for the unfolding of social life'.[31] This book attempts to understand the life of people in such settings where the

---

[27] Ibid.
[28] Metz and Cuccia, *Defining War*.
[29] See Keith F. Otterbein's definition—Keith F. Otterbein, *How War Began* (College Station, TX: Texas A&M University Press, 2004).
[30] Stephen C. Lubkemann, *Culture in Chaos: An Anthropology of the Social Condition in War* (Chicago, IL: University of Chicago Press, 2010).
[31] Ibid.

conflict has become endemic and prolonged, and generations have grown up amid violence. While there have been several efforts at the international level to mitigate the effects of armed conflict or war on civilians by regulating the conduct of warring parties, yet the civilians continue to bear the brunt of war.

INTERNATIONAL LAW ON CIVILIANS IN ARMED CONFLICT

The first systematic codification of the restraints on the means and methods of warfare was *Instructions for the Government of the Armies of the United States in the Field* prepared by Professor Francis Lieber in 1863 during the American Civil War.[32] However, the regulation of the means and methods of warfare in treaty law dates back to the 1868 St. Petersburg Declaration, the 1899 and 1907 Hague Conventions and the 1925 Geneva Gas Protocol.[33] Lieber Instructions or the Lieber Code was used as the primary basis for the development of the Hague Conventions of 1899 and 1907 which in turn influenced later developments.[34]

The 1899 and 1907 Hague Conventions 'focus on the prohibition to warring parties to use certain means and methods of warfare'.[35] Some provisions pertaining to 'the protection of

---

[32] Waldemar Solf, 'Protection of Civilians against the Effects of Hostilities under Customary International Law and Under Protocol I', *American University International Law Review* 1 (1986): 1–17.

[33] ICRC, 'Customary IHL' (2015), https://www.icrc.org/customary-ihl/eng/docs/v1_rul_in_puofthst

[34] Louise Doswald-Beck and Sylvain Vite, 'International Review of the Red Cross', https://www.icrc.org/eng/resources/documents/misc/57jmrt.htm (accessed on 25 January 2015).

[35] United Nations, 'Genocide Prevention and the Responsibility to Protect', https://www.un.org/en/genocideprevention/war-crimes.shtml

populations against the consequences of war and their protection in occupied territories' are included in the Regulations relating to the laws and customs of war on land, annexed to the 1899 and 1907 Hague Conventions.[36] Although Article 25 of the Hague Regulations prohibits 'the attack or bombardment, by whatever means, of towns, villages, dwellings, or buildings which are undefended', and is based on the principle of distinction between civilians and combatants, the Regulations do not as such state that the parties to the armed conflict make a distinction between the civilians and combatants.[37] The 1899 and 1907 Hague Conventions respecting the Laws and Customs of War on Land are applicable only to international warfare.[38]

The Hague Conventions proved to be inadequate during the First World War, considering the dangers emanating from air warfare and of the problems pertaining to 'the treatment of civilians in enemy territory and in occupied territories'. The International Conferences of the Red Cross held during the 1920s made the initial efforts towards setting forth additional or supplementary rules for the protection of civilians during war.[39] These efforts, after a great deal of struggle, culminated in the Geneva Convention of 1949 which provides protection to civilians, including in occupied territory.[40]

---

[36] ICRC, 'Convention (IV) Relative to the Protection of Civilian Persons in Time of War. Geneva, 12 August 1949' (2015), https://www.icrc.org/ihl/INTRO/380
[37] Jean-Marie Henckaerts, L. Doswald-Beck, C. Alvermann, K. Dörmann, and B. Rolle, 'Distinction between Civilians and Combatants', in *Customary International Humanitarian Law*, eds. Jean-Marie Henckaerts and Louise Doswald-Beck (Cambridge: Cambridge University Press, 2005).
[38] James G. Stewart, 'Towards a Single Definition of Armed Conflict in International Humanitarian Law: A Critique of Internationalized Armed Conflict', *International Review of the Red Cross* 85, no. 850 (2003): 313–350.
[39] ICRC, 'Convention (IV)'.
[40] Ibid.

INTERNATIONAL HUMANITARIAN LAW

Also referred to as the laws of war, International Humanitarian Law protects those who are not participating in combat (medics, aid workers and civilians) as well as those who can no longer fight (such as wounded soldiers and prisoners of war). International Humanitarian Law also places restrictions on the kind of weapons that can be used.[41] The 1949 Geneva Conventions and their 1977 Additional Protocols form the cornerstone of International Humanitarian Law, which seeks to regulate armed conflict and protect the civilian population.

The Geneva Conventions are contained in four international treaties and their Additional Protocols. While the first Geneva Convention (1864) protects wounded and sick soldiers on land during war, the second Convention (1906) protects wounded, sick and shipwrecked military personnel at sea during war. Further, the third Convention (1929) relates to prisoners of war and the fourth Convention (1949) provides protection to civilians, including in occupied territory. While the 1977 Additional Protocol I of the Fourth Convention strengthens the protection of victims of international armed conflict, the Additional Protocol II strengthens the protection of victims of non-international armed conflict. These protocols further define limits on the way conflicts are fought.[42]

The Geneva Conventions, which were adopted prior to 1949, focused merely on combatants and not civilians. The Second

---

[41] New Zealand Red Cross, 'What Is International Humanitarian Law?' https://www.redcross.org.nz/what-we-do/in-new-zealand/international-humanitarian-law/international-humanitarian-law/
[42] ICRC, 'The Geneva Conventions of 1949 and Their Additional Protocols' (2010), https://www.icrc.org/eng/war-and-law/treaties-customary-law/geneva-conventions/overview-geneva-conventions.htm

World War laid bare the catastrophic repercussions of the absence of a convention for the protection of civilians during combat. The 1949 Convention which comprises 159 articles took account of the devastating experiences of the Second World War. It contains a brief section relating to 'the general protection of populations against certain consequences of war'.[43] However, laws regulating the conduct of hostilities in the Geneva Conventions still dated back to the Hague Conventions of 1907. Military aviation did not even exist when the Hague Conventions were negotiated. These laws were updated by the 1977 Additional Protocols of the 1949 Geneva Conventions.

Since the 1899 and 1907 Hague Conventions are still the basis of the law governing the conduct of hostilities, it has become customary to state the 'law of the Hague' to describe the set of rules pertaining to the conduct of hostilities, while the term 'law of Geneva' is used to explain the set of rules pertaining to the protection of war victims, as laid down in the Geneva Conventions in particular. Although victims are as much the key focus of one set of rules as of the other, 'the means used to protect them under the law of The Hague differ, to some extent, from those of the Geneva Conventions'.[44]

Unlike the Geneva Conventions, which essentially aim at protecting the victim once affected (the wounded, the shipwrecked, prisoners of war or civilians in the power of the adverse party), the law of The Hague aims primarily at protecting combatants and non-combatants by restricting the

---

[43] ICRC, 'Civilians Protected under International Humanitarian Law' (2010), https://www.icrc.org/eng/war-and-law/protected-persons/civilians/overview-civilians-protected.htm

[44] François Bugnion, 'The International Committee of the Red Cross and the Development of International Humanitarian Law', *Chicago Journal of International Law* 5, no. 1 (2004): Article 14.

means and methods of warfare. In a sense, one might consider the law of The Hague 'as working "upstream" from the law of Geneva' and highlighting primarily the prevention. Both the law of The Hague and the law of Geneva converged with the adoption of the two Protocols Additional to the 1949 Geneva Conventions, which brought up to date and developed not just the rules pertaining to the protection of war victims, but also those regulating the conduct of hostilities.[45]

APPLICATION OF INTERNATIONAL HUMANITARIAN LAW

The sources of the Law of Hague and the Law of Geneva are both customary and codified in treaties.[46] Under international law, a treaty is usually described as an agreement entered into by states and international organizations. There exist challenges of applying the treaties to contemporary armed conflicts, since treaties apply merely to the states that have ratified them. Therefore, different treaties of International Humanitarian Law are applicable to 'different armed conflicts depending on which treaties the states involved have ratified'. While all the states have ratified the Geneva Conventions, Additional Protocol I has not yet attained worldwide adherence. Since the Protocol applies only between parties to an armed conflict that have ratified it, its efficacy remains limited since a number of states that 'have been involved in international armed conflicts are not a party to it'.[47]

Unlike treaty law, which merely applies to those states that have ratified the particular treaty, customary law is binding

---

[45] Ibid.
[46] Judith Gail Gardam, *Non-combatant Immunity as a Norma of International Humanitarian Law* (Dordrecht: Martinus Nijhoff Publishers, 1993).
[47] ICRC, 'Customary IHL'.

upon all states, irrespective of whether they have ratified the agreement or treaty. It is defined as a 'general and consistent practice of states followed by them from a sense of legal obligation'.[48] Customary law forms the fundamental benchmark of conduct in armed conflict acknowledged by the world community. It is universally applicable irrespective of the application of treaty law and is based on extensive and almost uniform state practice considered as law.[49]

The Martens Clause safeguards customary law while upholding the argument that what is not prohibited by treaty may not necessarily be lawful. It is applicable to all the parts of international humanitarian law, not merely to belligerent occupation.[50] The International Court of Justice, in its advisory opinion, acknowledged the relevance of the Martens Clause for considering the legality of methods and means of warfare and of particular weapons. However, it did not resolve the principle controversies concerning its interpretation. Nonetheless, it is generally agreed that the clause signifies, at the minimum, that the adoption of a treaty regulating specific aspects of the law of warfare does not deny the affected individuals the protection of those norms of customary humanitarian law that were not incorporated in the codification.[51]

Considering the universality of the Geneva Conventions, Waldemar Solf observes that it may be argued that their general principles, even though not all the detailed rules

---

[48] Jack L. Goldsmith and Eric A. Posner, 'A Theory of Customary International Law', 66 *The University of Chicago Law Review* 66, no. 4 (1999): 1113–1177.
[49] ICRC, 'Customary IHL—Helping to Improve the Protection of Victims of Armed Conflict' (2014),https://www.icrc.org/eng/resources/documents/interview/2014/07–29-customary-international-humanitarian-law-cihl.htm (accessed on 25 August 2015).
[50] Theodor Meron, 'The Martens Clause, Principles of Humanity, and Dictates of Public Conscience', *The American Journal of International Law* 94 (2000): 1.
[51] Ibid.

implementing these principles, have now become a customary law binding on non-parties.[52] Besides, the status of the Geneva Conventions as customary law has been recognized by the International Court of Justice and is rarely contested.[53] Despite the presence of International law on the conduct of hostilities and the protection of war victims including civilians, all parties in different armed conflicts frequently flout or violate the law. Besides the indiscriminate firing and shelling which have an adverse physical and psychological impact on the civilian population, the warring parties across conflict zones have frequently targeted non-combatants. This often leads to colossal destruction and engenders terror among the civilians. Let us turn to how ordinary people who endure these hardships experience or view war.

WAR THROUGH THE EYES OF PEOPLE

WAR AS DESTRUCTION

'War means destruction, destruction of your life, right and identity. War means disappearance of humanity,' explained Mona Araste, a researcher from Afghanistan—a country which has seen decades of brutal war.

Similarly, referring to the India–Pakistan conflict over Kashmir, Syed Zubair, who belongs to Srinagar in Kashmir, told me, 'War is *barbadi* (destruction) for both India and Pakistan. It destroys future, nature, it breaks dreams, war makes us handicapped. It is not good for anyone. *Chahe woh Muslim ho, chahe Sikh ho, Hindu ho, Christian ho, marta kaun hai,*

---

[52] Solf, 'Protection of Civilians against the Effects of Hostilities'.
[53] Meron, 'The Martens Clause'.

marta insaan hi hai (Whether it is Muslim, Sikh, Hindu or Christian, it is the human being who is killed).'

Junaid, a musician from the downtown area of Habba Kadal in Srinagar, described the conflict in Kashmir as destruction and chaos. He spoke to me about the turmoil in the valley through his song. He explained, '*Main kehna chahta hoon ki chahe woh CRPF jawan ya policeman ho, chahe woh stone pelter ya civilian ho, marta toh insaan hi hai* (I am trying to say whether it is the CRPF person or policeman, whether it is the stone pelter or civilian, it is the human being who dies).'

Similarly, Rishab Chaku, another musician from Habba Kadal in Srinagar, described war or conflict as destruction and the Kashmir Valley as 'heaven transformed into hell'.

Maher, a carpet trader in Beirut, who has lived through the war in Lebanon (1975–1990), told me, 'War means death and destruction.' All these explanations of war are evocative of Lowes Dickinson's description of war in his book *War: Its Nature, Cause and Cure* published in 1923. Dickinson writes,

> My theme may be put in a sentence: If mankind does not end war, war will end mankind. This has not been true in the past. But it is true in the present. For the present has produced something new. It has produced science. And if science is the principal hope of mankind, it is also the principal menace. For it can destroy as easily as it can create; and all that it creates is useless, if it creates only to destroy. But destruction is what war means; and all its other meanings are made meaningless by this.[54]

---

[54] G. Lowes Dickinson, *War: Its Nature, Cause and Cure* (Abingdon: Routledge, 1923).

As pointed out by all the people I met in conflict and 'post-conflict' zones, war does imply destruction—material and non-material—which engulfs the entire matrix of human existence in the troubled or affected zone. Destruction may entail obliteration of people or damage to their psychosocial well-being, destruction of landscape, cities or villages and 'normal' life. Further, the destruction or annihilation of people, cities or villages and cultural spaces maybe an attempt to annihilate a certain race, group or community, culture as well as collective memories. In this context, collective violence may transform into genocide when a specific group is systematically and deliberately targeted for destruction.[55]

Some examples of collective violence or genocide include the annihilation of a large number of Europe's Jews during the Holocaust of 1939–1945, the carnage of almost half a million people in Indonesia during 1965–1966, genocide in Bangladesh (1971), Burundi (1972), Cambodia (1975–1979), East Timor (1975–1979), Rwanda (1994), Bosnia (1995)[56] and Darfur in Sudan.

The description of war by Maher, Zubair and Mona which focuses on destruction of life is also reminiscent of Carolyn Nordstrom's following account of a local during the war in Mozambique.

> Our life has been taken from us: A life where people go to their fields to work, produce the foods that nourish our families, build the houses where we will raise our children—a good life, a healthy life. People

---

[55] James E. Waller, *Becoming Evil: How Ordinary People Commit Genocide and Mass Killing* (Oxford: Oxford University Press, 2007).
[56] Ibid.

just want to eat, to play with their children, to be able to buy a chair for their house if they can, to visit with their family and friends. These are things we can't do now, we suffer too much—our lives are suffering. The life here, the life in the world, is no good now, it has been broken by war. We eat suffering for dinner. We can't walk freely, we can't work freely, we can't eat freely, we can't live freely. The life of war is a damaged {estragado} life.[57]

In the above paragraph, words such as 'broken' and 'damaged (*estragado*)' echo the destruction caused due to war. Other themes in the above account are loss of freedom and productivity, and above all loss of 'normal life'. Many poets in war zones have described the futility and wantonness of war and the immense destruction it causes. In *Farewell to My Dying Land*, Tom P. Cauuray, a Sierra Leonean poet who was forced to leave his country during the conflict, poignantly describes the destruction caused by the war:

When the sky played the rain song, And the showers danced with you,

I remember the rhythm and the tune, The whirring waltz which lulled my eyes to sleep.

These woes of war belabour sleep.

When you washed your dark-brown skin, I smelled your spray of earth-perfume, but now the scent of smouldering human flesh. Your forests are scorched. Your fauna crushed. Your cheerful twigs on the bush-road edge,

---

[57] Carolyn Nordstrom, 'Terror Warfare and the Medicine of Peace', *Medical Anthropology Quarterly* 12, no. 1 (1998): 103–121.

whose playful sprinkle washed my head, Are all dead, now weevil's bed.[58]

An enormous appetite for imbecile violence among the combatants, particularly the rebels Revolutionary United Front (RUF), was the defining feature of the armed conflict in Sierra Leone that lasted for over a decade from March 1991 till January 2002. During my visit to Sierra Leone in 2011, most former combatants I interacted with, spoke of the wanton violence and devastation during the Sierra Leone war. Akim, a former child soldier, told me, 'RUF gave me drugs in different forms. They mixed my food with drugs. They gave me injections. They gave me coke. With coke in my head I don't know how many people I killed. I burned all the things—villages, children, everybody. I had three weapons—pistol, AK-47 and mortar. Later I became a commander. I gave orders to kill enemies.'[59]

Interestingly, while war destroys it may also create new systems, identities, rules, groups and factions. However, the impact of destruction and devastation it causes is colossal which often surpasses or overshadows what it creates. During my trip to Lebanon in January 2019, I met two ex-combatants Ziad Saab and Badri who had fought during the Lebanese War (1975–1990). Ziad Saab had transformed from a fighter into a 'fighter for peace' and so did Badri as they realized the futility of war. It was my friend Firas who helped me get in touch with Ziad Saab. During our conversation, Firas had mentioned that Ziad Saab runs an organization called Fighters for Peace and I could perhaps contact him for the research on my book.

---

[58] https://theafricanbookreview.com/category/55-poems/senegal-togo/
[59] Name changed.

The next morning as I sat in a cafe sipping Turkish coffee and watching the raindrops gently tap the windowpane, I decided to call Ziad. It was a rather husky voice which greeted me from the other side of the phone. I asked if it was Ziad Saab from Fighters for Peace?

'Yes. It's Ziad,' he said. I explained to him the purpose of my visit to Lebanon and asked if I could meet him to learn about the organization. 'Perhaps within two hours' time,' he responded. As I reached his office building, a tall and robust man greeted me with a warm smile and said, 'It's Ziad.' After we entered his office, he introduced me to Badri, his friend and colleague.

Despite being ex-fighters themselves during the war, Ziad and Badri highlighted the futility and depravity of war and of course the immense destruction it causes. Talking about his transformation, Ziad said, 'I didn't change suddenly. The change happened by answering many questions. The main and important question was: Is it possible to achieve a positive change in society by violence? The answer is No. It doesn't matter how noble the cause is, violence will give you the opposite result.'

Disturbed by the 2013 clashes between Sunni and Alawite sects in Tripoli, Lebanon's second largest city, they decided to set-up an organization called 'Fighters for Peace'. For Ziad, Badri and other ex-fighters who are part of the 'Fighters for Peace', these clashes seemed like flashbacks of the Lebanese war. These ex-fighters got together and wrote an open letter to the youth to not let the country slip into a civil war:

> From the depth of our pain at what our country is going through and the pain we feel watching our country slip into a civil war like the one we lived

through for many long years of our lives, and from our pain watching the youth of today getting dragged into carrying weapons and choosing violence instead of dialogue, like we did at the start of and during the civil war when we carried weapons and participated in the fighting, thinking that only we were right. We destroyed our humanity more than anything else, and we killed our souls with every soul that fell because of us. We kidnapped many, we participated in battles on the frontlines, we sniped and shelled areas, we destroyed, we burned down buildings and entire neighbourhoods without that changing the equation in the slightest.... Don't repeat the mistakes that we made. Everyone loses a civil war—even whoever thinks has won. There is nothing other than death and destruction.

WAR AS TERROR: A BRUTAL AND ANTI-HUMAN ACT

Raja Atif Hayat from Karachi, Pakistan described 'war as terror and a brutal anti-human act'. According to him, 'The idea of war germinates when a human being experiences power and becomes self-centred. Unable to handle criticism, he/she may declare war on the "enemy"'. During our conversation a year ago, Raja told me, 'I live in Karachi where I have experienced political fascism, racism and religious fanaticism. The groups advocating such ideologies impose war for their self-interest which is often supported by the state'. Raja was referring to the crime wars or gang wars of Karachi, which have long dominated the political landscape of Pakistan's largest city.

The city's gangsters are 'openly linked to Pakistan's national politics, in an ecology that runs from the street-side "*bhatta*" extortions up to the highest corridors of state office', wrote Matthieu Aikins.[60] In a traditional sense, these conflicts may not be termed as 'wars'. However, as previously mentioned, since the end of the Cold War, non-traditional conflicts involving non-state actors have burgeoned. This triggered a debate as to whether the nature of war had experienced transformation. Concepts such as 'new' and 'hybrid' war have emerged to refer to these kinds of conflicts. Robert Muggah and John P. Sullivan argue, 'The future conflicts will mostly be waged by drug cartels, mafia groups, gangs and terrorists.'[61] They note, mostly these warring groups are themselves 'highly fragmented, and today's warriors are just as likely to be affiliated with drug cartels, mafia groups, criminal gangs, militias, and terrorist organizations as with armies or organized rebel factions'.[62] These are the kind of crime wars Karachi has experienced for decades.

It was not just Raja but others as well in conflict zones who view war as 'terror and a brutal anti-human Act'. A number of people I met in conflict or 'post-conflict' zones in South Asia, Middle East and Africa also mentioned how the state and the rebel groups use terror techniques against the local population. There are various methods and means of spreading terror during war, one of them being rape. Carolyn Nordstrom notes, 'Rape is one of the most common terror tactics employed in war.'[63] The UN observes,

> Rape committed during war is often intended to terrorize the population, break up families, destroy

---

[60] Matthieu Aikins, 'The Gangs of Karachi' (2014), https://pulitzercenter.org/projects/pakistan-peoples-party-karachi-national-politics-amn-committee-pashtun-sindhi-MQM
[61] https://foreignpolicy.com/2018/09/21/the-coming-crime-wars/
[62] Ibid.
[63] Carolyn Nordstrom, 'Rape: Politics and Theory in War and Peace', *Australian Feminist Studies* 11, no. 23 (1996): 147–162.

communities and, in some instances, change the ethnic make-up of the next generation. Sometimes it is also used to deliberately infect women with HIV or render women from the targeted community incapable of bearing children.[64]

For a long time, sexual violence in conflict was tacitly accepted as inevitable. A 1998 UN report on sexual violence and armed conflict observes that historically, armies viewed 'rape as one of the legitimate spoils of war'. It was not until 1992, with the reports of widespread rapes of women in the former Yugoslavia, that the issue caught the attention of the UN Security Council. In December 1992, the Council declared the 'massive, organized and systematic detention and rape of women, in particular Muslim women, in Bosnia and Herzegovina' an international crime that needed to be addressed. In Rwanda, reportedly between 100,000 and 250,000 women were raped during the three months of 1994 genocide. UN agencies estimate that over 60,000 women were raped during the war in Sierra Leone (1991–2002), over 40,000 in Liberia (1989–2003), at least 200,000 in the Democratic Republic of the Congo since 1998 and up to 60,000 in the former Yugoslavia (1992–1995).[65]

A number of ex-girl soldiers in Sierra Leone who were part of the rebel groups or militias during the civil war in the country (1991–2002) narrated to me their accounts of torture and rape. They mentioned how war for them was synonymous to terror. During the conflict, girls in Sierra Leone were recruited in various military factions such as RUF, the Armed Forces

---

[64] United Nations, 'Sexual Violence: A Tool of War', https://www.un.org/en/preventgenocide/rwanda/assets/pdf/Backgrounder%20Sexual%20Violence%202014.pdf
[65] Ibid.

Revolutionary Council (AFRC) and the pro-government Civil Defense Forces (CDF) which included the Kamajors. A large number of girls were abducted to work as cooks, porters, spies and fighters and were often used as sex slaves.

It was the spring of 2011. While I was based out of Freetown in Sierra Leone, I was also visiting other districts of the country. After travelling to Makeni, the capital of Bombali district, I decided to visit the diamond-rich Kono district located in the Eastern province of Sierra Leone to interview former child soldiers, including girls. I set out for Kono early morning and passed through some of the most charming villages enveloped in lush-green forests. By late afternoon, I was in Kono and headed towards the office of a community-based local non-governmental organization (NGO), which had arranged my interviews with the former child soldiers. While in Freetown I interacted with most people in English with some words and phrases of Krio thrown in, most ex-child soldiers in Kono spoke Krio and were not well versed in English. One of the staff members of the local NGO translated their response to my questions. All the ex-girl soldiers (including few boy soldiers) mentioned that they were frequently sexually exploited by the soldiers or the rebels.

Aminata, from Kono, narrated her horrid ordeal during the war. 'When I was 10, the RUF abducted me in Kono district. I was made to cook, clean, fetch water and food. I was also given a gun but it was too heavy for me. My food and tea were often spiked with drugs,' she said poignantly, 'I was frequently gang-raped, and at 13, I became pregnant. Soon, my baby died.'[66]

---

[66] Name changed.

WAR AS A GAME

Sierra Leone (2011): At around 6:30 in the evening, as the tangerine sun peeped through the grey blue clouds and the trees gently swayed in the wind, I made my way towards the Lumley car wash in Freetown. I entered the car wash through the streets buzzing with traffic, and heard the music grew louder. Some young men were washing cars, others were smoking weed, while few were singing and gyrating to the rhythm of Bob Marley's *Africa Unite*. As I approached a group of young men, some asked me the purpose of my visit to the car wash. 'I am here in Sierra Leone to conduct research on the post-conflict reintegration of child soldiers in the country,' I responded. As mentioned previously, a large number of children and youth had participated in the conflict in Sierra Leone.

One of the boys called others as well. Most of these young men had been involved in the Sierra Leonean conflict as child soldiers. They had joined the Lumley car wash as part of the disarmament, demobilization and reintegration (DDR) process. Most were quite willing to share their experiences of the conflict. Interestingly, some described their experiences as if it were a fast-paced thriller. One of them, in an extremely casual tone, said, 'I was on drugs all the time. I don't know how many people I killed.' Another jumped in, 'I killed a lot of people and burnt villages.' The one who stood next to a car said, 'We don't know what we were doing; we were on drugs all the time.' While many shared how terrified they were as children when they were abducted by the RUF and other militias, some spoke of their fascination with guns.

The idea of war as a game may be linked to romanticization of war. Henning Eichberg observes, associations between war and play have earlier been discovered and reflected upon.

They have been observed from various perspectives such as those of cultural history, military history and philosophy.[67] Toy soldiers are documented among the oldest known toys, excavated from ruins throughout the ancient world, in Asia, Egypt and Syria. Miniature soldiers and miniature weapons are said to have been used to train future generations of warriors the art of war. Antonia Fraser notes, 'Where girls had their dolls, the boys also had their soldiers.' The lands and islands of the Mediterranean have all offered evidence of 'ancient making of model warriors in metal or clay, and tiny Roman war-like figures have been found in Spain, Germany, Britain and even Abyssinia'. According to Fraser, 'The toys of children often reflect a nation's notion of a hero, as children as far back in Greek times have had a penchant for war games as reflected by a clay war chariot from Athens.'[68]

At the turn of the 18th to the 19th century, soldier games became a standard role-play for young boys. Among the children of the industrial society, the sabre, wooden rifle, drum, helmet, hobby horse and flag became popular play toys as well as typical Christmas gifts. Tin soldiers also became popular toys at that time and later during the 20th century, toy soldiers were created in plastic and followed by fantasy warriors.[69] In contemporary times, war toys such as guns or other weapons and even video games (where war actions and shooting became a main genre) have, as argued by many authors, have taken forward the legacy of glorifying war.[70]

---

[67] Henning Eichberg, 'Playing War-playing with Fire: About Dark Games', in *Philosophical Perspectives on Play*, eds. Malcolm MacLean, Wendy Russell, and Emily Ryall (Abingdon: Routledge, 2015).
[68] Antonia Fraser, *A History of Toys* (London: Weidenfeld & Nicolson, 1966).
[69] Eichberg, 'Playing War-playing with Fire'.
[70] Ibid.

Brown (1990) has written a history of toy soldiers, focusing particularly on 19th and early 20th century Britain. According to him, 'War games contributed to a build up of aggression that resulted in enthusiasm for World War I.' He identifies two ways in which war and toy soldiers were linked at the turn of the century. First, 'toy soldiers formed part of a continuum of militaristic influences to which boys were exposed.' Second, toy soldiers were insidious as they helped in reinforcing a particular view (romanticized and heroic) of the nature of war. Brown, however, adds,

> In the last resort, it is impossible to prove conclusively that playing with toy soldiers had any influence at all on subsequent behaviour. Nor was any relationship necessarily a straightforward causal one. Some individuals doubtless took to the soldiers because their enthusiasm for martial matters had already been fired by other aspects of contemporary militarism.[71]

Although, the study by Brown illustrates a relationship between war and war toys, yet as Brown argues, it does not imply causality. A study of Hawaiian children after the bombing of Pearl Harbor by Bonte and Musgrove (1943), however, shows a causal relationship between war and war play. They observed that soon after the bombing of Pearl Harbor, Hawaiian school children began to create more toy weapons and play more war games. Girls also participated in this play, performing the roles of military nurses and creating buildings to be destroyed or 'bombed'.[72]

INTERPRETING WAR

---

[71] Jeffrey Goldstein, 'Immortal Kombat: War Toys and Violent Video Games', in *Why We Watch: The Attractions of Violent Entertainment* (Oxford: Oxford University Press, 1998).
[72] Ibid.

Lisa L. Ossian, referring to the American children during the Second World War, notes that regardless of the world's conflicts, 'children found time to play as children always have done'. During these years, however, 'they mostly played war from impromptu neighbourhood battles attacking Hitler's Nazis to board games bombing the Japanese'. Due to the rationing of materials, commercial toys and games were few, however, both boys' and girls' playtimes often underscored militaristic themes. Ossian continues that another form of children's recreation was 'Saturday matinees of newsreels and war films, which both fascinated and horrified children as they gazed for hours at the depiction of war heroes and internalised the constant military bombardment'.[73]

Whether or not, war or militarization of society has a direct impact on the young people's proclivity towards war games or vice versa and even aggressive behaviour is much debatable. However, the prevalence or prominence of war influences the inclination for war play, as a number of studies have illustrated. My interactions with hundreds of people both male and female, male in particular, in conflict or 'post-conflict' zones across South Asia, Middle East and Africa revealed that during their childhood, adolescence or youth, many were fascinated by guns and grenades.

Some of the expressions I heard too often from the locals who grew up during the conflicts in Lebanon, Kashmir, Afghanistan, and Sierra Leone were: 'We saw war as a game'; 'We played war all the time'; 'We used to play with grenades'; 'We would play with bullets'; and 'There were times when, as children, we danced to the sound of gun shots.' Some of the

---

[73] Lisa L. Ossian, *The Forgotten Generation: American Children and World War II* (Columbia, MO: University of Missouri Press, 2011).

locals who grew up during the war in Lebanon said that when they witnessed the gun fighting they wanted to participate because it was like play. Interestingly, while many of these people expressed that as children sometimes war seemed like a game, they also shared the terrifying side of war.

As described above, people across different conflict or 'post-conflict' zones defined war in various ways—destruction and death being the dominant metaphors for war. Many who either live or have lived in war zones said—war is death; war is destruction. Others saw it as terror that kills or devours everything including humanity. Some even mentioned that as children they were fascinated with guns and bullets, and associated war with thrill and excitement, at the same time emphasizing the dark side of war—unbridled violence, countless deaths and endless destruction.

Even if historically, and to a lesser extent today, war and victor are glorified and the dead honoured, it has always been at the expense of colossal destruction and human suffering. Beneath the glory of war, lurk everyday anxieties, fears, pain and suffering of those entrapped in conflict. As Leila, a free-lance writer from Beirut in Lebanon, who grew up during the prolonged and deadly war in her country (1975–1991), told me, 'War is devastating. War is misery. War is chaos. It causes instability and uncertainty. There is no future. Nothing. You cannot see anything outside it because you are stuck in the middle. You cannot fancy anything. You cannot even plan for the next day. This is war.'

CHAPTER 3

NORMALIZING MILITARIZED VIOLENCE

A loud explosion echoed through the streets. As she played with her doll, Kainath (age four) began to imitate the sound. Suddenly she exclaimed in Dari, 'I am no more scared of these sounds and explosions.'

—Kabul, Afghanistan (4 January 2018)

It was a freezing winter morning when I left for the dry fruits bazaar in Kabul with Ahmad Fareed, a local who originally belongs to Logar province in Afghanistan. The narrow lanes of the crowded bazaar snaked through the vibrant shops exuding an old-world charm. The cheerful smiles of the shopkeepers and pulsating energy of the bazaar reflected a semblance of peace and 'normalcy'. It was hard to tell that in the last week the city had been jolted with a series of suicide bombings.

After spending a couple of hours in the bazaar, Ahmad and I took a shared taxi to go to another market, closer to his home, to buy traditional Afghan kurtas. We got caught in a traffic jam and Ahmad suggested, 'We should postpone our visit to the market for the next day.' I agreed reluctantly.

When we reached home, Ahmad's family members greeted us with warm smiles. His mother then offered us saffron tea and some biscuits. Kainath, Ahmad's four-year-old niece, came running towards me and quickly gave me a hug. As I sipped the tea, there was a loud explosion. Kainath began to imitate the sound and said something in Dari (Afghan variant of Persian). Unable to clearly decipher what she said, I asked Ahmad to translate it for me. 'She is saying that she is no more scared of these sounds and explosions,' Ahmad explained.

'Where exactly did the explosion take place?' I asked. 'Suicide bombing took place in PD9,' Farhad, Ahmad's brother, responded. PD9 was the police station close to the market where I had decided to go after visiting the dry fruits bazaar but eventually postponed the plan. As I talked about the suicide attack with Ahmad and his family and curiously browsed my phone in anticipation of any updates of the bombing, Kainath continued to play unfazed.

In the various provinces I visited or travelled through in Afghanistan (Kabul, Herat, Nangarhar, Kapisa, Parwan and Lagman), the locals continued with their everyday life amid frequent violent attacks and suicide bombings. It was apparently difficult to distinguish between 'wartime' and 'peacetime'.

NORMALIZING VIOLENCE

Violence is a critical element of war. Carolyn Nordstrom notes,

> War comes into existence when violence is employed. Political aggressions may become flamed, threats may be flung back and forth, military exercises may take place, but it is only when bullets are fired and people are maimed and killed, when bombs destroy strategic targets that war is said to exist.[1]

---

[1] Nordstrom, *A Different Kind of War Story.*

Referring to the centrality of violence in war, Shroeder and Shmidt note that the concept of war describes a state of confrontation wherein the likelihood of violence is constantly present and considered 'legitimate by the perpetrating party, and in which actual violent encounters occur on a regular basis'.[2] Although structural violence may become deeply embedded in conflict zones, while mentioning about normalization of violence, I am essentially implying actual violent attacks.[3]

Let us now understand the term 'normal'. 'Normal' comes from the Latin word *norma*, which means 'a "rule" or "pattern" and was originally derived from the name of a mason's tool, a square by means of which his work and his designs were standardized'.[4] Normality implies the state of being normal and the verb normalize denotes 'to make normal'.[5] While referring to the term 'normal', Phillip Davis and John Bradley rightly note, 'while the definition varies with the referent', it largely describes 'some commonly held understanding, a culturally accepted belief' regarding what is usual, typical and natural.[6]

In war or conflict zones, 'normal' life or what is commonly believed to be normal (for instance, going to school, university, work, carrying on with daily tasks without any constant

---

[2] Ingo Shroeder and Bettina Shmidt, 'Violent Imageries and Violent Practices', in *Anthropology of Violence and Conflict*, eds. Bettina Schmidt and Ingo Schroeder (Abingdon: Routledge, 2001).

[3] The term 'structural violence' is generally ascribed to Johan Galtung, which he introduced in his 1969 article 'Violence, Peace, and Peace Research'. It refers to a form of violence wherein some social structure or social institution may harm people by preventing them from meeting their basic needs.

[4] C. Daly King, 'The Meaning of Normal', *The Yale Journal of Biology and Medicine* 17, no. 3 (January 1945): 493–501.

[5] Keith L. Moore, 'Meaning of "Normal"', *Clinical Anatomy* 2, no. 4 (1989): 235–239.

[6] Phillip V. Davis and John G. Bradley, 'The Meaning of Normal', *Perspectives in Biology and Medicine* 40, no. 1 (1996, Autumn): 68–77.

threat to one's life or the lives of family members and friends) is frequently disrupted. Violent attacks or militarized violence, which are otherwise considered an anomaly, often become a part of everyday life or a 'normal' life condition.

Speaking of Somali journalists in her book *Getting Somalia Wrong? Faith, War and Hope in a Shattered State*, Mary Harper notes, 'From time to time they call me in great excitement to tell me there has been no fighting that day, something so unusual that, for them, it is "news"'.[7]

Teresa Koloma Beck in her book *The Normality of Civil War: Armed Groups and Everyday Life in Angola* notes that what seems natural, obvious and 'normal' in an individual's perspective is indeed 'the result of a historical, evolutionary process, in which this particular reality prevailed over possible others'. Therefore, normalities are contingent, what is viewed as 'normal changes with the evolution of man and society, in processes involving interest, power and politics'.[8]

Violent attacks and fighting may become 'normal' or commonplace in conflict zones, so much so that spells of 'peace' or 'no fighting and violent attacks' may seem unusual to those living in these areas. During my interaction with Saima from Kashmir on the militarization of the valley, she remarked, 'Death, killings and forced disappearances are so common here that the day there is no news on the same, we feel that there is something wrong or "abnormal"'.

---

[7] Mary Harper, *Getting Somalia Wrong? Faith, War and Hope in a Shattered State* (London: Zed Books, 2012).
[8] Teresa Koloma Beck, *The Normality of Civil War: Armed Groups and Everyday Life in Angola* (Frankfurt: Campus Verlag, 2013).

'WE ARE USED TO IT'

When I had returned to India from my first trip to Afghanistan in December 2016, just few days later, on 10 January 2017, multiple bombings and attacks ripped through Afghanistan. In Kabul, the Taliban suicide attack killed over 30 and wounded at least 70 people. On the same day, at least 14 people were killed and scores wounded in separate incidents in Helmand and Kandahar.[9] Anxious and horrified, I called my friend Hanif to check if he and his family were doing fine. 'We are used to it,' Hanif quipped.[10] Perhaps it is about adapting to the 'everyday conflict', which could be similar to how our senses may gradually adapt to certain alien smells, sounds and images if exposed to them for a sustained period.

Hanif's response to war and violence echoed what most people who had lived through the war in Lebanon told me during my visit to the country in January 2019. Most said that they got used to the fighting after a while. To offer an example, on my way to Tripoli in North Lebanon, the taxi driver pointed out that he was a soldier during the latter part of the war and fought on the side of the Lebanese army. 'What made you participate in the war?' I asked. 'My country, I fought for my country,' he quickly remarked. 'For instance, initially you are scared because you do not know how much power you have, but when you know your power, it becomes normal. Like in shooting and fighting, initially you are scared then it becomes normal,' he explained.

In hundreds of interviews I have conducted for over a decade with people in conflict zones in different parts of the world,

---

[9] https://www.reuters.com/article/us-afghanistan-blast-idUSKBN14U1DL?il=0
[10] Name changed.

of people living in extreme poverty, or those affected by violence for a sustained period of time, 'We are used to it' has been a significant response to how they cope with their situation. It may be pertinent to point out the report titled *It's Wrong ... but You Get Used to It: A Qualitative Study of Gang-associated Sexual Violence towards, and Exploitation of, Young People in England* by Beckett et al. One of the key findings was that young women's responses to sexual victimization were mostly fatalistic. 'I'm used to it.... It's normal.... It's wrong, but you get used to it.... Welcome to our generation' (young women's focus group).[11]

Here, the sexual violence seems to have become normalized. For a number of these young people, sexual violence is considered a fact of everyday life, something which is inevitable and cannot be avoided. Likewise, many people whom I interviewed in conflict zones mentioned that they have adapted to the conflict and unstable security situation, which has become a part of their existence. Interestingly, most of them used the word 'we' rather the 'I' as if implying a collective sense of everyday violence.

As Derek Summerfield notes, when conflict so routinely entails the destruction or terrorization of entire communities, 'even survivors of individual acts of brutality' are likely to view their wounds as social rather than psychological.[12]

---

11 http://uobrep.openrepository.com/uobrep/bitstream/10547/305795/1/Gangs-Report-final.pdf
12 Derek Summerfield, 'The Impact of War and Atrocity on Civilian Populations: Basic Principles for NGO Interventions and a Critique of Psychosocial Trauma Projects', Relief and Rehabilitation Network Paper 14 (London: Relief and Rehabilitation Network, 1996).

'WE ARE TIRED OF WAR'

It was January 2018, when one evening in Kabul I was buying a ticket to Herat (North Western province of Afghanistan bordering Iran), Asad, a travel agent, after seeing my passport remarked enthusiastically, 'I love India and Indians too.'[13] We got talking about the extremely warm relations and cultural ties between India and Afghanistan. After a while, I asked him what he feels about the situation in Afghanistan and how he copes with the frequent violent attacks and bombings in his country. 'We are used to it,' he responded and in the same breath, said, 'We are tired of this endless war, and there will be a time when all of us in Afghanistan will lose our mental balance.'

In 2014, when I was teaching at the University of Kashmir, I had the opportunity to travel to 9 out of 10 districts in the Kashmir Valley, which is heavily militarized. Some of these districts such as Pulwama and Shopian in South Kashmir are the hotbed of insurgency. Most locals in the valley, like Asad from Afghanistan, would point out that they are 'tired of the situation' while also mentioning that they are 'used to it now'. During my interactions with scores of locals in both Kashmir and Afghanistan on the security situation, one key thing, which stood out, was that most locals are 'tired or exhausted of conflict' as it has become a part of their everyday existence. Yet it has become normalized.

In 2019, the conflict fatigue in the Kashmir Valley had seemed to deeply penetrate all sections of the Kashmiri society. It was the time when the Indian State revoked the autonomy of Kashmir, imposed 'curfew-like' restrictions

---

[13] Name changed.

and communication blockade in the valley. The strict restrictions were imposed at a time of *Bada* Eid (major festival of Muslims) and the wedding season; at a time when the tourist season was in full swing; during the apple growing season; and around the time when students were preparing for their exams in the upcoming months. This move by the Indian State not just crippled the economy of Kashmir, it also seemed to affect the local population psychologically.

For one and half month, since the Indian State revoked the autonomy of Kashmir on 5 August, I interacted with hundreds of people in Pulwama, Anantnag, Baramulla and Srinagar districts on the abrogation of Articles 370 and 35A and the 'curfew-like' restrictions in the valley. In Srinagar, besides visiting Rajbagh, Dalgate, Lal Chowk, Sonwar, Hazratbal, Nowpora and Khyam Chowk, I spent one month interacting with families including children and youth in the extremely sensitive downtown areas of Aanchaar, Rainawari, Nowhatta, Soura, Hawal, Alimgiri Bazaar, Habak, Habba Kadal, Fateh Kadal, Bohri Kadal and Gojwara.

Most Kashmiris I met said that besides being tired of the conflict, they are frustrated and helpless like never before. The anger and rage I noticed among the locals against the Indian government ensuing the abrogation of Articles 370 and 35A was unprecedented. In August 2019, during a conversation with a family whose one member (17-year-old boy) had been severely hit by pellets in Fateh Kadal one of the family members indignantly said, 'People are exhausted of the conflict. We neither want to be with India nor Pakistan. We Kashmiris just want to be left alone.'

Several people across different conflict zones including Kashmir, referring to the security situation, have often told

A Street Vendor during Lockdown Post Abrogation of Article 370,
Bohri Qadal, Srinagar, Kashmir

me that 'they have no choice but to live with it'. When I asked them how they cope with the threat of everyday violence, some pointed out, 'Whatever has to happen will happen.' Therefore, fatalism or acceptance of the situation is yet another response to conflict (especially intractable conflicts) which I have observed among many people in these regions.

Despite everyday militarized violence, most people in conflict zones continue to go about their daily lives or practice 'normalcy', unless the schools and/or universities are closed, there are shutdowns or curfews (like in Kashmir) or they have been displaced from their homes, or the villages and cities are under siege. Robert McNamara from Sierra Leone, who witnessed the brutal war in his country during the 1990s and early 2000, told me, 'Initially the war was confined to the provinces, and it was much later that the RUF captured the capital Freetown. I used to stay in Freetown and had not seen any armed violence.'

He explained, 'But when I was 12 years old, in 6th standard, I decided to visit my village Kabalain in Koinadugu district and saw atrocities committed by the RUF. When I returned from my village, the rebels soon after took control of the capital as well. For a long time we could not go to school. People had to stay indoors for long periods due to the fear of the rebels. They would step out only to find food.'

I asked Robert if during the war he was perpetually scared of the armed groups and militias. 'Well it was not constant fear; I would be scared whenever I heard the sound of jets, gunfire and fighting on the streets. On other occasions, I would try and be normal,' he said.

DEFINING EVERYDAY IN WAR

Mary A. Favret, in her article *Everyday War*, writes, 'For all its spectacular trappings, modern warfare rarely escapes intimacy with the prosaic everyday.'[14] How does one define 'Everyday'? Ben Highmore, in his book *Ordinary Lives: Studies in the Everyday* explains, 'The everyday is the accumulation of "small things" that constitutes a more expansive but hard to register "big thing"'. He continues,

> But like fissures in a stream of constancy the everyday is also punctuated by interruptions and irruptions:

---

[14] https://s3.amazonaws.com/academia.edu.documents/31721411/EverydayWarELH.pdf

a knock on the door, a stubbed toe, an argument, an unexpected present, a broken glass, a tear, a desperate embrace.[15]

In conflict zones, violent attacks and bombings often seem to become subsumed in the everyday 'small things' or routines of the people, so much so that armed violence seems to become normalized.

Many contemporary conflicts are, in fact, protracted conflicts in which people seem to live in a twilight zone wherein it becomes difficult to distinguish between wartime and peacetime. Short spells of 'peacetime' maybe interrupted by extreme violence such as suicide bombings, firing and shelling or armed attacks. Some of the examples include Afghanistan, Syria, Palestine, Kashmir and armed conflicts in Africa. In case of Afghanistan, there have been times when peace seemed to return or the conflicting parties came close to a peace deal, the country was jolted with bomb attacks. Militarization of daily life has been a constant feature in these areas for a prolonged period.

DEFINING MILITARIZATION

The terms militarism and militarization have sometimes been used synonymously. Militarism is usually much narrower in scope than militarization, however, 'identifying a society's emphasis on martial values'. It also focuses on the political realm and suggests that martial or warlike values have an independent ability to propel social change, while

---

[15] Ben Highmore, *Ordinary Lives: Studies in the Everyday* (Abingdon: Routledge, 2010).

militarization focuses on the simultaneously discursive and material nature of military dominance.[16]

Michael Geyer defines militarization as 'the contradictory and tense social process in which civil society organises itself for the production of violence'.[17] According to Cynthia Enloe, militarization is a step-by-step process by which an individual or a thing 'gradually comes to be controlled by the military or comes to depend for its well-being on militaristic ideas'. The more militarization transforms a person or a society, the more that person or society comes to consider military needs and militaristic presumptions to be not just valuable but also normal.[18] In the context of gender, Anuradha Chenoy notes that patriarchal values and attitudes are, expectedly, entrenched in the ideology of militarism, just as patriarchal practices will be evident in the process of militarization.[19]

In conflict zones, each act 'is affected by, dependent on and mobilised by militaristic values'.[20] In areas such as Kashmir, Palestine, Afghanistan and parts of Syria, militarization has become a part of life, to the extent that it seems to have become normalized. Carolyn Nordstrom rightly notes, 'Cultures of militarization and the ontological experiences of being victimized by militarized actions span cultural divisions based on

---

[16] Catherine Lutz, 'Making War at Home in the United States: Militarization and the Current Crisis', *American Anthropologist* 104, no. 3 (2002): 723–735.
[17] Michael Geyer, 'The Militarization of Europe, 1914–1945', in *The Militarization of the Western World*, ed. John R. Gillis (New York, NY: Rutgers University Press, 1989), 79.
[18] Cynthia Enloe, *Maneuvers: The International Politics of Militarizing Women's Lives* (Berkeley and Los Angeles, CA: University of California Press, 2000).
[19] Anuradha Chenoy, 'Militarization, Conflict, and Women in South Asia', in *The Women and War Reader*, eds. Ann Lois Lorentzen and Jennifer Turpin (New York, NY: New York University Press, 1998).
[20] Nadera Shalhoub-Kevorkian, *Militarization and Violence against Women in Conflict Zones in the Middle East: A Palestinian Case Study* (Cambridge: Cambridge University Press, 2009).

national and ethnic identities' to connect people in war zones throughout the globe.[21] However, it may be argued here that women, children, men or even different ethnic groups may experience war or militarized violence differently or have certain similar experiences as they belong to a specific category, yet each individual may have some experiences, which are unique. Besides, each individual while belonging to a certain group or category may react and respond differently to her/his war experience.

MILITARIZED SPACES

Militarization of life across conflict zones may be reflected through palpable presence of the military or security forces on the streets and public places, security checks, roadblocks, curfews, emergency laws, barricades, concertinas and frequent firing, shelling, attacks and bombings. However, the level and intensity of militarization may vary from one conflict zone to another.

KASHMIR: 'FEELS LIKE A PRISON'

'Do you see how every few hundred metres, there are check-points and barricades in the city?' 'We have grown up in this environment—Kashmir is nothing but a prison,' Umer, one of my martial arts trainers, said dejectedly as we walked towards Lal Chowk after the Wushu class at Sher-e-Kashmir stadium in Srinagar. Several others in the valley have also frequently echoed this sentiment.

---

[21] Nordstrom, *A Different Kind of War Story*.

Besides frequent security checkpoints and deployment of security forces on streets, in a number of places in Kashmir, Central Reserve Police Forces (CRPF) camps are located within civilian areas. In the case of Srinagar, some of the CRPF camps are located within the residential areas of Zaldagar and Nowpora; near Sheera cinema within the vicinity of tuition centres; around Neelam cinema in proximity to the market; and near SP College. Clearly, civilian spaces have been militarized.

Just after the abrogation of Article 370, I happened to meet Rishab Chaku, a Kashmiri Pandit from Habba Kadal, Srinagar, who told me, 'At Berbershah bridge, when there was no bunker of the security forces, the situation was much better. Stone pelting began around the area after the bunker was set-up. I do not even take that route anymore. People feel threatened and insecure due to the camps of the security forces in the civilian areas. While I do not support Azaadi, I feel civilian areas should be demilitarized.'

Rishab, who is a musician, explained, 'Kashmir is like an invisible prison. It feels like a graveyard. All of us are dead souls here.' On the abrogation of 370, he said, 'Kashmir is a political issue not a developmental issue. While Kashmiri Pandits in the downtown area of Habba Kadal have mixed opinion on the abrogation, I am against it. We have been forcefully integrated.' 'Due to the communication blockade my upcoming music projects have been stalled. I was about to collaborate with a Pakistani music producer Ghauri but now that has been put on hold,' he lamented.

'Caged or imprisoned'—that is how most Kashmiris describe their life in Kashmir, their home. Further, the brutal restrictions and the communication lockdown that ensued the abrogation of Article 370 in August 2019 came as a rude shock.

Just when the valley seemed to be limping back to 'normalcy', soon it went into a lockdown again due to the Coronavirus pandemic. While for most of the world, lockdown or long periods of curfews are anomalous, Kashmiris will tell you, 'We are used to it.' While the ordeals of Kashmiri Pandits who had to flee Kashmir in 1990 as militancy swamped the region are extremely poignant, those who live in the valley are subjected to heavy militarization reflected in draconian laws, frequent security checks and a large presence of the security forces.

The militarization of everyday life including constant or frequent presence of the security forces in the civilian areas, is likely to have an adverse psychological impact on the civilian population, children and youth in particular. After the abrogation of Article 370, I met Shaheen in the downtown area of Nowhatta, at a time when a large number of troops were deployed in the valley, the downtown area in particular. She exasperatedly said, 'When you look out of your window, you see security forces; if you step out of home, you see forces; if you walk outside even in the residential areas, there are forces; there are forces everywhere.' 'This is the environment we have grown up in. I don't feel comfortable walking outside with my daughter when there are forces with guns all round, nor do the children feel safe,' she continued as her face cringed with anger.[22]

On the other hand, most of the security forces and police officers I interacted with in the valley around the same time expressed how strenuous their job is. Suresh, from the CRPF, wearily said, 'We wake up at 3 in the morning and are deployed at our respective locations at 6 AM.'[23] Mahesh, also from the CRPF added, 'All day we stand for hours, clad in

---

[22] Name changed.
[23] Name changed.

heavy uniforms, helmets and jackets. We just sleep for three to four hours in a day.' Few days later during my visit to the downtown area of Srinagar, Javed, from the CRPF, who was deployed at Rainawari when I met him, said, 'All day we stand in the heat, unaware from which side we may be hit my stones. We have to be vigilant and constantly alert of the stone pelters, particularly in the downtown area of Srinagar.'[24]

Towards the end of August 2019, I met Abdul from the CRPF, who originally belongs to Jammu. He mentioned that he has completed 28 years of service with the CRPF and has served in Gadchiroli (Maharashtra), Balaghat (Madhya Pradesh), Vaishno Devi (Jammu), and Srinagar (Kashmir).[25]

'I was also deployed in South Kashmir (Anantnag, Kulgam and Pulwama) for a month during 2019 elections,' he pointed out. 'Which place offered you the best work environment?' I asked. 'Nagaland. I was deployed there for three years from 1992–1995. Arunachal Pradesh was also quite good in terms of work,' he added. 'And the most difficult one?' I asked. 'Kashmir! I have been here for one and half years. When the situation is tense or during curfew, we are on duty for 15–16 hours a day. If the security situation is under control, we leave for our camps between 6 and 7 in the evening. Thereafter, every alternate day we have to serve for two hours in the night at our camp,' he responded.

'In times of curfew, we may sleep for merely three to five hours at night. The weight we carry—jackets, boots and other equipment—is at least 12 kg. Besides, we also have to deal with the stone pelters, particularly in the downtown area of Srinagar.'

---

[24] Name changed.
[25] Name changed.

Around the same time, I met Majid Dar, from the J&K Police, who is originally from the Old Town Baramulla. He spoke to me about the challenges his job throws up.[26]

'In times like these, when there is curfew, every day we wake up at 3 in the morning and leave for our duty between 5 and 6 AM. We are deployed through Police Control Room. We reach our location between 6:30 to 7 in the morning,' Majid explained.

'By 7:30 to 8 in the night we leave for the camp. Our job is extremely strenuous. There is also a threat of being targeted by the militants. Our families are always worried about us,' he said anxiously.

The Kashmir Valley is one of the most heavily militarized zones in the world. For almost a decade, most Kashmiris (civilians) I met or interviewed in nine districts (Srinagar, Pulwama, Anantnag, Shopian, Kulgam, Ganderbal, Baramulla, Bandipora and Budgam) of Kashmir, expressed anger and frustration with the heavy militarization of the valley. When I had travelled to Kashmir for the first time in 2010, it was going through an uneasy and unstable phase of bandhs (shutdowns) and curfews, which lasted for over four months. During that time, I spoke to a number of people from different districts in the valley regarding the turmoil. Sajad from Shopian told me, 'Kashmir should be demilitarized and it would be 90 per cent safe.' Around the same time, Mohammad Wani, a *shikarawala* (boatman) said, 'The security forces should move towards the border, and out of the civilian spaces.'[27]

The early 1990s witnessed growing militarization of the valley. After decades of political discontent and excesses of

---

[26] Name changed.
[27] Name changed.

the Indian State, during the early 1990s, several Kashmiri men crossed over to Pakistan Administered Kashmir for arms training, with an aim to fight the Indian State. While Pakistan fomented trouble in the Indian Administered Kashmir, the Indian security forces reportedly led a brutal campaign against the insurgents and their families. The militarization of the valley is well reflected in a number of emergency provisions, particularly the Armed Forces (J&K) Special Powers Act (AFSPA), which was imposed in 1990 to deal with militancy.

This draconian law provides legal protection from prosecution to the armed forces stationed in the disturbed areas. AFSPA grants extraordinary powers to the security forces, including power to detain and enter property without warrant and to 'fire upon or … or otherwise use force, even to the causing of death, against any person who is acting in contravention of any law or order for the time being in force in the disturbed area' if that officer considers it essential 'for the maintenance of public order'.[28]

In the aftermath of Burhan Wani's killing, a militant commander of Hizbul Mujahideen, by the security forces on 8 July 2016, militarization of the valley was further intensified. A large number of Kashmiris took to the streets in several parts of the valley to denounce Wani's death. As a result of the unrest which followed his death, scores of people on both sides were injured or killed. Many children were also injured and some killed by 'non-lethal' or crowd control weapons (CCW) such as pellet guns, rubber bullets and tear gas shells used by the security forces to handle the violent crowd. Following widespread outrage against the use of

---

28 https://www.hrw.org/reports/2008/india0908/5.htm

pellet guns, in September, the Union Home Minister Rajnath Singh said that the chilli-filled grenades or Pelargonic Acid Vanillyl Amide will replace pellet guns for crowd control and latter will be used only in the rarest of rare cases.

The pellet gun was first introduced in Kashmir in 2010 during the unrest. It has been used as a CCW in only few countries such as Bahrain, Egypt and Tunisia. When fired, the pellets or iron balls spray into multiple directions and do not follow a singular trajectory. Therefore, the pellets may also hit a passer-by. Nasir Ahmad Bhat, a 16-year-old from Halmatpora, Kupwara was among eight pellet victims I met at Shri Maharaja Hari Singh (SMHS) hospital in Srinagar towards the end of August 2016. He told me, 'On 13 August, the CRPF opened fire on the protesters who were pelting stones on the security personnel in Halmatpora. At that time, I was heading home after Namaz when pellets struck me in my eyes.' 'I have had three surgeries so far. However, I can hardly see clearly,' he said poignantly.

On the other hand, a number of security personnel and even civilians have been injured during the stone-pelting incidents. Altaf, a Kashmiri Businessman who is based out of Sweden, pointed out, 'It is not just the security personnel who have been injured during the stone-pelting incidents, my colleague from Delhi was severely injured when some boys were pelting stones in the downtown area of Srinagar,' he explained.[29] In fact, at the time of abrogation of 370, when I was travelling to Soura from Nowhatta in Srinagar on a two-wheeler with Ayaan, a local, someone randomly flung a huge stone from the park. However, we managed to cross the park unhurt.

---

[29] Name changed.

Besides, the disproportionate use of force by the security forces to handle violent crowds, which has injured or killed not just the protesters but also bystanders, has further enraged and alienated the civilian population in the Valley.

While many civilians in the Kashmir Valley have spoken to me about human rights violations committed by the security forces and the J&K Police, the latter shared with me the challenge of dealing with a large crowd of stone pelters. Most of the CRPF personnel mentioned that it is extremely humiliating to hear the stone pelters shout 'Indian dogs'. One of them said, 'Whenever the stone pelters call us dogs and shout "go back to India", I get extremely angry.' On the other hand, many Kashmiris, particularly in the downtown area of Kashmir, pointed out that the security forces often verbally abuse them. One of them told me, 'Why do we have to keep showing our IDs, go through frequent frisking and searches even in our homes?' Many, in the rural areas in particular, have frequently spoken to me about the atrocities committed by the security forces and the police against the civilian population. Since the early 1990s, human rights groups have reported rampant rights violations by the security forces against the people of Kashmir reflected in arbitrary arrests and detentions, forced disappearances, mass graves, and rape or sexual abuse of women and girls.

Few months after Burhan Wani's killing, I met Saba Khan from the downtown area of Idgah who spoke about the militarization of Kashmir. 'When I was a child (perhaps in 2nd standard), I would feel that this place (Kashmir) is different from other places.' 'We would see the security forces as alien, some people from different land asking for our IDs,' she pointed out. 'In Kashmir, violence, protests and bandhs (shutdowns) have become mundane—everyday fact of life,' Saba continued,

In such a situation, we need to divert ourselves to remain sane and avoid becoming desensitized.[30]

Next, I returned to Kashmir in May 2019 during Ramadan, at a time when there were hardly any tourists in the valley. After Ramadan, however, tourists began trickling in. In the beginning of August 2019, at a time when the hotels and tourists sites in the valley were brimming with people, the annual Amarnath Pilgrimage was in full swing, the Home Ministry released an advisory for the tourists to leave Kashmir citing a terrorist threat. As mentioned previously, thousands of more troops were deployed in the valley.

Around that time, I was on a field visit to several villages and towns of Pulwama such as Noorpora, Tral, Dadsara, Awantipora and Padgampura. After my visit to Noorpora on 3 August, where I spent the entire day interacting with the locals, I returned to Srinagar in late evening. The streets were dark and almost barren. Most shops were closed. Security forces outnumbered the civilians. The city seemed nothing short of a garrison. Next, on the 5 August, the Government of India revoked the autonomy of J&K. A large number of people from the mainstream including politicians, activists and lawyers, as well as separatists were detained by the Indian State, mostly under the Public Safety Act and various sections of Criminal Procedure Code. Scores of young boys were also detained.

Strict restrictions were imposed in parts of J&K, particularly in Kashmir, with some relaxation from time to time. The last WhatsApp message of my mother before the phone lines and the Internet were snapped on 5 August was 'Please come back'. Agitated and stressed, like many other Kashmiris in the valley

---

[30] Name changed.

as well as outside it, I had no idea how I could contact my mother who had a brain surgery the previous year. Few days later, some locals told me that I could perhaps go to the police station and contact my family through the satellite phone.

Just a week after the revocation of Kashmir's autonomy, it was *Bada* Eid on 12 August. As I headed towards Dal gate in the evening (a key tourist spot in Srinagar) along with Omar, a local, until 8:00 PM some people and vehicles were seen outside on the streets. Soon after, Dal gate turned as dark as the night. 'It is *Bada* Eid, but it seems the valley is in a state of mourning,' Omar said movingly.

AFGHANISTAN: 'SUICIDE BOMBINGS AND ARMED ATTACKS ARE A PART OF OUR LIVES'

As I landed at the Hamid Karzai airport in Kabul in December 2016, I had to go through multiple security checks, many more than any country or conflict zone I had visited. When I stepped out of the airport, Kabul seemed like any other city. People seemed to move about their daily tasks, the crowds thronged the local markets and malls, the local vendors dotted the city streets and local cafes brimmed with people. However, frequent security checkpoints, which punctuated the vibrant city streets, acted as a reminder of the conflict in Afghanistan.

SUICIDE BOMBINGS AND EVERYDAY VIOLENCE IN AFGHANISTAN

On 25 December 2017, just few days after I landed in Kabul, a security check post in the city was struck by a suicide blast. According to Afghan officials, the suicide blast 'killed two intelligence officers and four civilians, while injuring two people'.[31] Najib Danish, the Interior Ministry spokesman, said, 'The bomber apparently wanted to target Afghan security forces and instead hit a civilian car.' The Islamic State group claimed responsibility for the explosion through its Amaq news agency.[32]

After I returned to Kabul from my visit to Nangarhar province in Afghanistan, on 28 December 2017, a suicide bombing struck the Tebyan centre, a Shiite cultural centre in Pul-e-Sukhta area of Kabul. According to the health officials, over 40 people were killed and more than 80 were wounded in the attack.[33] These included women and children. The Islamic State claimed responsibility for the attack.[34] Just a few days after the Tebyan bombing, on 4 January 2018, Kabul was struck by another suicide bombing. This time I witnessed the jarring sound of the explosion. It was the same incident I have described in the beginning of this chapter. A suicide bomber blew himself up close to a group of security personnel who were conducting an operation against illegal drugs and alcohol dealing, stated Afghan officials. According to the spokesperson for the Ministry of Public Health, 11 dead and 25 wounded had been brought to city hospitals after the blast. This attack too was claimed by the Islamic State.[35]

Just a few days after I returned to India, on 27 January 2018, a deadly suicide bombing killed at least 95 people and injured

---

[31] https://www.voanews.com/a/report-explosion-kabul-intellegence-agency/4177967.html
[32] Ibid.
[33] https://www.tolonews.com/afghanistan/explosion-reported-kabul-city-0
[34] https://www.nytimes.com/2017/12/28/world/asia/afghanistan-suicide-attack.html
[35] https://www.reuters.com/article/us-afghanistan-attack/blast-hits-police-in-afghan-capital-kabul-dozens-of-casualties-idUSKBN1ET22Z

scores in Kabul. The militants drove an ambulance loaded with explosives past a police checkpoint in a 'secure' zone of the city, home to government offices and foreign embassies. The Taliban claimed responsibility for the attack, the deadliest in several months.[36]

A 2018 BBC study had observed that the Taliban had become openly active in 70 per cent of Afghanistan. The study claimed that the insurgents controlled or threatened much more territory than when foreign combat troops left the country in 2014. According to the study, around 15 million people, half the population of Afghanistan, reside in areas that are either controlled by the Taliban or where the group is openly present and regularly launches attacks.[37] The BBC research also noted that the Islamic State is more active in the country than ever before, although it remains substantially less powerful than the Taliban.[38]

The Afghan population is stuck between the ongoing conflict in the country between the Taliban, the Islamic State, other militant factions and the government security forces. Civilian casualties are at an unprecedented level. From 1 January to 31 March 2018, United Nations Assistance Mission in Afghanistan (UNAMA) documented '2,258 civilian casualties (763 deaths and 1,495 injured), reflecting similar levels of civilian harm documented in the first three months of 2017 and 2016'.[39]

According to UNAMA, civilian casualties from suicide improvised explosive devices and complex attacks are the primary

36 https://www.bbc.com/news/world-asia-42843897
37 https://www.bbc.co.uk/news/world-asia-42863116
38 Ibid.
39 https://unama.unmissions.org/latest-un-update-records-continuing-record-high-levels-civilian-casualties-2018

cause of civilian casualties, a new development observed in 2018. The Mission found that ground engagements were the second most important cause of civilian casualties, 'followed by targeted and deliberate killings, explosive remnants of war, and aerial operations'.[40] The situation in Afghanistan reflects how locals try to continue with their everyday lives in the face of looming threat of suicide bombings, attacks and various other kinds of violence.

In late December 2017, while planning a trip with Ahmad Fareed, a local, to the Nangarhar province (bordering Pakistan), one of my friends from Kabul suggested that I take a shared public vehicle rather than a private taxi. 'On the way to Jalalabad (the capital of Nangarhar) the Taliban is often seen on the checkpoints in the evening,' he pointed out. 'Therefore, it is better to travel in a public vehicle and wear a hijab so that you can melt in the crowd,' he suggested. His family members advised me to avoid talking during the entire journey.

Dressed in hijab, I headed to a public taxi stand along with Ahmad, and around noon we got a taxi for Jalalabad. During the entire journey of about four hours, I did not speak and, whenever required, communicated through gestures. It began to get a little warm as we approached Laghman province, parts of which had been captured by the Taliban. After travelling through the rugged mountains and dusty landscape of Laghman, we reached Jalalabad in the evening.

The city appeared markedly different from Kabul which is a delightful amalgam of the traditional and the modern. Mostly rustic, Jalalabad's quaint streets, were alive and buzzing with

---

[40] Ibid.

the sound of rickshaws. Unlike Kabul, I could spot only a few women on the streets and none with their faces visible. After passing through the narrow lanes and traffic jams, Ahmad and I reached the office of the local NGO,[41] which had agreed to assist me on my research on the status of Afghan returnees from Pakistan and drug addiction in the Nangarhar province. Since the interviews and the field visits were to take place the next day, I asked the NGO staff if Ahmad and I could visit the local market.

'Jalalabad is on high security alert and it is not advisable to step out after 4 in the evening, especially for a woman who is an Indian national,' the Director of the NGO explained. 'Since Nangarhar is close to the Pakistan border, it is dangerous for an Indian to move around the province,' he added.

Due to the tense security situation, the NGO arranged for my accommodation at some training hall. I spent the next few days researching on drug addiction in Nangarhar, visiting a day care centre at Jalalabad for Afghan returnees from Pakistan, and talking to the locals about the militarization of everyday life in the province. I also visited a gurdwara in Jalalabad and spoke to the Sikhs, a minority community in Afghanistan, which has received frequent death threats from the Islamic State. Prakash Singh, a member of the gurdwara, mentioned that the entire Sikh community in Nangarhar has been living in fear, particularly since the time the Islamic State established its stronghold in the province.[42] 'I had to send my family to Delhi in India because I didn't want my children to grow up in this environment of constant insecurity and fear,' he explained as his voice trailed off.

PIECE OF WAR

---

[41] The name of the NGO has been kept confidential.
[42] Name changed.

Next, I travelled to the Landi Kotal–Torkham border in Nangarhar (bordering Pakistan) along with Ahmad, and two medical staff members including a female doctor from the same NGO. It was over one-hour drive to the border. During the journey, we passed through territories controlled by the Taliban. As our vehicle moved through the parched mountains, I quietly looked outside through the glass. After a while, I asked the medical staff accompanying me about the Taliban and ISIS control over the territories in the Nangarhar province. The male doctor responded, 'You see these barren fields on both sides? Just after a kilometre on both sides is the Taliban territory.'

'What about the ISIS territory?' I interrupted. 'ISIS? That's further ahead—At least 25 kilometres. I will show you the road which leads to the ISIS territory,' he responded. I asked the doctor if he has ever had any personal experience with the Taliban or ISIS. 'Taliban, yes. In fact many times. But ISIS, no, not yet,' he said.

'Can you describe few of those encounters with the Taliban?' I requested, looking at him curiously. After glancing at me thoughtfully and then staring into the distance, as if to recall something, the doctor narrated his encounters with the Taliban:

'Couple of years back, I would regularly visit a Taliban-controlled village in Nangarhar province for treating patients. One day some villagers told me that two members of the Taliban would like to meet me'.

'What was your reaction,' I interjected.

He looked at me and said, 'I was petrified,' his eyes widened. 'But when they finally met me, it was alright; they actually came for the medical treatment.' After a brief pause he said, 'Before leaving, they said that I should continue visiting their village for treating patients. Thereafter, they would visit me frequently to check if the villagers were doing fine.'

Soon we reached the medical centre at the Torkham border. As we entered the Centre, we were greeted by the medical staff who then showed us the facilities for the Afghan returnees and explained about the functioning of the Centre. There were no patients at that time. Subsequently, we visited a local hospital near the border, which treats the locals as well as the Afghan returnees.

The next visit was to the International Organization for Migration's (IOM) Torkham Transit Centre for undocumented Afghan returnees from Pakistan. The staff explained to us the situation of Afghan returnees and mentioned that in the past year, a large number of Afghans have returned to Afghanistan. More than 55,000 undocumented Afghans returned from Pakistan through mid-May in 2017—'double the number of returns during the same period in 2016, the highest return year on record'.[43]

According to the United Nations High Commissioner for Refugees (UNHCR), there were '1,405,715 registered Afghan refugees and 210,465 Afghan families in Pakistan as of 3 June 2019'. The IOM reported that 10,720 Afghans have returned home from Pakistan since the beginning of 2019. 'Of the total figure, 8,421 have returned spontaneously, while 2,299 others were deported.'[44] Most of the Afghan returnees I spoke to at a day care centre in Jalalabad the previous day, said they returned voluntarily.

[43] https://afghanistan.iom.int/press-releases/iom-transit-center-pakistan-border-expands-cope-influx-afghan-returnees
[44] https://www.tolonews.com/afghanistan/pakistan-allows-afghan-refugees-stay-another-year

Afghan Girl At the Day Care Centre, Jalalabad, Nangarhar, Afghanistan

Some mentioned that they just wanted to return home while others said that the police in Pakistan would unnecessarily trouble them, which compelled them to return to their own country. They belonged to some of the worst conflict-affected districts in the province such as Achin, Khogyani and Shinwar. All of them fled to Pakistan due to everyday brutalities committed against the local population either by the Taliban or the Islamic State. Hamid Khalili, from Khogyani, said anxiously, 'Due to the presence of the Islamic State in my village, I cannot go home. I will have to stay with my family at the day care centre till the situation normalizes.'[45]

After our visit to the Torkham border, the medical facility, a local hospital and the IOM Transit Centre at the border

---

[45] Name changed.

for the Afghan returnees from Pakistan, we headed towards the NGO office. It was already evening when we reached. The NGO Director asked, 'So how was your trip to Torkham border?' I narrated the entire experience to him.

As Ahmad and I got up to leave, the Director reached for the drawer and took out a pistol. He caught me looking bewildered and quickly said, 'The situation in Nangarhar is tense. It is quite dangerous to move about. Suicide bombings and armed attacks are a part of our lives. Each day when I leave for work in the morning, I do not know if I will return home safely. I am a doctor but, unfortunately, I am compelled to carry a gun.'

BEIRUT, LEBANON: 'WE WOULD SLEEP IN THE CAR DUE TO FEAR OF BULLETS LANDING INSIDE THE ROOM'

During the war in Lebanon (1975–1990), political parties and organizations developed into militias and Beirut's neighbourhoods transformed into recruiting grounds. The Green Line of Damascus Road, which began downtown near the waterfront and extended southward, divided Beirut into a mostly Muslim west and a mostly Christian east.[46] Kristin V. Monroe in her article 'The Insecure City: Space, Power, and Mobility in Beirut' notes, 'During the protracted conflict, everyday life was subject to the episodic fighting that erupted among the militias.'

Monroe describes the militarization of space in Beirut:

---

[46] Kristin V. Monroe, 'The Insecure City: Space, Power, and Mobility in Beirut', *Anthropology Faculty Book Gallery* (Lexington, KY: University of Kentucky, 2016).

Both the public and private built environments were shaped by daily fighting in Beirut and acquired new geopolitical meanings. Exterior walls of buildings became the protective cover for residents trying to stay out of the line of sight of snipers, and inside these buildings metal vault-like security doors were affixed over the doorways to the apartments. During the war's worst phases, life became entirely insular, as residents left the streets for the safety of the interior.[47]

In Lebanon, I had a chance to meet a number of people who either grew up during the war or who had lived through the war. Leila Hamdan was one such individual. During dusk, as I was walking through the streets of Sanayeh in Beirut, I came across a puppy, extremely playful and effervescent, accompanied by a woman. I bent down and smiled as the puppy began to bounce in excitement. Then I looked up at the woman and asked the puppy's name. 'That's Ringo,' the woman responded. We got talking and she introduced herself as Leila, a freelancer, who works for news websites and sometimes does translations for NGOs. 'What about you?' she asked.

I told her that I am researching on ordinary lives in conflict zones and intend to interview people who have lived through the war in Lebanon. 'I would also be visiting Lebanon–Syria border for interviewing the Syrian refugees at the settlements,' I explained. 'Ah! Ok.' looking at me thoughtfully, she continued, 'I grew up during the war; those were difficult times, but I would prefer to go back to the wartime.' Puzzled and curious, I asked her why she feels that way. 'Now the country is so unstable; there is so much corruption; it's a

---

[47] Ibid.

total chaos.' I asked if I could speak to her sometime about her experiences of the war. She agreed. After a few days, we decided to meet at a cafe at Hamra Street. It was a cosy, dimly lit cafe which served Lebanese food and some other cuisines as well. 'Shall we sit outside?' she asked. 'Sure, it is not very cold today so it should be fine,' I responded.

We comfortably seated ourselves in the corner and ordered for coffee and herbal tea. As I sipped the tea, relishing its delightful floral flavours, Leila asked, 'Could you first tell me a little about yourself?' I told her about myself and then asked if she could share her experiences of the war. 'In Lebanon, it was foreign intervention,' she began. 'From a human perspective how do you see war?' I interjected.

'War is devastating. War is misery,' Leila explained. She then went on to talk about militarization of Beirut. She described, how during the war, Beirut was divided into East and West. Almost breathless, she continued, 'When the war started I was little. We were eternally displaced from place to place. I remember once there was a loud explosion very close to our house.' She paused to remember and carried on, 'My mother used to go to the public booth near our house every day to call family members. Once she was at the booth and suddenly there was an explosion. She had, in fact, gone to the booth to talk to my brother in the United States to tell him that we were alright. The moment she went in, there was an explosion.'

Leila looked away and gazing at the street said, 'I am just trying to remember.' 'At night we would frequently sleep in our car at garage in the basement. We could not sleep in the room since the bullets or shells could land inside the room through the windows.' She paused to take a sip from her coffee and then continued, 'We had to be in the shelter most of the time during the night since the militias or armed groups would start shelling at night.'

Then Leila talked about other everyday struggles. She told me that to get bread, they had to stand in a long queue every day. 'Despite the struggles,' Leila said, 'We did not move outside Lebanon, except my brother. Many families went outside the country such as Syria.' She mentioned that her father sent her brother to the United States since he did not want him to get involved in any political party.

'Then he was just 18 years old,' she mentioned, 'I still remember my mother stood at the balcony and her heart was coming out of her body.' Leila's eyes became moist and her voice shuddered. She spoke in a stream of consciousness, her words flowing spontaneously as she reminisced about her life during the war. 'I was 16 when my brother left for the United States. At that time, my father used to work in Kuwait as a pharmacist. He used to come to Lebanon to see us, to check on us.' After a brief pause, she mentioned that when the US marines would bombard them, the shells used to land in the streets and homes of the civilians. 'Everyday there was devastation,' Leila spoke in a guttural voice.

'What about school? Was it irregular?' I asked. 'We did not go to school for two years,' Leila responded. 'Really. Two years?' Astonished I reconfirmed. 'Yes, but there was a programme by the Ministry of Education to complete the curriculum. Later I enrolled in another school which was close to my house,' she replied. 'My mama used to take me to the school every day,' Leila's face appeared tense and her voice sombre as she said, 'We used to go walking to the school. There were times when we would encounter shelling on our way to school. During 1975 or 1976, I did not go to school because of the war. We could not do anything. We couldn't go out and play.'

The tenor of her voice lightened as she continued, 'But our house was big so we could go to the balcony at least.'

'Did you constantly feel scared because of the war or were there phases?' I asked. My voice seemed to drown in the music and chatter from the adjacent table. 'I beg your pardon,' Leila said. 'Did you continually feel scared due to the war or were there phases?' I repeated. 'Ah! Ok. There wasn't constant fear. There were phases of fear. We got used to the war. Also we were little so we got used to it,' she explained. Interestingly, the statement about children adapting easily in general including adjusting to the war situation, was something I heard from people across conflict zones.

'What kind of coping mechanisms did you adopt, if at all, to deal with the war situation?' I asked. 'Coping was basically— just move from place to place. When fighting is intense in one place we would move to another place. This is a kind of coping,' Leila smiled and said, 'As kids we were not sad.' 'Wouldn't you get scared of the bombing, shelling and firing,' I enquired. 'Of course we would get scared. But we got used to it *khalas* (that's all) because it was part of everyday life. It was routine. *Yaane* (meaning) if there was no shelling we felt there was something wrong,' she quipped and continued, 'Many people went to Syria. It was safe and stable there. We weren't *yaane* miserable. Maybe because we were children. Children don't feel the suffering for too long, their memory is short.'

Virtually interrupting Leila's thoughts, I asked hesitantly, 'Can you tell me if there were times when you felt really scared and anxious?' Appearing shaken from her thoughts, she replied, 'The scariest incident was when the Israeli planes hit a building very close to us. And they didn't stop shelling.' Leila closed her eyes and creasing her forehead said, 'Let me try to think, I am trying to recollect.' I told her it is all right if she cannot remember.

After a while Leila said, 'In one incident, my father's cousin lost his wife and daughter in the shelling in Beirut. They were just crossing the street and going to their house. A shell took their lives.' I looked at her, unsure of what to say. Both of us were silent for a few minutes while the music and chatter of the people at the cafe grew louder.

Suddenly Leila said, 'I remember once some men from one of the militias-Amal faction[48] came to occupy one of the floors in our building. I had a fight with them and they wanted to kill me because I confronted them.' 'When was this?' I asked. 'Maybe 1983 or 1984; I was in school that time. Finally they occupied one of the floors, maybe for months or one year,' she explained. I asked her if she has any 'happy memories' of growing up during those tumultuous times. 'Of course yes, regardless of the war, life went on. There were five to six movie theatres. It was better then. Now there is nothing. We would go to the theatre whenever we had the chance or the time,' she responded.

Just when I was replenishing the cup from the teapot, a woman with a dusky complexion adorning a scarlet bindi (a small decorative mark between the eyebrows), entered the area where we were seated. 'Hey, she is Indian I suppose,'

---

[48] The Amal Movement is a Lebanese political party associated with Lebanon's Shia community.

I said in excitement and continued, 'I hardly see any Indians here in Lebanon.' Leila smiled and remarked, 'I don't think so. She is faking it.' 'Faking it? Meaning?' I chuckled. 'Alright. Let's ask her,' Leila suggested. I asked the lady in bindi if she were from India. 'No I am not but I have travelled to India many times. I just love going there,' the lady smiled and said, 'Many people think I am Indian.' After she narrated her experiences of India, Leila mentioned that she herself has visited India a few times. Both of them enthusiastically shared their experiences of their stay in India.

After the lady left, I said to Leila, 'The first day when I met you on the Sanayeh Street I remember you had mentioned that you would like to go back to the wartime. I was extremely puzzled.' 'Why would you say that?' I asked. Leila immediately responded, 'Now it's chaotic; there is no stability.'

'But wasn't there chaos during the war?' I asked. 'Yes there was, but chaos then was organized, now we are fed up.' Still a little puzzled, I mentioned to her, a gentleman from Lebanon told me few days back that wartime was freedom. He said, 'We were free.' 'Do you also feel the same?' Her eyes widened and nodding her head she reiterated what I had just told her. 'Yes. That is it. We were free; I was just searching for the right words. In fact many people my age will tell you the same thing,' she exclaimed.

It was a time of political crisis in Lebanon when I visited the country in January 2019. For around nine months, there was no stable government. Prime Minister Saad al-Hariri sparked a significant political crisis in 2017, when he announced his resignation on a visit to Saudi Arabia in a televised address, mentioning that he feared an assassination attempt. However, two weeks later, he suspended his own resignation after speaking to President Michel Aoun in Lebanon.[49] During my visit to Lebanon in 2019, the country was grappling with severe economic crisis and high unemployment rate; the national debt stood at about 150 per cent of GDP.

'Can you tell me when the war ended, what transition did you see?' 'When the war was declared over or when there was a ceasefire,' Leila said, 'It was the first day after years of war when I could peacefully sleep in my room at night.' She had mentioned earlier during our conversation that she was unable to sleep in her room at night due to the shelling. 'But that day when the war ended, I still remember, I slept in my room peacefully. I was very relaxed,' Leila expressed. Her countenance seemed at ease and her voice elated as if she were re-living those moments. Leila mentioned that in 1990, around the time the war ended, she had taken up her first job at a news agency. 'Even then there were skirmishes sometimes. But more or less things were moving smoothly,' she said, 'I got into a routine. Another routine.'

SIGHTS AND SOUNDS OF MILITARIZATION

Quite often people who live in conflict zones are inundated with sights and sounds of militarization or militarized violence. The sight of security forces with guns, pools of blood, charred bodies, ramshackle vehicles, buildings blown to pieces, sounds of gunfire and bombings become commonplace or are a frequent occurrence in conflict settings. Saba Khan, a student from Idgah, Kashmir, spoke to me movingly about everyday militarization in the valley. Referring to the security forces,

---

[49] https://www.bbc.com/news/world-middle-east-47080597

she said, 'When I was a child, the sound of the boots and the uniform were symbols of horror to me.'[50]

Similarly, Muzamil Maqbool, a Developmental Practitioner, from Srinagar, Kashmir, poignantly said, 'Few years back I stopped going out of the house, after a while I realised it was depression. How it all began? I had been watching videos of encounters by the security forces where young boys who had turned to militancy were killed.' 'Every other day there would be news of attacks and firing in the valley, I was petrified of stepping outside. The sight of the security forces in the civilian areas makes one feel, things are not normal,' he paused and wearily continued, 'I was trying hard to get out of the valley, out of my home. My home did not feel safe anymore. Then I got a job with the UN in Cox's Bazar, where I felt safe.'

As J. Martin Daughtry in his book, *Listening to War: Sound, Music, Trauma, and Survival in Wartime Iraq* rightly notes, 'armed violence, through its sensory and affective intensity, brings injury to a far larger population than those whose bodies are penetrated by flying metal'.[51] Militarization of everyday or militarized violence often cripples 'normal' functioning of a society, yet ironically sights and sounds which symbolize militarization may become normalized.

During my trip to Afghanistan (2017–2018) when I visited a gurdwara (Sikhs' place of worship) in Kabul, one of the members at the gurdwara quipped, 'Suicide attacks now seem like firecrackers.' 'There are times when the outside world may be aware of the bombing through the media, but the

---

[50] Name changed.
[51] J. Martin Daughtry, *Listening to War: Sound, Music, Trauma, and Survival in Wartime Iraq* (Oxford: Oxford University Press, 2015).

locals who are in a different location in Kabul may not even hear about it,' he explained.

In another instance, in January 2019, during my visit to Lebanon, I met Sabrina, a Communications Manager in Beirut, who grew up during the war in Lebanon (1975–1990).[52] She narrated to me some of her childhood experiences. 'There were times when, as children, we danced to the sound of gun shots,' she smiled, 'We were so used to them.'

Around the same time, I spoke to a number of Syrians in Beirut; near the Lebanon–Syria border at Masna crossing; and at the settlements in Tripoli in North Lebanon, around 100 km from Homs in Syria. They narrated gruesome tales of militarized violence in the Syrian cities of Homs, Raqqah and Idlib. However, one personal experience, which stood out, was an interaction with the Syrian children in Beirut, which exemplifies how frequent sights and sounds of violence may slowly become normalized.

One winter night, walking through the streets of Hamra in Beirut, I came across three children, one boy (possibly 5 or 6 years old) and two girls (both between 7 and 9 years of age) who asked me if I could get them something to eat or drink. I stopped and asked in Arabic, '*hal ant min Suria?* (Are you from Syria?).' They smiled and quickly nodded their heads. I looked around and spotted a juice shop. 'Would you like to have juice with me?' I asked. Excited, they accompanied me to the shop. In my broken Arabic and through gestures, I asked, '*Mama baba?* (Where are your father and mother?), *Ayn tuskan?* (Where do you stay?).'

---

[52] Name changed.

One of the girls with a vacant expression said, '*Baba maut* (Father is dead)' and something else as well in Arabic which I could not decipher. One of the words I could catch was '*Al harb*' which means war in Arabic. As I turned to offer them juice, I saw the same boy, pretend to hold a gun and mimic the sound of gun fire. Suddenly he covered his face with his hands and appeared to sob. Baffled and concerned, I approached the little boy and asked him, '*hal ant bakhyar? (are you alright?)*' He looked up at me and chuckled. As he mimicked the sound of the gunfire again and cackled, the two girls accompanying him moved and danced playfully.

Frequent violence in conflict zones, protracted conflicts in particular, may slowly become normalized. Most conflicts today are prolonged or protracted, wherein militarized violence has increasingly penetrated civilian spaces; and the boundaries between the realm of combat and civilian life have collapsed. People in these regions seem to live in a twilight zone where everyday life of violence and despair is juxtaposed with everyday routines of people, and even celebrations.

CHAPTER 4

FOOTPRINTS AND AFTERMATH THROUGHOUT GENERATIONS

It was December 2019; around 10 in the morning, I left for Ukhia, a small town in Bangladesh's Cox's Bazar district and now a home to many Rohingya refugees who reside in the world's largest refugee camp, Kutupalong. After crossing the beaches of Himchori and Inani, the CNG, the auto in Bangladesh, traversed through the dusty roads, intermittently lined with tall palm trees. It was more than an hour drive to Ukhia from the city of Cox's Bazar.

I asked the driver to take me to the Kutupalong camp in Ukhia. 'Yes this—Rohingya camp,' he said in broken English. 'Are you sure? I cannot see the signboard. Please stop the auto and ask someone.' I said agitatedly. As he stopped the vehicle, a lean man with a long flowing beard said, '*Kya mein apki madad kar sakta hoon?* (Can I help you?).' Excited to have finally found someone who spoke Hindi, I asked him about the Rohingya camp. '*Yehi hai* (This is the camp).' I introduced myself and asked if I could interact with a few Rohingyas. 'My name is Nafeez. I am also Rohingya. I stay in this camp,' he explained in fluent Hindi.

Rohingya Children playing in Kutupalong Camp, Ukhia, Cox's Bazaar, Bangladesh

Later, he asked if I want to visit a local NGO field office where he could introduce me to some more Rohingyas. I agreed. As we navigated through the dusty lanes of the crowded Kutupalong camp, I saw some children peeping through their shelter, others trotting across a barren field and some even had their faces painted with *thanaka*, a yellowish-white paste made with ground bark. Suddenly, Nafeez lifted his hand and pointed towards a signboard, and said, '*Yeh dekhiye, yehi Kutupalong hai* (look, this is Kutupalong).'

As we reached the NGO field office, Nafeez introduced me to more Rohingyas; some of them even spoke Hindi. The one, standing next to a table overlooking the window, introduced himself as Zonun in English. He mentioned that besides his native language, he also speaks English and Hindi.

'I am from Toung Bazaar village of Buthidaung in the Arakan (Rakhine state) in Myanmar and currently residing in Camp 1 of Kutupalong,' said Zonun with a smile.[1] A senior police officer from community policing of Rohingya had told me that there are 27 camps for Rohingya refugees at Kutupalong.

When I asked Zonun whether he was studying or working in Myanmar, he said that he had completed high school. I enquired about his family. 'My mother is here with me in this camp. I have four sisters and one brother. While my sisters reside in another camp, my brother is currently working in Yangon,' Zonun explained.

'When did you come here?' I asked.

'My mother and I left the village on Friday, just few days before 25 August 2017—the Rohingya genocide day.' 'This is before the Burmese military began burning houses in our village. *Mera basti bhi jala diya* (My colony was also burnt). So we left for another colony in Toung Bazaar but soon had to flee from there as well.'

Nafeez who had brought me to the local NGO's field office began to browse through his phone and showed me some photographs and videos of their journey through the mountains of Myanmar into the territory of Bangladesh. People in large numbers, young and old, women, children and elderly, were seen traversing through the arduous terrain of Myanmar's jungles, some even carrying children and elderly on their backs. The next photograph showed mutilated and burned corpses of Rohingyas. Then a video of a Rohingya

---

[1] During the 1990s, the Myanmar military junta changed the name of the Arakan state to Rakhine state, which reflected the dominance of the Rakhine people in the region. The Rakhine people who constitute the majority in the Rakhine state are predominantly Theravada Buddhists.

being thrashed by the Myanmar security forces as several other Rohingyas lay prostrate with their hands tied behind their backs.

The next photograph was even more dreadful and indescribable. The moment I looked at it, I politely told them that I couldn't see those pictures anymore. Appalled and upset with what I had just seen, I became still. The entire hall got silent for a few minutes. Interrupting the silence, Zonun said, 'Please control yourself. *Humko toh ab in sab ki aadat ho gayi hai* (We are used to all this now).' *'Hum log ek kapada tak nahi laye* (We did not bring even a single pair of clothes). We came almost empty-handed, with just some biscuits and nuts to survive through our journey to Bangladesh,' Zonun explained.

'How many people left with you for Bangladesh?' I asked.

'Around 5,000 of us. It took us 15 days to reach here,' Zonun responded. 'During my journey to Bangladesh, I came across a corpse of someone I knew from my village,' he recalled and continued, 'His wife resides in this camp. Sadly, her one-year-old child passed away last year.' After a brief pause, I asked, 'Did you ever had any personal encounter with the military?'

'I never had any personal experience with the military but few days before we left our colony in Toung Bazaar, I saw them burn villages and shoot randomly.'

'Do you know anything about Arakan Rohingya Salvation Army (ARSA)?' I asked.

'There is no ARSA,' he quickly responded. Saeed, a Rohingya, sitting across the table jumped in, 'Burmese (Myanmar) military calls everyone ARSA.'[2] Naseem, another Rohingya sitting

---

[2] In 1989, the military junta changed the name of the country from Burma to Myanmar.

next to me reiterated in Hindi, '*ARSA kuch hai hi nahi. Military sab Rohingya Muslim ko ARSA kahti hai* (There is no ARSA. The military calls all the Rohingya Muslims ARSA).'

'Alright,' I said and queried, 'I heard from state officials that Rohingya are not allowed to move out of the camp and are also prohibited from working in Bangladesh. Is that right?'

'Yes, we are not allowed to work. But few months back I was volunteering with a US-based organization within the camp and would receive some stipend. I worked with them for two years. Soon the Government of Bangladesh banned the organization. I don't work anymore,' Zonun responded.

'What about the basic amenities—food, water and healthcare?' I asked. 'Each month the World Food Programme (WFP) provides us (me and my mother) 30 kg of rice, 1 litre oil and some nuts.' 'We are just two of us here, but large families receive more. Another project provides gas,' he said.

'And the medical facilities? Are there any organizations within the camp which provide medical aid?' I enquired.

'Basic medical healthcare is free in the camp. There is Médecins Sans Frontières (MSF) and other NGOs which offer healthcare services.' 'For serious medical cases which cannot be treated in the camp, we need permission by the Camp In charge to refer the case outside,' Zonun answered.

'What are the facilities for education inside the camp? One senior state official had told me Rohingya children cannot enrol themselves in schools in Bangladesh,' I mentioned. 'Organizations like BRAC, United Nations Children's Fund (UNICEF) and Mukti provide education within the camp. But it is just informal education,' Zonun explained.

Mohammad Salam, a Rohingya from Maungdaw in the Rakhine state, was the next person with whom I interacted. Salam, who was residing in Camp 7 of Kutupalong, mentioned he was in class 9th when he had to flee in 2017. 'I have six brothers and one sister. One brother works in Malaysia in a hotel,' he said. I asked him about his parents to which he responded, 'My father is a farmer and mother housewife.'

'What made you flee Myanmar?' I queried.

'I decided to leave home because the military began burning villages. I reached Bangladesh on 26 August 2017 along with around 7,000 people. My entire family is here. Initially, we stayed in no man's land between Bangladesh and Myanmar for a few months. We made our own shelter,' he explained in a feeble tone.

'Do you work inside the camp? What about your food and other basic amenities? Do you get enough food from WFP?' I asked.

'Yes I am volunteering with BRAC. My work is related to side management. I receive some stipend as well. Since my family is large, we get kgs of rice and 3 litres of oil and some nuts as well,' Salam responded and mentioned that he would have to leave urgently.

Next was Nur Islam, a Rohingya from Yimmakyaung Toung in the Rakhine state, who spoke to me about his journey to Bangladesh. '*Mein Hindi mein zyada comfortable hoon* (I would be more comfortable to talk in Hindi),' he mentioned. 'Were you studying in Myanmar?' I asked in Hindi.

'I was in class 9th,' he said.

'When did you come to Bangladesh?' I queried.

'I came here in 2017 along with my mother and father. We were around 10,000 of us who fled the village,' Nur Islam responded while also adding, 'We did not carry anything along, except some food for our journey.' He also mentioned that his father died sometime back in the camp because of asthma and few months ago he got married due to his mother's ill health.

I asked him what made him flee home. 'Because of the military. They used to trouble us and also extort money.'

'How long did it take you to reach Bangladesh and where did you first stay in the country?' I queried.

'12 days. We stayed at No Man's Land (between Bangladesh and Myanmar),' Nur Islam said in a helpless tone. He mentioned that they had made their own shelter and after spending a few months at the No Man's Land, they shifted to Camp 1 where I met him.

Do you work inside the camp? I queried.

'For over two years, I have been working with Relief International in the child protection group,' he responded.

'Would you want to go back to your village?' I asked.

'Yes of course, if the Myanmar government is willing to respect our human rights.'

As I finished interacting with Nur Islam, Zonun asked, 'Would you like to visit my place? I will make you meet my mother.'

'Sure,' I said. While Nur Islam, Nafeez, and others left for some work, Zonun and I set off for his place.

We walked past some shops run by Rohingya, through the narrow lanes criss-crossing towards a rickety bridge surrounded by thick palm trees. A group of children, boys and girls, trotted across the bridge, their chatter filling the air. A young girl, her face painted with *thanaka*, smiled at me. Soon all the children began waving at us, some running in circles, as their laughter glistened against the gloomy backdrop of the camp. I stopped to interact with these children, some of whom accompanied us halfway through Zonun's shelter. As we reached his place, he introduced me to his mother who said something in Bengali. 'She is asking you to eat lunch,' Zonun translated. 'Thank you so much. But we have to go to other camps as well,' I responded.

Soon we left to visit a few more camps in Kutupalong. Dusty and crowded, the camps sprawled across the hills, housing over 600,000 Rohingyas. As we walked through the camps, I saw two young girls peeping out of the bamboo and tarpaulin shelter, young boys and men gathered around the shops run by Rohingyas, and children playing near a small pond, their laughter echoing through the dusty field. It was almost 4 in the evening and I had to leave before it got dark. Zonun accompanied me to my vehicle and soon I left for Cox's Bazar.

In 2019, Human Rights Watch reported that over 730,000 Rohingya residing in Myanmar have fled to neighbouring Bangladesh 'since the military campaign of ethnic cleansing began in August 2017. The government denied extensive evidence of atrocities, refused to allow independent investigators access to Rakhine State, and punished local journalists for

Rohingya in Kutupalong Camp, Ukhia, Cox's Bazaar, Bangladesh

reporting on military abuses'.[3] The Rohingya, who numbered around one million in Myanmar at the beginning of 2017, is one of the ethnic minorities in the country, majority of whom had been living in the Rakhine state.[4] While Myanmar is predominantly a Buddhist country, most of the Rohingya population is Muslim and the rest is Hindu.

The violent military campaign has been reported to have begun after the events of 25 August 2017, when fighters from ARSA which states its aims are to 'defend, salvage and protect' the Rohingya against state (Myanmar) repression, carried

---

[3] https://www.hrw.org/world-report/2019/country-chapters/burma
[4] https://www.bbc.com/news/world-asia-41566561

out a series of attacks on 30 Myanmar security posts. ARSA is led by Atta Ullah, a Rohingya Muslim, born in Karachi, Pakistan to a Rohingya migrant family, which fled Myanmar sometime in the 1960s.[5] While ARSA says it is fighting on behalf of the Rohingya people, who have been denied basic rights, the Myanmar authorities view the group as a Muslim 'terrorist' organization wanting to impose Islamic rule.

Also known as Harakah al-Yaqin, ARSA rose to prominence in October 2016 after launching similar, although smaller-scale, attacks 'on border police posts in northern Rakhine State, prompting a disproportionate military response also amounting to crimes against humanity'.

The group was reportedly established ensuing the violence between Buddhist and Muslim communities in Rakhine State in 2012.[6] In 2016, International Crisis Group reported, the insurgent group is led by 'a committee of Rohingya émigrés in Saudi Arabia and is commanded on the ground by Rohingya with international training and experience in modern guerrilla war tactics'.[7]

The 25 August attacks by the insurgent group prompted 'an unlawful and grossly disproportionate campaign of violence by Myanmar's security forces', Amnesty International reported.[8] Human Rights Watch noted that Rohingyas who fled to

---

[5] Christine C. Fair, 'Arakan Rohingya Salvation Army: Not the Jihadis You Might Expect', *Lawfare* (2018), https://www.lawfareblog.com/arakan-rohingya-salvation-army-not-jihadis-you-might-expect
[6] https://www.amnesty.org/en/latest/news/2018/05/myanmar-new-evidence-reveals-rohingya-armed-group-massacred-scores-in-rakhine-state/#_ftn6
[7] https://www.crisisgroup.org/asia/south-east-asia/myanmar/283-myanmar-new-muslim-insurgency-rakhine-state
[8] Amnesty International, 'Myanmar: New Evidence Reveals Rohingya Armed Group Massacred Scores in Rakhine State', https://www.amnesty.org/en/latest/news/2018/05/myanmar-new-evidence-reveals-rohingya-armed-group-massacred-scores-in-rakhine-state/

Bangladesh in 2018 reported ongoing abuses by Myanmar security forces, including killings, enforced disappearances, arson, extortion, lack of food and healthcare, and severe restrictions on movement. They also reported sexual abuse and abductions of girls and women in villages and at checkpoints along the route to neighbouring Bangladesh. Returnees to Myanmar faced torture and arrest by state authorities. The organization also stated that over 4,500 Rohingya remained caught in the 'no-man's land', of Myanmar–Bangladesh border subjected to harassment by the officials of Myanmar and regular threats through loudspeaker to induce them to cross over to Bangladesh.[9]

The Rohingya, who say they are descendants of Arab traders and other groups, have for decades experienced systematic discrimination by the government of Myanmar. The government denies the Rohingya citizenship and views them as illegal immigrants from Bangladesh. Rohingya were even excluded from the 2014 census. Referring to the military campaign of ethnic cleansing against the Rohingya in August 2017, Amnesty International observed, 'these crimes and violations reached a peak, with unlawful killings, rapes, and burning of villages on a large scale', prompting the majority of the Rohingya population to flee Myanmar.[10]

As stated by the UN (2019) report, Myanmar's military, referred as the Tatmadaw, revealed its genocidal intent against the Rohingya population:

> Through the widespread and systematic killing of women and girls, the systematic selection of women and girls of reproductive ages for rape, attacks on

---

[9] https://www.hrw.org/world-report/2019/country-chapters/burma
[10] Amnesty International, 'Myanmar'.

pregnant women and on babies, the mutilation and other injuries to their reproductive organs, the physical branding of their bodies by bite marks on their cheeks, neck, breast and thigh, and so severely injuring victims that they may be unable to have sexual intercourse with their husbands or to conceive and leaving them concerned that they would no longer be able to have children.[11]

Shall I say 'most reported assaults?' were directed at girls and women who were beaten, slashed with knives, burned with cigarettes, raped and held as sexual slaves on military bases. The cases of forced nudity, rape and the sexual torture of men and boys were also documented. The UN report further stated, 'Extreme physical violence, the openness in which it is conducted ... reflects a widespread culture of tolerance towards humiliation and the deliberate infliction of severe physical and mental pain or suffering on civilians.'[12]

On 27 December 2019, just one day before my visit to the Rohingya Muslim refugee camps where Zonun, Nafeez, Nur Islam and others spoke of their ordeals and the brutality of Myanmar military campaign, I visited a Rohingya Hindu camp at Ukhia, where 475 Rohingya were reported to be living.[13] Shishupal, a barber from Chikanchori village at Mungdaw township, Arakan or Rakhine state, told me that he, his wife and his four-year-old child fled Myanmar along with some 600 Hindus in August 2017. Some of the Hindus have returned to Myanmar. When I asked him what made

---

11 United Nations, 'UN Fact-finding Mission on Myanmar Calls for Justice for Victims of Sexual and Gender-based Violence' (2019), https://www.ohchr.org/EN/NewsEvents/Pages/DisplayNews.aspx?NewsID=24907&LangID=E
12 Ibid.
13 Unlike the Rohingya Muslims, the Hindus have the green card citizenship which is meant for 'naturalized citizens', essentially immigrants.

Rohingya in Kutupalong Camp, Ukhia, Cox's Bazaar, Bangladesh

him flee, he said that ARSA had encircled their village and did not allow Rohingya Hindus to step out of their homes for a couple of days.

'From three villages of Arakan (Chikanchori, Ballibazar and Balukali), Rohingya Hindus had to flee because of ARSA,' Shishupal explained in Hindi. According to him, all Rohingya Muslims of these villages began to support ARSA. 'Why do you think this happened?' I asked.

'Rohingya Muslims felt that we (Rohingya Hindus) were supporting the Myanmar government.' However, Shishupal was quick to add, 'Prior to 2017, Hindu–Muslim Rohingyas would live together as brothers.' The person standing on my right, referring to Rohingya Muslims added, '*Baaki log bhi ARSA hogaye* (other people also turned ARSA).' Another person mentioned that ARSA militants attacked Rohingya Hindus with guns and swords and that is why they had to flee.

Next, I interacted with Bonawala, a middle-aged woman from Chicanchori village whose husband is a priest. 'What made you flee?' I asked in Hindi. 'She speaks Bengali,' Shishupal interjected. He repeated in Bengali what I had just asked her. Bonawala said something, which I could partially decipher.

'She says it was because of ARSA. She fled Myanmar in 2017 along with her husband and four children to escape the brutality of the militant group,' Shishupal translated in Hindi. He continued, 'She is saying that ARSA had encircled Chicanchori for eight days and the people were unable to step out to even buy food and other essentials. After eight days, a Rohingya Muslim from her village intimated her husband of an impending attack by ARSA. She also says they don't have any personal rivalry with ARSA. She does not understand why they did this?'[14]

Upon my enquiry, they told me that it had taken them three days to reach here. Through the mountains and the jungles, they had reached the Naf river dividing Myanmar and Bangladesh. They hadn't even carried food with them. After my further prodding, I got to know that on reaching Bangladesh, they had stayed with a Bangladeshi Hindu family in Kutupalong for first few months and in 2018, they had shifted to this camp.

---

[14] ARSA has categorically denied killing the Hindus. It has been reported that the Rohingya Hindus have changed their statements on who attacked them, initially blaming the army and the Rakhine Buddhists.

Amnesty International, after conducting a detailed investigation inside Rakhine State, observed that a Rohingya armed group brandishing swords and guns is responsible for 'at least one, and potentially a second, massacre of up to 99 Hindu women, men, and children as well as additional unlawful killings and abductions of Hindu villagers in August 2017'. Based on dozens of interviews conducted in the Rakhine State and in Bangladesh, as well as photographic evidence analysed by forensic pathologists, the organization concluded how ARSA militants sowed fear among Hindus as well as other ethnic communities with these ruthless attacks.[15]

According to Amnesty International, while some Rohingya Muslim villagers participated in the attacks by ARSA, the overwhelming majority did not. It further stated that ARSA's horrendous attacks 'were followed by the Myanmar military's ethnic cleansing campaign against the Rohingya population as a whole'. Amnesty International concluded, 'Both must be condemned—human rights violations or abuses by one side never justify abuses or violations by the other.'

CIVILIANS IN CONFLICT

Civilians have always borne the brunt of war ever since its very beginnings. Yet the post-Cold War period witnessed far greater impact on civilians' lives than the earlier times. The end of the Cold War spawned an era of civil wars or intra-state armed conflicts in various parts of the globe. However, even these so-called internal conflicts have regional as well as international dimensions.[16] Parts of Africa, Asia, Latin America, Middle East and Europe are still experiencing

[15] Amnesty International, 'Myanmar'.
[16] Graca Machel, *The Impact of War on Children* (Hyderabad: Orient Blackswan, 2001).

armed conflicts leading to high civilian casualty rates, mostly women and children. Wars today have increasingly penetrated everyday lives of the ordinary people, thrusting them amid all the chaos and misery.

According to the UN report titled *Impact of Armed Conflict on Children*,

> Civilian fatalities in wartime climbed from 5 per cent at the turn of the century, to 15 per cent during World War I, to 65 per cent by the end of World War II, to more than 90 per cent in the wars of the 1990s.[17]

The report further states,

> More and more wars are essentially low-intensity internal conflicts, and they are lasting longer. The days of set-piece battles between professional soldiers facing off in a field far from town are long gone. Today, wars are fought from apartment windows and in the lanes of villages and suburbs, where distinctions between combatant and non-combatant quickly melt away.[18]

Although, in today's conflicts, distinguishing between combatants and non-combatants or perpetrators and victims may be a difficult task, I use the term civilian to refer to ordinary people caught in between the conflict.

Civilians are frequently killed and maimed in targeted or indiscriminate attacks by the warring parties. In some conflicts, as in the case of Rohingya, a certain community may be a deliberate target of attack. Some states and armed groups continue to use indiscriminate weapons such as landmines and

---

[17] https://www.unicef.org/graca/patterns.htm
[18] Ibid.

cluster munitions, which have been prohibited under international law for jeopardizing the lives of civilians. Others, such as Sudan and Syria, have also used chemical weapons.[19]

In today's conflicts, from Afghanistan and Syria to South Sudan, hospitals and schools are deliberately attacked. United Nations Office for the Coordination of Humanitarian Affairs (UNOCHA) states that humanitarian and medical personnel are injured, killed, kidnapped or even prevented from reaching those in need. They are exposed to legal hurdles and even forms of punishment for impartially aiding people who require it to survive.[20] People may be deprived of food, water and other basic amenities. Civilians in some conflicts have also been starved as a deliberate tactic of war. Children are frequently recruited as soldiers by the armed groups and the state forces. Armed groups have also used them as suicide bombers. In several conflicts, rape and sexual violence have been used as a deliberate strategy of armed conflict.

Millions of people have fled their countries due to war, violence and persecution or have been internally displaced, and many continue to be at risk of displacement. In case of Muslim-dominated Kashmir Valley, a large number of Kashmiri Pandits who formed one of the main minorities left the valley in 1990 as militancy mired the region. It has been reported that they were compelled to flee the Kashmir Valley as they were being targeted by the militants groups including Islamic insurgents.[21] Sanjay Tickoo, a Kashmiri Pandit who heads

[19] Amnesty International, 'UN: Catastrophic Failure as Civilians Ravaged by War Violations 70 Years after Geneva Conventions' (2019), https://www.amnesty.org/en/latest/news/2019/05/un-catastrophic-failure-as-civilians-ravaged-by-war-violations-70-years-after-geneva-conventions/
[20] UNOCHA, '5 Ways to Better Protect Civilians in Conflict Zones' (2018), https://www.unocha.org/story/5-ways-better-protect-civilians-conflict-zones
[21] There are activists and writers who say that both Muslims and Pandits who were thought to be close to the ruling establishment or the armed forces were being targeted.

KPSS, an organization that deals with the issues relating to Kashmiri Pandits who continue to live in the valley, told me, 'Pandits were being viewed as Indian agents by the militants. Many left because they felt threatened.' 'However, there were Pandits who after fleeing their homes, temporarily stayed with the Kashmiri Muslim families in the Valley,' he added. 'As the militancy began, detestable slogans against the Pandits blared from the loudspeakers of mosques. There seemed to be a change in attitude towards Hindus which was exploited by politicians on both sides,' he explained.

Once displaced, many refugees may not return home for months, years or even decades as in the extremely poignant case of Kashmiri Pandits. Then there are those such as Rohingyas from the Rakhine state in Myanmar, who may not be able to return home at all. Also known as the stateless people, the government of Myanmar does not recognize them as citizens, therefore, the prospects of them returning to their homeland are rather bleak.

The Rohingya population has experienced decades of statelessness, systematic discrimination, and targeted violence in Myanmar's Rakhine State. Such persecution has compelled them to flee into the territory of Bangladesh for many years, with major spikes ensuing violent attacks in 1978, 1991–1992 and in 2016. However, it was August 2017 that prompted undoubtedly the most rapid and largest refugee inflow into Bangladesh.[22]

Appalling militarized violence, which frequently manifests in killings, torture, rape and sexual abuse is likely to cause severe psychological pain among the ordinary people living

---

[22] UNOCHA, 'Rohingya Refugee Crisis', https://www.unocha.org/rohingya-refugee-crisis

in conflict zones. It may not be easy to separate the physical repercussions of conflict from psychological suffering.

EMOTIONS, WAR STRESS AND TRAUMA

'Growing up in Kashmir has meant living amid curfews, hartals and encounters. For me, It all began with the uprising of 2008 (Amarnath shrine board incident), followed by Asiya and Nelofar rape case in 2009, then the Uprising of 2010 where hundreds of Kashmiri youth were killed,' said Muzamil Maqbool exasperatedly.

'Next it was the hanging of Afzal guru in 2013, followed by floods in 2014 and the Burhan Wani incident in 2016. In 2017, blasts took place, followed by the Pulwama attack in February 2019. Subsequently the autonomy of Jammu and Kashmir was revoked in August 2019 and harsh restrictions and communication blockade were imposed. Now it is the lockdown due to the Coronavirus pandemic.'

Muzamil, who is a Developmental Practitioner, pointed out, 'I feel Kashmiris are always the worst hit in entire India. I have been part of the 2018 survey by Rumi Centre for Global Peace, which observed that 3 in 10 people (mostly women) in Kashmir have PTSD.'

'The prevalence of depression is 63.77 per cent. It is highest among the age group of 15–25 years. Followed by 69.21 per cent in the 26–38 years of age group. Depression is higher in rural areas (89.31%) as compared to urban areas (26.35%). In rural areas the prevalence of depression among females is higher (96.1%) as compared to males (4.99%),' he added.

Referring to heightened emotions and stress, Muzamil said, 'Fear including perceived fear, anxiety and stress are pervasive in Kashmir. If I leave my home at 7:30 pm in the evening to take a stroll, my parents would call me continuously. If I get late and cross the deadline of 9:00 pm, my parents get anxious.'

'I would never risk going outside without an ID due to the presence of the security forces who may ask you to show it any time. I would not even drive late at night. These perceived fears have also prevented me to work in many parts of India. Besides, I also see that hatred towards Muslims or Islamophobia is on the rise in the country,' he added wearily.

Next, he spoke about his struggle with anxiety: 'Although, I train people in Peace Education, Peace Psychology and Life skills, yet I had to visit a counsellor many times due to my constant fears and anxiety. It worked for me; however, there must be scores of young people as well as elderly who do not get any opportunity to visit a psychiatrist or a counsellor.'

Referring to the plight of mental healthcare in Kashmir, Muzamil concluded, 'Despite tremendous increase in the psychiatric illnesses due to the ongoing conflict, unstable security situation, and stressful environment, mental health in Kashmir has been neglected for far too long. I hope that people in the valley are able to live freely without their fears and anxieties.'

> Emotional phenomenon are non-instrumental behaviors and non-instrumental features of behaviors, physiological changes, and evaluative, subject-related experiences, as evoked by external or mental events, and primarily by the significance of such events. An emotion is either an occurrence of phenomena of these three kinds or the inner determinant of such phenomena; the choice will be made later.[23]

[23] Nico H. Frijda, *The Emotions* (Cambridge: Cambridge University Press, 1986).

Emotions often get heightened in situations of armed conflict. People living in conflict zones may experience a range of intense emotions such as constant fear, anxiety and anger due to war stress, which could affect their mental and psychological well-being. The term war stress refers to the multiple stressors that individuals 'are exposed to when they have experienced war, either directly or indirectly'. These stressors can be psychological, biological, chemical, mechanical, social, cultural, economic and so forth, and are often experienced simultaneously, which reflects the intense and complex quality of war stress.[24] Violence, bombings, death, and separation from family are some of the key stressors during situations of armed conflict.

The scientific study of civilian victims of armed conflict is a relatively recent phenomenon in psychology. Most of the early research as well as clinical work on war trauma until the Second World War focused on combatants, barring the holocaust experience. Since the 1970s, psychiatrists, psychologists and sociologists have studied the repercussions of Northern Ireland conflict on civilian lives. Another conflict situation that has been studied intensively in terms of impact on civilians has been the Israeli Yom Kippur War, particularly its impact on children, adolescents and family life. The impact of the Israel–Lebanon war on civilians also generated extensive research and intervention. Since the 1990s, there has been proliferation in research on the psychological impact of armed conflict on ordinary lives.[25] Besides, terms such as war trauma and post-traumatic stress disorder (PTSD) have become popular in the parlance of psychology.

---

[24] Stanley Krippner and Teresa M. McIntyre, *The Psychological Impact of War Trauma on Civilians: An International Perspective* (Westport, CT: Greenwood Publishing Group, 2003).
[25] Ibid.

DEFINING TRAUMA

Salamuttwah explained when I met him in Teknaf, Bangladesh, which shares a border with Myanmar, 'The Myanmar military along with some Buddhist Rakhine people locked us in our house and then burnt it down. Along with my six children and wife, I somehow managed to escape. Around 15,000 of us (Rohingyas) who were also victims of arson, decided to leave for the Bangladesh border.'

Salamuttwah, who was a shopkeeper in Maungdaw, Rakhine state in Myanmar, further said, 'All 15,000 of us left after 25 August 2017. When we reached the border, Bangladesh border guards offered us food and showed us the route to Teknaf. Soon after I came to the Camp 26 of Nayapara along with my family.'

He anxiously expressed, 'We (Rohingyas) have continuously experienced persecution in Myanmar. We have been denied citizenship. There are no opportunities for us in our home country. We witnessed our houses being burnt down. Finally we were compelled to flee our country. All this has left an indelible scar which we still carry with us.'

Extreme suffering or witnessing a 'terrible event' may lead to shock or trauma. The American Psychological Association (APA) defines trauma in the following manner:

> Trauma is an emotional response to a terrible event like an accident, rape or natural disaster. Immediately after the event, shock and denial are typical. Longer term reactions include unpredictable emotions, flashbacks, strained relationships and even physical symptoms like headaches or nausea. While these feelings are normal, some people have difficulty moving on with their lives.[26]

---

[26] American Psychological Association, *Trauma* (2013), http://www.apa.org/topics/trauma/

Allan Young notes that in the 19th century, a new type of painful memory emerged.[27] It was different from the memories of earlier times as 'it originated in a previously unidentified psychological state', termed as 'traumatic', and was 'linked to previously unknown kinds of forgetting', known as 'repression' and 'dissociation'. The new memory is most notable today with reference to a psychiatric malady, Post Traumatic Stress Disorder (PTSD). In 1980, the American Psychiatric Association adopted PTSD as part of its official nosology, and it swiftly attracted the attention of researchers and clinicians throughout the Americas, Britain, Scandinavia, Australia and Israel.[28] PTSD has been described as an anxiety disorder characterized in part by such phenomena as flashbacks, intrusive memories, numbing of effect, memory and attentional impairment, adjustment difficulties and hyperalertness.[29]

The term war trauma implies 'the effects of war as an extreme stressor that threatens human existence', acting upon an individual or a group of people. At an individual level, this may involve physical or psychosocial consequences, such as the inability to speak to or relate to other individuals. The terms battle fatigue, shell shock and PTSD have been used 'to describe the aftereffects of war trauma'. At a collective level, war trauma includes all the health, political, economic, social and cultural consequences of war stress.

The terms such as war trauma and PTSD have come to dominate the discourse on psychological impact of war. However, psychologists and psychiatrists have often engaged in a debate

---

[27] Allen Young, *The Harmony of Illusions: Inventing Post-traumatic Stress Disorder* (Princeton, NJ: Princeton University Press, 1995).
[28] Ibid.
[29] C. M. Chemtob, H. L. Roitblat, R. S. Hamada, J. G. Carlson, and C. T. Twentyman, 'A Cognitive Action Theory of Post-traumatic Stress Disorder', *Journal of Anxiety Disorders* 2, no. 3: 253–275.

over the universality of such terms and other trauma-related disorders. There are those who attempt to 'validate PTSD as a universal and cross-culturally valid psychopathological response to traumatic distress' which may be ameliorated or even cured with (Western) clinical and psychosocial therapeutic measures. On the contrary, others assert that the Western discourse on trauma is relevant only in the context of a specific cultural and moral framework and, hence, becomes problematic in the context of other social and cultural settings.[30]

Whether or not, the prolonged or chronic stress experienced by individuals living in conflict zones can be characterized as war trauma, PTSD or other trauma-related disorders, it may be argued that conflict-induced stress or prolonged stress may have a long-lasting negative impact on the psychological well-being of people. Further, not all who experience war stress go on to develop severe psychological disorders. In fact, various sociocultural, environmental and psychosocial factors play an instrumental role in aggravating or alleviating the impact of war stress on individuals.

Those who experience direct impact of war or are exposed to violence are more likely to be affected psychologically. This is reflected below in the case of Roshan Lal from the Indian side of the India-Pakistan border, whose leg was severely injured during firing and shelling from across the border. However, individuals may react differently to even similar situations in conflict zones and the capacity to cope may vary from individual to individual. This is contingent on the individual's environment, the intensity, duration and abruptness of the

[30] Hanna Kienzler, 'Debating War-trauma and Post-traumatic Stress Disorder (PTSD) in an Interdisciplinary Arena', *Social Science and Medicine* 67 (2008): 218–227.

conflict-related experience, family and community support and the individual's disposition or psychobiological makeup.

FEAR AND ANXIETY IN CONFLICT ZONES

The word 'fear' relates to such words as Old English 'fear', Old High German *fara* and Old Norse *far*, all of which imply danger or its consequences.

Oxford Dictionary notes that fear is 'an unpleasant emotion caused by the threat of danger, pain, or harm'. According to *Cambridge Dictionary*, fear is 'an unpleasant emotion or thought that you have when you are frightened or worried by something dangerous, painful, or bad that is happening or might happen'. Fear is also described as 'a primary emotion evoked by impending danger and accompanied by the wish to flee'. It is 'sometimes defined as "objective" anxiety'. On the other hand, 'anxiety is sometimes defined as irrational fear.'[31] As per Oxford Dictionary, anxiety is 'a feeling of worry, nervousness, or unease about something with an uncertain outcome'. The word 'anxiety' is etymologically connected to Latin *angor* (tightness of the chest) and *angustus* (narrow) and therefore signifies a manifestation of the emotion.[32]

Michael E. Kerr makes a distinction between acute and chronic anxiety. He notes,

> Acute anxiety generally occurs in a response to a real threat and is experienced as being of limited duration. People usually adapt to acute anxiety fairly successfully. Chronic anxiety generally occurs in

---

[31] Hanna Kienzler, 'Debating War-trauma and Post-traumatic Stress Disorder (PTSD) in an Interdisciplinary Arena', *Social Science and Medicine* 67 (2008): 218–227.
[32] Paul Hodiamont, 'How Normal Are Anxiety and Fear?' *The International Journal of Social Psychiatry* 37, no. 1 (1991): 43–50.

response to imagined threats and is experienced as having no end in sight. Chronic anxiety often strains or exceeds people's ability to adapt. Acute anxiety is fed by fear of what is, chronic anxiety is fed by the fear of what might be. While there are learned or inborn elements in both acutely and chronically anxious responses, learning plays a more important role in chronic anxiety. While everyone experiences acute and chronic anxiety, the difference between people in the amount of chronic anxiety they experience seems to be based primarily on learned responses.[33]

Like 'chronic anxiety often strains or exceeds people's ability to adapt', a prolonged experience of fear contributes to several observed effects. For instance, fear sensitizes attention to threatening cues, gives priority to processing information regarding potential threats, extends associative networks of information regarding threats, leads to overestimation of dangers and threats, aids the selective retrieval of information about fear, raises expectations of threat and danger, and augments accessibility of procedural knowledge which was 'effective in coping with threatening situations in the past'.[34]

During my interaction with the people in conflict zones, fear and anxiety due to unstable security situations, violent attacks, suicide bombings and militarized violence emerged as the primary emotions experienced by them. In Afghanistan, while some locals told me that they no longer fear frequent violent attacks and suicide bombings and are used to them,

---

[33] http://ftp.columbia.edu/itc/hs/nursing/m4050/baker/8571Su03/Kerr.pdf
[34] Daniel Bar-Tal, 'Why Does Fear Override Hope in Societies Engulfed by Intractable Conflict, as It Does in the Israeli Society?' *Political Psychology* 22, no. 3 (2001): 601–627.

many mentioned that they lived in a constant state of fear and anxiety.

In May 2012, while conducting research in the militarized Maoist-affected district of Malkangiri in Odisha, I sensed a certain degree of fear among the locals when confronted with questions related to the Maoist issue and the presence of security forces in the region. In Malkangiri district, where I visited seven villages in five (Kalimela, Korukonda, Kudumuluguma, Malkangiri and Mathili) of its seven blocks, some local activists pointed out that even the 'discussion' on the Maoist issue could jeopardize the security of the locals.

Reportedly, Maoists have engaged in killings of locals suspecting them of being police informers. I also sensed fear of the security forces among the villagers. Local activists have frequently highlighted cases of innocent civilians being detained by the security forces for being 'Maoist'. In a remote village in Korukonda block, where I was accompanied by a local activist who had been working in that area for over a decade, the local tribals explicitly spoke about human rights violations committed by both the security forces and Maoists.

In Kashmir Valley, many locals (across the nine districts) have spoken to me about their constant battle with anxiety, some of whom also had to seek medical help, due to militarized violence, frequent curfews, bandhs and a challenging security situation. Some Kashmiri Pandits in the downtown area of Habba Kadal, Srinagar shared with me their fears and anxieties of belonging to a minority community in the valley.

Further, in 2015, during my visit to the border villages at the disputed LoC and working IB in J&K, most residents said that the constant threat to their lives, property and belongings due to frequent and indiscriminate firing by Pakistan from across the border contributes to invariable fear and anxiety among them.

Evelin G. Lindner in *Emotion and Conflict: Why It Is Important to Understand How Emotions Affect Conflict and How Conflict Affects Emotions* writes that in 1998, she had interviewed Adam Bixi in Somaliland. Lindner states,

> He described growing up in the Somalian semidesert, learning as a very small boy to be constantly alert, even at night, for dangerous animals and 'enemies' from other clans. He learned to be ready for fight or flight in a matter of seconds, at any time, day or night. Continuous emergency preparedness meant that all other aspects of life had to wait. Emergency trumped everything else. Bixi felt he had not lived life.[35]

This account resonates with the accounts of most villagers I interviewed in August 2015 in seven villages of J&K along LoC and IB between India and Pakistan. At that time, the tension between the two belligerent neighbours culminated in intense firing and shelling from both sides. The worst-affected areas were Balakot, Sabjiyan, Mandi, BG and KG along the LoC in the Poonch district; and Akhnoor, Suchetgarh, RS Pura, Arnia (all these sectors are in Jammu district), Samba district and Kathua district along the IB.

The firing and shelling from both sides along the Indo-Pakistan border poses a constant threat to the lives, belongings and

---

[35] Evelin G. Lindner, 'Emotion and Conflict: Why It Is Important to Understand How Emotions Affect Conflict and How Conflict Affects Emotions', in *The Handbook of Conflict Resolution: Theory and Practice*, eds. Morton Deutsch, Peter T. Coleman, and Eric C. Marcus), 2nd ed. (San Francisco, CA: Jossey-Bass, 2006), 268–93.

livelihood of the residents of the border villages. Many villagers reside in *Kaccha* huts instead of concrete houses, which are more vulnerable to being damaged during the cross-border tensions. Many locals told me that they experience constant fear and anxiety due to the possibility of the splinters of mortar shells landing inside their huts.

In mid-August 2015, during my visit to the Sabjiyan sector of Poonch district along the LoC, an aged woman from Bandi village anxiously said, 'During the recent shelling my relatives were injured and their houses damaged. The shelling also destroyed my maize crop.' 'The government must do something. Where will we go during the shelling?' she asked helplessly.

Due to cross-border firing, scores of people who live in zero-line villages or in proximity to the border are rendered homeless. Many get temporarily displaced until the firing subsides which could mean weeks or even months. Most inhabitants of the border villages depend on agriculture and cannot leave their farms and settle somewhere else permanently.

In the first week of August 2015, when I travelled to Sidherwan in Akhnoor sector, the locals who are mostly farmers recalled that during the Kargil war, from 1999 to 2003, there was no farming in the village. One of them added, 'The entire village was deserted. The villagers mostly took shelter in schools, government buildings and tents in the "safer" areas provided by the state.'

The uncertainty of the security situation along the IB in Jammu and the LoC in Kashmir poses a huge threat not just to the physical and economic security of the border people but psychosocial security as well.

The term 'psychosocial' underscores the close relationship between the psychological and social effects of armed conflict, the one type of effect continually influencing the other. 'Psychological effects' are defined as those experiences that affect emotions, behaviour, thoughts, memory and learning ability and the perception and understanding of a given situation. 'Social effects' are defined as the effects that the various experiences of war (including death, separation, estrangement and other losses) have on people, in that these effects change them and alter their relationships with others. 'Social effects' may also include economic factors. Many individuals and families become destitute because of the material and economic devastation of war, losing their social status and place in their familiar social network.[36]

LIFE ALONG THE BORDER

In August 2015, along with Dinesh, I travelled to the Akhnoor sector of Kashmir. It was a bright day and the clear blue skies appeared to be gazing down at the sprawling fields. We passed through clusters of huts, along a trail dotted with sparse trees, which led us towards Gakhriyal, a village close to the Pakistan border.

As we got off the vehicle, I saw a young woman standing outside her cement hut along with her two children. She gave me a warm smile. Soon a conversation began about the security situation in her village, which has witnessed frequent firing and shelling from across the border. Introducing herself

[36] Cape Town Principles, 'Cape Town Principles and Best Practices' (1997), http://www. unicef.org/emerg/files/Cape_Town_Principles(1).pdf

as Jyoti, she asked us to come inside her house. As we entered, I noticed two partially broken glass windows with multiple cracks. She pulled out two chairs for us in the Veranda and headed towards the kitchen. Soon she returned with ginger tea and some biscuits. After offering us tea she sat next to us, while her children played inside.

'When did your village last witness firing and shelling?' I asked.

'Four days back. Because of the firing, I had gone to my mother's place in another village along with my children. I returned home yesterday,' Jyoti responded in Hindi. She continued in an anxious voice, 'For days, this village saw frequent firing and shelling from across the border. The situation got worse few days back when all night we heard shelling. My children were extremely terrified and the younger one cried all night. Seeing my children horrified, I decided to leave for my mother's village. My husband was also not here with us. I was alone with my children.'

She pointed towards a half-broken glass window, which had multiple cracks and fretfully said, 'Look at this window; it broke that day due to shelling and firing. A shell landed inside our home.' Her voice seemed to shudder as she said, 'We are not safe even in our homes. We do not know what may happen next minute. Firing and shelling from across the border starts any time. Children suffer the most. They begin to cry whenever there is shelling which makes me feel extremely helpless.'

After spending few hours at Jyoti's place, we decided to return to Jammu city. Driving through the meandering lanes, irregularly peppered with olive green bushes, we came across a group of young boys and men near a small shop. As Dinesh stepped out of the vehicle to ask for directions, I started a discussion with the locals on what was it like to be confronted with frequent firing and shelling from across the border. One young boy said in an impassive tone, 'We have to live with it. There is no other way. In this last month, we have seen such intense firing and shelling affecting our daily lives. People and cattle have suffered injuries. Our houses have been damaged. Children have not been able to go to school. We are living in a state of constant fear and anxiety.'

Another added, 'In this village, firing and shelling start any time. It could even start now as we stand talking near this shop.'

Some other locals who were passing by also joined the conversation. As the murmurs of two boys behind us grew louder, one local anxiously said, 'The frequent shelling and firing cause perpetual anxiety and insecurity among us.' Our conversation continued for another half an hour. Soon it began to get dark. As the evening sun dipped below low-hanging clouds and the sky deepened to an ash-grey, we decided to leave for Jammu.

Around 10 AM the next morning, Dinesh and I left for Suchetgarh. It was over an hour drive from the Jammu city. As we reached Flaura village, after parking our vehicle under thick trees, we walked towards a cluster of huts where some locals stood talking. We stopped and asked them about the situation in their village. 'Just two days back, this village saw intense firing,' one of them said. Another, who introduced himself as Neeraj, told us about Roshan Lal whose one leg was severely injured during shelling in 2014. Neeraj agreed to accompany us to Roshan Lal's hut.

We walked past some huts, stray cattle and few locals sauntering across the wide fields. Soon we entered a narrow lane lined with thick trees on both sides, and into an even narrower path leading towards Roshan Lal's hut. Dressed in white pyjamas, Roshan Lal was seated on his bed. After Neeraj introduced us to him, Roshan Lal narrated how he was injured in 2014 when splinters of a mortar shell landed in his hut during cross-border tensions between India and Pakistan.

'I had my leg operated in RS Pura. The government provided me with some compensation,' Roshan Lal said in Hindi. 'There was not much recovery. Therefore, I went to a private hospital in Amritsar and ended up spending over three lakh rupees on my treatment. I had to mortgage my land to pay the hospital bills and some amount was provided by my relatives.' Roshan Lal mentioned that physically he felt much better. Yet the trauma of his leg injury due to cross-border firing and the distress of shelling out huge amount of money for his treatment still persists, and he was still a long way from full recovery.

Many border residents across the seven villages of J&K along the Indo-Pakistan border told me they were unable to sleep at night for the fear of mortar shells landing inside their huts. Sahiba from Jowrafarm at Suchetgarh poignantly said, 'We cannot sleep at night. For past 10 days, this village has seen intense firing and shelling during the night-time. Even when the shelling stops, its sound continues to resonate within our minds.'[37]

EVERYDAY ANXIETY OF AN 'IMPENDING WAR' IN LEBANON

Beirut 2019: After dinner, when I was walking towards my hotel at Hamra Street, I came across a young woman, sitting

---

[37] Name changed.

on the pavement close to a baby in a pram. She looked at me and smiled, her eyes reflecting traces of grief and hope at the same time. '*Min ayn ant?* (Where are you from?)' I asked in Arabic. 'Raqqa in Suria (Syria is Suria in Arabic),' she responded. '*Aeyila, zawj* (family, husband),' I queried. She said something, which I could barely decipher, except *al harb* and la, which mean 'war' and 'no', respectively.

Soon I saw another Syrian woman accompanied by her three children whom I had met near a shop, approaching us. Almost an hour back, when I had stepped out of that shop, two of her daughters possibly between the ages of 6 to 8 years, looked at me in anticipation and asked, '*haleeb* for baby (milk for baby)'. They were asking for milk to feed their little brother.

The young Syrian woman who was seated on the pavement, interrupting my thoughts said, 'Money for *haleeb* (milk)', as she pointed towards her baby in the pram. I went towards the baby who lay peacefully with a bottle in his mouth, which was empty.

The next morning, I visited Sabrina, communications manager in Beirut.[38] Still disturbed by the last night's incident, I spoke to her about the plight of Syrian refugees in her country and the war in Syria, which Lebanon also witnessed few decades back. Visibly perturbed Sabrina said, 'Our country has experienced what Syria is going through now,' and donning a thoughtful expression continued, 'Considering Lebanon's long war and its strategic location—with the country being surrounded by volatile areas or states such as Syria, Palestine, Israel and Iraq, it always feels that the war is at Lebanon's doorstep.'

---

[38] Name changed.

After a brief pause, she said in an uneasy tone, 'Those who can, always have their passports ready, so that they can leave the country in case war breaks out. We Lebanese are always looking for an exit strategy.'

Although the war in Lebanon was declared over in 1991 with the signing of the Taif Agreement, yet many people I met there in 2019, expressed anxiety about an 'impending' or a possible war and uncertainty over the political situation in the country. They mentioned that persistent anxiety led them to always search for an 'exit strategy'—exit from their own country to a 'safer' place or perhaps 'an exit from constant anxiety'.

Anxiety of war may outlive the war itself, in both an individual as well as collective sense. It may even persist long after the war is over, leading to severe psychological disorders among some people.

Physical repercussions of war-killings, deaths, displacement, separation from family, damage to property and belongings and loss of livelihood are intrinsically linked to war's psychological impact on people. The former may trigger a response in an individual's psyche, inimical to her/his well-being in the long run. At the same time, in a conflict zone awash with weapons and militarized violence, ordinary people may eternally sense fear or anxiety, even if there is no personal experience of the conflict-related violence. This may manifest in debilitating psychological problems. Yet, not all individuals living in conflict zones will react similarly to perceived or real threats. Some may exhibit greater levels of war stress induced by intense fear, anxiety or even anger, and even in similar situations, some may be able to cope better than the others.

Despite everyday violence or attacks, most people try to continue with their routine or daily lives, unless schools and universities are closed, there are shutdowns and curfews (like in Kashmir) or they have been displaced from their homes, or the villages and cities are under siege. Some of the statements I have frequently heard by common people living in conflict zones are as follows:

'We are used to the situation.'
'We have no choice but to go on with our lives.'
'We have adapted ourselves.'
'This is our fate. We have to live with it.'
'The situation doesn't worry or scare us anymore.'
'We have now become resilient.'

All these statements exude a sense of fatalism, adaptability and even resilience. Yet, as I have mentioned previously, the same people have also told me how tired they are of the situation, and on other occasions some of them have mentioned about the fears they are confronted with. This reflects that the emotions experienced by these people are in flux depending on their immediate situation and circumstances. In some cases, fear, anxiety or even inexplicable pain lie buried underneath the semblance of adaptability, fatalism and resilience.

Heightened emotions of fear, anxiety and anger may resonate in the psyche of people even if they learn to adapt to everyday or frequent armed violence. As Linda Green notes,

> While it is true that, with repetitiveness and familiarity, people learn to accommodate themselves to terror and fear, low-intensity panic remains in the shadow of waking consciousness. One cannot live in a constant

state of alertness, and so the chaos one feels becomes infused throughout the body. It surfaces frequently in dreams and chronic illness.[39]

Yet, in conflict-affected regions, individuals and communities often improvise or develop ingenious coping mechanisms to deal with negative emotions induced by war stress. Some people I met exhibited a zest for life and remarkable resilience despite constant threat of violent attacks. Life in war zones is a life of contradictions, straddling hope and despair, weakness and strength, and vulnerability and resilience.

---

[39] Linda Green, 'Fear as a way of Life', *Cultural Anthropology* 9, no. 2 (1994): 135–178.

CHAPTER 5

CHILDREN OF WAR

Barren and nearly deserted, the streets were tense. The air was thick with rumours. As we stood talking along the pavement of one of the main streets in Tral, known as the hotbed of militancy in Kashmir, Umar, who was possibly in his late 20s, ardently said in Urdu, '*Humko ab maut ka bhi khauf nahi hai* (We are no longer scared of death now).'[1] He was referring to his willingness to sacrifice his life for the freedom of Kashmir.

It was 1 August 2019, and all sorts of rumours were doing the rounds regarding Article 370 which provided special status to the state of J&K. Tral was among several other places in South Kashmir I visited along with Sana, a local from Srinagar, just before the abrogation of Article 370 on 5 August.[2] Some of the other places were Noorpora, Pulwama, Dadsara and Nawdal. During my interactions with the young boys in South Kashmir, many mentioned that they no longer fear the security forces. Some, like Umar, even said that they were prepared to sacrifice their lives for Kashmir's freedom. The reaction of Umar and some other boys in South Kashmir to the turmoil in Kashmir was in stark contrast to that of

---

[1] Name changed.
[2] Name changed.

Sana's cousin, Amir, from Padgampura who was in his early 20s.[3]

It was 2 August, the day the Government of India issued an advisory for all tourists including the Amarnath pilgrims to leave the Kashmir Valley, citing a terrorist threat from across the border. Sana and I had just returned from Pulwama to her cousin's (Amir) place in Padgampura and found Amir's parents glued to television in anticipation of updates on the situation in Kashmir.

'What will happen to Kashmir? Will the Article 370 be abrogated?' Ayesha, Sana's aunt asked anxiously in half Urdu and half Kashmiri.[4] 'We heard some rumours in Pulwama. Can't say anything,' Sana responded in Kashmiri.

Zubair, Sana's uncle continued to browse different news channels.[5] As Ayesha went into the kitchen to get some tea for us, Sana, Zubair and I entered into a conversation on what could be the next big announcements by the Government of India. Amir and Ayesha soon joined us. Our discussion on Article 370 continued over dinner as well.

After dinner, Sana, Amir and I went to the living room to watch the news. While Sana browsed through her phone, Amir and I began a discussion on the turmoil in Kashmir. After a while, I asked him about his views on the situation and if he ever had any personal encounter with the security forces. 'Yes. I did. It was quite an excruciating experience,' Amir responded as his face turned pale.

---

[3] Name changed.
[4] Name changed.
[5] Name changed.

'Over a year ago when I was going towards Awantipora for some work in the evening, the security forces stopped me and asked for my ID. I showed it to them. They refused to give it back and said that I should take it from their camp the next day.' 'I visited their camp the next evening, yet they refused to return it on the pretext of suspicion. They asked me which militant organization do I belong to? My father had to intervene and somehow I was able to get my ID back.' He took a deep breath as he looked at his phone and said, 'After that day, I started to avoid going out. It has been over a year and I mostly stay at home. I have stopped meeting my friends too.' All the while as he narrated this incident, his eyes revealed a sense of fear mixed with sadness.

After a brief silence, Amir said, 'Few months back I would go for my computer classes every day in Awantipora but I have stopped going there too.' 'Why is that?' I asked. 'Although I would leave quite early for the class, I was always late due to the military convoy.' 'When a military convoy is on the road, all the public vehicles have to stop to let the convoy pass. Therefore, I decided not to continue with the classes,' he said as he looked down at the floor. He paused for a while and with a half-smile flickering on his face, carried on, 'Every few hundred metres, you find security forces; once you step out of home, you may be stopped, interrogated and asked for an ID. From the crack of dawn until night, we have to live with the presence of the security forces.' He paused to catch a breath and said, 'From the time we leave home and step into the streets, the market, other public areas, we are surrounded by the forces.'

Each time a question would arise in my mind, I would hold myself back to avoid interrupting Amir, his thoughts and emotions that seemed to flow effortlessly. It was already

10:00 PM. Zubair, Amir's father who had just come out of his room reminded me that I had to leave early in the morning. As I bent down to pick up my phone and spectacles from the table, Amir said, 'Thank you very much for listening to me patiently.' I looked at him hesitantly, not knowing how to respond.

Over a month after my conversation with Amir, I happened to meet Asif (early 20s), a rap artist from the downtown area of Srinagar.[6] By that time, Article 370 had been scrapped and the valley was in a state of lockdown. Rishab, a Kashmiri Pandit from Habba Kadal, had introduced me to him along with his other musician friends at their music studio in Srinagar. Since the caretaker had to close the studio by 6 that evening, we

Image 5.1

Lockdown, Post Abrogation of 370, Habbal Kadal, Srinagar, Kashmir

---

6 Name changed.

decided to meet at Habba Kadal in the downtown area the next day. Rishab said he would pick me up at 2:00 PM from the Residency road, which was quite close to my hotel. I reached the Residency road well in time. At 2:20 PM, I saw Rishab walking towards me with his two friends, Sami and Asif.

'Situation is tense in the downtown area. Perhaps we should just sit somewhere here and talk,' Rishab said frantically. We decided to sit by the Jhelum near the footbridge. It was a mildly warm afternoon of endless blue skies and soft breeze gently swaying the trees. As the Chinar leaves seem to fall rhythmically in the muddy park, I sat talking to Rishab on his work and his thoughts on the situation in Kashmir. It seemed like a perfect day, but for an imperfect time-the entire valley was in a state of lockdown. Next, Asif began to talk about music and his experiences of the turmoil in Kashmir. 'My grandfather was a poet. He would write in Persian. He inspired me to only speak the truth. He would often narrate a lot of stories on the militancy in Kashmir.' 'I was in 5th standard when, inspired by him, I wrote these couplets on the situation in the valley':

Walvantam mikhanich khan cha khabra dil panun
behlava khudaya ndwitnam ne ijasat zuw panun
muklava (aaj aa kisi mekhane ki khabar de jisse
main apna dil behlaunga. Allah ne iski ijajat nahin di
khudko khudi maarneki).

'I am trying to convey—never harm anyone, not even your-self,' he explained in Urdu. From poetry, to music, our conversation shifted to his personal encounter with the security forces and the police. As Sami and Rishab stood by the bench, Asif told me how he was detained and interrogated by the security forces and J&K Police a few times.

'The first incident took place when I was in the 8th standard. It was a winter evening when I was going towards Harwan. The Special Task Force (STF) stopped me.' Asif described how one of members of the STF screamed, '*Arre tujhko kab se dhoond rahe hai hum, tu wahi hai na jisne kuch din pehle petrol bomb maara tha* (We have been looking for you for so many days, aren't you the one who had thrown a petrol bomb at us?).'

He looked up at the clear blue sky and said, 'I still remember it was Arfa that day (a day before Eid).' He paused and continued, 'I told them I haven't come this side towards Harwan in a long time. They refused to believe me and took me to the police station. For hours, I was interrogated, thrashed and beaten up by the J&K police.' 'I even wrote a rap song on the entire incident. It was called *ghamand* (arrogance) exemplifying the arrogance of the police officers.'

'After sometime my father turned up at the police station,' Asif said. 'How did he get to know that you were at the police station?' I asked. 'When I was stopped at Harwan, there was another friend behind me on the bike who was not questioned by the STF. He informed my father.' 'After speaking to me about the incident, my father had a long conversation with the police and I was finally let off,' he explained.

'The next time when I was detained by the police I was in the 12th standard. It was Arfa again.' 'Ever since I have stopped going out on Arfa,' he said with a playful half-grin on his face. Sami, Rishab and I began to cackle. 'At that time I used to work as a salesman in a shop at Nowhatta. When I was taken to the police station, a constable checked my clothes and found one cigarette in my pocket.' 'The constable asked *tu piyega ya main pi loon?* (Would you like to smoke or shall I take it?),' he added humorously. '*Aap pi jiye* (You have it please),' I told him. Next, Asif described the sequence of events, which followed his detention: After a while, the SHO entered the police station and headed towards his cabin. Just after few minutes, I and another boy who had also been detained the same day were called inside SHO's cabin. The SHO was seated in his room and staring into his laptop. Both of us kept standing as the SHO continued to watch something. The boy who stood next to me tried to peep into his laptop, which of course irked the SHO. He told me *beta tu bethja* (child you sit down), and looking at the other boy said, *aur tu, tu khada rahe* (and you, you keep standing). After that, SHO showed us the pictures he had been looking at on his laptop, and pointing towards an overweight boy who had his half face covered with a scarf asked—isn't this you?

'I have always been as lanky and skinny as I am right now. How could it be me?' Asif looked at me as his face grimaced. Sami, Rishab and I began to laugh again. 'Thankfully the SHO's driver who had just entered his cabin recognized me and whispered in his ear. He mentioned that he has seen me as a salesman at a shop in Nowhatta,' Asif said with a sigh of relief and continued, 'The SHO turned towards the other boy and said, "*Par tu toh hai pathharbaj* (but you are a stone pelter)." He asked his driver to first cut his long hair short. The boy pleaded and said that he has been growing his hair for his wedding. However, the SHO refused to listen to him. Then he looked at me and said, "*Beta tu jaa* (Child you can leave)."'

After the narration of his encounters with the STF and the police, Asif mentioned, 'Having been detained and interrogated twice and even thrashed once by the police, I no longer fear the police or the security forces.' 'At the same time, despite these experiences, I have never resorted to stone pelting and I want to make a career in music,' Asif said. Rishab intervened, 'I have known him for a long time, he has never been involved in any violent activity including stone pelting despite being detained or interrogated two or three times.'

Even while describing some of the poignant moments of his life, in contrast to Amir, Asif kept the entire narration light, every now and then adding some humour to it. He had also mentioned during our conversation that the first time he was beaten up by the police, he was filled with fear and had even cried a lot. However, the next time he was detained, he no longer had the same kind of fear.

During my visit to Kashmir in 2019, just over two months after the Pulwama attack in which 40 CRPF personnel were killed, I interacted with hundreds of children and youth across the Kashmir Valley on how they view and cope with the conflict in Kashmir; there was no uniform response. While most of the youth expressed anger against the policies of the Indian State, heavy militarization in particular, and many asserted that they no longer fear the pellet guns and bullets and will fight relentlessly for a free Kashmir, some even expressed fear. At the same time, a number of them spoke about their battle with anxiety.

There were some who mentioned that they never had any unpleasant encounter with the security forces. Sahil, who is originally from Sopore, was among one of them. When I met him in Srinagar few days after the abrogation of Article 370, he said, 'I have never been harassed by the security forces. They have always just asked for my ID.' Sahil, an 11th standard student, also spoke about his father who was killed by the militants.

He explained, 'My father was an SHO when he was killed by militants 13 years ago. At that time, he was posted in Pampore. I was really young then but I got to know later that the militants attacked him when he had gone to buy sheep on Arfa (a day before Eid). He had been attacked several times before but somehow he always escaped.'

'I was in LKG and my sister was just few months old. I went into depression for a long time. It was a very difficult time for us. My mother who is a medical practitioner in a government dispensary in Srinagar has brought us up with great difficulty.'[7]

Zainab from Srinagar, who works in a salon, also told me that she has never had any unpleasant experience with the security forces. 'In fact, I feel bad to see them standing all day in heavy uniforms, far away from their homes.'[8] Some young Kashmiris, particularly in the cities, also told me, while they have not had any bad experience with the forces, they have heard other people talking about their unpleasant encounters.

Further, few young people, both boys and girls, were reluctant to talk about militancy and abrogation of 370. While some Kashmiri Pandits in Habba Kadal, Srinagar, comfortably shared their views, few seemed to hesitate when I asked them about militancy and revocation of Kashmir's autonomy. Like the Pandits, some young people from the minority Sikh community were unwilling to talk to me about these issues, others unflinchingly shared their views. None of the Pandits and Sikhs I met supported Azaadi of Kashmir. Besides, all the

---

[7] Name changed.
[8] Name changed.

Pandits I interacted with in the Valley were against the revocation of Kashmir's autonomy arguing that Article 370 reflected Kashmir's separate identity. As far as Sikhs are concerned, while some supported abrogation of Article 370 for various reasons, others felt Article 370 meant a separate Kashmiri identity. Mannat, who was pursuing Masters in Public Administration when I interacted with him in June 2020, said he supports the abrogation of Article 370. 'Now there will be more employment opportunities,' he remarked. During my visit to Tral in early 2020, the hotbed of militancy in the valley, I met Randeep, a young boy from the minority Sikh community. Randeep, who is from Basantpora village, refused to talk about militancy and the abrogation of 370. 'I cannot respond to your questions. You will go, but I have to live here,' he said.[9]

During an armed conflict that consumes immeasurable lives, children and youth are among the worst affected. The wanton violence usurps the spaces for normal life and their peaceful existence. Besides physical hazards, children and youth may experience lasting psychosocial damage. War or conflict is likely to evoke different emotions among them, which may affect their overall well-being in the long run. Emotions may range from fear, horror, anxiety and rage to even amusement and excitement. The cases of Amir, Asif and others discussed above reflect that not all young people will react and respond to the conflict situation in the same manner.

Similarly, not each one of them would exhibit the same kind of resilience, some may be more resilient to suffering and pain than the others. In conflict zones, while there may be a sense of collective suffering or even collective fear among certain communities, however, the usage of the term 'collective' also

---

[9] Name changed.

entails a risk of overlooking the nuances of how different individuals may react differently to a similar situation or what can be described as 'an individual's unique reality'.

DEFINING CHILDHOOD, ADOLESCENCE AND YOUTH

CHILDHOOD

The United Nations Convention on the Rights of the Child (UNCRC), a universal legal device, defines a child as every person who is below 18 years of age 'unless, under the law applicable to the child', majority is reached earlier.[10] Proponents of cultural relativism have raised criticism against this definition, maintaining that childhood is a relative concept that changes according to local culture, historical time, socio-economic conditions and geographical environment.[11]

Barbara A. Hanawalt argues that the second half of the 20th century witnessed greater interest in the idea of childhood and its history. Several factors influenced the historical study of childhood. The popularity of Freudian psychoanalysis and Jean Piaget's study of child development played a huge role.[12] In Piaget's theory, child development has a specific structure that consists of a series of predetermined stages, leading towards the ultimate achievement of logical competence, that is, from the immaturity of a child towards adult rationality. Within such a theoretical design, children are marginalized

---

[10] UNCRC, 'United Nations Convention on the Rights of the Child' (1989), http://www.un.org/documents/ga/res (accessed on 11 March 2009).
[11] Afua Twum-Danso, 'The Political Child', in *Invisible Stakeholders: The Impact of Children on War*, ed. Angela McIntyre (Pretoria: Institute for Security Studies, 2004).
[12] Barbara A. Hanawalt, 'Medievalists and the Study of Childhood', *Speculum* 77, no. 2 (April 2002): 440–460.

persons 'waiting temporal passage, through the acquisition of cognitive skill', into the social landscape of adults.[13]

Phillipe Aries's *Centuries of Childhood* triggered a debate on the historical development of the notion of childhood. Aries notes,

> In medieval society, the idea of childhood did not exist; this is not to suggest that children were neglected, forsaken or despised. The idea of childhood is not to be confused with affection for children: it corresponds to an awareness of the particular nature of childhood, that particular nature which distinguishes the child from the adult, even the young adult. In medieval society this awareness was lacking.[14]

Although Aries was not the first historian to propose a radical critique of the concepts of childhood, his work had a strong influence on the social sciences.[15] Aries argues that it was only between the 15th and 18th centuries that the notion of childhood emerged in Europe.[16] On the contrary, Barabara A. Hanawalt argues, in medieval and renaissance art, artefact and dress, the phase of childhood was discernible from the stages of adolescence and adulthood.[17]

Like Aries, John Holt states that institutions such as childhood, motherhood, home, family, as we know them, are essentially

---

[13] Alan Prout and Allison James, 'A New Paradigm for the Sociology of Childhood/ Provenance, Promise and Problems', in *Constructing and Reconstructing Childhood: Contemporary Issues in the Sociological Study of Childhood*, eds. Allison James and Alan Prout (London: Routledge Falmer, 2003).
[14] Phillipe Aries, *Centuries of Childhood: A Social History of Family Life*, trans. Robert Baldick (New York, NY: Vintage Books/Random House, 1962), 128.
[15] Alan Prout and Allison James, 'A New Paradigm for the Sociology of Childhood'.
[16] Ibid.
[17] Barbara A. Hanawalt, 'The Child in the Middle Ages and the Renaissance', in *Beyond the Century of the Child: Cultural History and Developmental Psychology*, eds. Willem Koops and Michael Zuckerman (Philadelphia: University of Pennsylvania Press, 2003).

recent and local inventions, and not some universal part of the human condition.[18] Neil Postman argues, 'Childhood is a social artifact, not a biological category.... The idea of childhood is one of the great inventions of renaissance, perhaps its most humane one.'[19]

Many thinkers have argued that these 'new ideas' soon extended to the rest of the world through colonialism and globalization and were finally standardized in International Law. Despite different conceptions of childhood among diverse cultures and societies, a universal definition of childhood has been adopted by the international community. According to Alcinda Honwana, by traditionally representing 'the image of the dependent child and the potential victim, International Law has failed' to view childhood as ahistorical and social construction.[20] Further, it is important to acknowledge that even if common standards of childhood have been adopted by the international community and have found their way into the international treaties on child rights, in practice many non-western countries, especially African states continue to hold traditional concepts of childhood.[21]

ADOLESCENCE AND YOUTH

World Health Organization (WHO) defines adolescents as persons in the 10–19 year age group and 'youth' as the 15–24 year age group. These two intersecting age groups are

[18] John Holt, *Escape from Childhood* (Bhopal: Eklavya, 1974), 12.
[19] Neil Postman, 'The Disappearance of Childhood', *Childhood Education* 61, no. 4 (1985): 286–293.
[20] Alcinda Honwana, 'Children of War: Understanding War and War Cleansing in Mozambique and Angola', in *Civilians in War*, ed. Simon Chesterman (Colorado: Lynne Rienner Publishers, 2001).
[21] Afua Twum-Danso, 'The Political Child'.

combined in the group 'young people', encompassing the age range 10–24 years.[22] The most frequently used chronological definition of adolescence covers the ages of 10–18, but may incorporate a period of 9–26 years depending on the source.[23]

WHO states,

> Adolescence has been described as the period in life when an individual is no longer a child, but not yet an adult. It is a period in which an individual undergoes enormous physical and psychological changes. In addition, the adolescent experiences changes in social expectations and perceptions. Physical growth and development are accompanied by sexual maturation, often leading to intimate relationships. The individual's capacity for abstract and critical thought also develops, along with a sense of self-awareness when social expectations require emotional maturity.

WHO recognizes that 'adolescence' is a stage rather than a fixed time period in an individual's life. As mentioned above, it is a stage of development on many fronts:

> From the appearance of secondary sex characteristics (puberty) to sexual and reproductive maturity; the development of mental processes and adult identity; and the transition from total socio-economic and emotional dependence to relative independence.

[22] WHO, 'Orientation Programme on Adolescent Health for Health Care Providers' (n.d.), https://www.who.int/maternal_child_adolescent/documents/pdfs/9241591269_op_handout.pdf
[23] Alexa C. Curtis, 'Defining Adolescence', *Journal of Adolescent and Family Health* 7, no. 2 (2015).

It is important to note that adolescents are not a homogeneous group. Their needs vary with their sex, stage of development, life circumstances and the socio-economic conditions of their environment.[24]

As far as the term 'youth' is concerned, the UN Secretariat uses the terms youth and young people interchangeably to imply age 15–24 with 'the understanding that member states and other entities use different definitions'. The UN Secretary-General first referred to the current definition of youth on 1981 International Youth Year in his report to the General Assembly (A/36/215, para. 8 of the annex).[25] However, the Secretary-General also recognized that, besides that statistical definition, the understanding of the term 'youth' varies in different societies across the globe. Several UN entities, instruments as well as regional organizations define youth somewhat differently.[26]

The term adolescence came to be used extensively in the social sciences during the 20th century, ensuing the publication of G. Stanley Hall's two volumes: *Adolescence: Its Psychology and Its Relations to Physiology, Anthropology, Sociology, Sex, Crime, Religion and Education* (1904).[27] According to Stanley Hall, adolescence is a period of heightened 'storm and stress'.

Barbara A. Hanawalt states, 'The use of the term "adolescence" for any period other than the late 19th or 20th century has been much debated.' Phillippe Aries disagreed that the

---

[24] Curtis, 'Defining Adolescence'.
[25] https://www.un.org/esa/socdev/documents/youth/fact-sheets/youth-definition.pdf
[26] Ibid.
[27] Susan Shaefer Davis and Douglas A. Davis, *Adolescence in a Moroccan Town*' (New Brunswick, NJ: Rutgers University Press, 1989).

medieval era had a life phase that could be defined with such a term; others have argued that the term holds a particular, very modern connotation even if Augustine did use the term adolescentia. She argues, literature on the history of adolescence shows that the life stage was defined and well recognized through the Middle Ages and into the modern period. Although, the modern period did not invent adolescence, it did alter the definition. She continues, while cultural change alters the male definitions of adolescence, the medieval and 20th century definition of female adolescence remains closer to biological than social definitions of puberty.[28]

The two stages of adolescence and youth often overlap. Youth is generally viewed as a phase of transition between childhood and adulthood. Historians John Gillis and Michael Mitterauer observe that youth as a category first became significant in the West during the beginning of the 18th century.[29] Erik Erikson depicted the period of youth as a 'psycho-social moratorium' in his 1968 work *Identity: Youth and Crisis* and viewed youth as a transitory stage.[30]

Literature on adolescent and youth cultures has often argued that these categories lack clear definition and may be based on one's social circumstances and cultural position rather than biological age. In this book, I would be using the UNCRC definition to define a child and the WHO definition to define adolescence and youth.

---

[28] Barbara. A. Hanawalt, 'Historical Descriptions and Prescriptions for Adolescence'.
[29] Göran Bolin, 'Themed section introduction Research on youth and youth cultures', *Young: Nordic Journal of Youth Research*, SAGE 2004, Vol 12(3):237–243.
[30] Erik Homburger Erikson, *Identity: Youth and Crisis* (New York, NY: Norton, 1968).

HISTORICAL PERSPECTIVE ON YOUNG PEOPLE IN WAR

Children and youth have always been either directly or indirectly affected by conflict since the beginning of warfare. However, the scale and magnitude of the problem is much greater today than any time in history. Boys and girls have regularly contributed to home front war efforts, armies have recruited very young soldiers for centuries, and wartime experiences have constantly affected the manner in which grownup children of war view themselves and their societies.[31]

There is a large body of literature, which suggests that throughout history, in various cultures and societies, children and youth have participated in combat or military campaigns. However, the question of the degree and the nature of their participation in combat is debatable. David A. Bosworth notes, throughout history, children have been used as soldiers. Biblical narratives seem to reflect a practice known from other times in which children begin military service by carrying out non-combatant roles and, in an apprentice-like system, slowly acquire training and experience to become warriors. For instance, the expression that Goliath is 'a warrior from his youth' implies that Goliath (like other soldiers) began training for combat from a young age.[32]

Afua Twum-Danso notes, in Medieval Europe, 'children' were not merely economic actors, beginning apprenticeships at the age of 12 or even younger; they were active political agents

[31] James Marten and Robert Coles, *Children and War: A Historical Anthology* (New York, NY: New York University Press, 2002).
[32] David A. Bosworth, 'Daid, Jether and Child Soldiers', *Journal for the Study of the Old Testament* 36, no. 2 (2011): 185–197.

too, often initiating uprisings and resistance. She argues that the Children's Crusade of 1212, which began near Cologne, was a peaceful movement of the poor, mostly farm workers and shepherds and was initiated by a 12-year-old boy called Nicholas. He led a crowd of approximately 20,000 children and adults over 700 miles across the Alps to Italy.[33]

Gary Dickson notes, young people, both male and female, were the most visible element in the Children's Crusade. The recognized leaders of this crusade enthusiasm, the French shepherd boy Stephen of Cloyes and the German peasant boy Nicholas of Cologne, were described by the chroniclers as young people or children, in a word, pueri. However, not all who joined the Crusade were youths; soon the Children's Crusade became a mass movement. Dickson writes, 'Elderly folk and entire families, including mothers with babes in arms, found themselves swept up in the collective excitement.'[34]

David Rosen notes, beginning in the Middle Ages, boy soldiers were routinely recruited into the British military, and by the late 19th century, the recruitment of young people became systematic and organized through the efforts of various institutions that emerged during this period. Citing cases from Africa and Latin America, Rosen states, in preindustrial societies, there was no particular, fixed chronological age at which young people joined in the actions, rituals, and dramas of war. Anthropologists have frequently documented cases of children at war in these societies.[35]

[33] Afua Twum-Danso, 'The Political Child'.
[34] Gary Dickson, 'Massacre of the Innocents? Sacral Violence and the Paradox of the Children's Crusade', in *Under Fire: Childhood in the Shadow of War*, eds. Andrea Immel and Elizabeth Goodenough (Detroit, MI: Wayne State University Press, 2008).
[35] David Rosen, *Armies of the Young-Child Soldiers in War and Terrorism* (New Brunswick, NJ: Rutgers University Press, 2005).

Oliver Furley, however, notes that in pre-colonial African societies, it appears that employing children as soldiers was not a common practice. The child passed through various stages in status 'during his growth and adolescence, marked by solemn rites', and did not attain the position of a full-fledged 'warrior' until he was well past childhood. Citing the case of Maasai people in East Africa, Furley asserts that with his throwing stick and a heavy spear, the Maasai warrior was definitely not a child.[36] On the contrary, Susan Shepler argues that for generations in Africa, young men have armed themselves alongside their fathers to protect their villages, just as they herded cattle or tended fields in peacetime.[37]

Further, there is a body of literature that indicates the presence of young people (below 18s) in the American Civil War. Besides, in the beginning of the 20th century, during the First World War, despite official age restrictions on recruitment, young boys reportedly continued to enlist. During the Second World War which began in 1939, the Nazis unleashed terror among the Jewish population of Europe which led to the massacre of around six million Jews. As a result of the Nazi policy towards the Jews, several armed organizations were formed. For instance, groups of Jewish partisans or 'Ghetto Fighters' emerged in the cities of Eastern Europe, and individuals and groups of Jews throughout Europe fled into forests and rural areas where they either formed or joined the partisan forces. According to a study of a thousand

---

[36] Oliver Furley, 'Child Soldiers in Africa', in *Conflict in Africa*, ed. Oliver Furley (London; New York, NY: Tauris Academic Studies, 1995).
[37] Susan Shepler, 'Educated in War: The Rehabilitation of Child Soldiers in Sierra Leone', in *Conflict Resolution and Peace Education in Africa*, ed. Ernest E. Uwazie (Lanham, MD: Lexington Books, 2003).

Jewish soldiers of the Lithuanian division of the partisans, more than one-third of the division's Jewish soldiers were 15 to 20 years old.[38]

Lisa L. Ossian notes, during the Second World War, although children's experiences and perspectives were at variance from their parents, adults never protected them from 'the experiences of the home front but rather encouraged patriotism and a strong work time ethic'. 'Every man, woman, and child would become very much involved in the work of fighting the Second World War.'[39]

CHILDREN AND YOUTH IN THE POST-COLD WAR ERA

Graca Machel in the UN Report (2001) titled *The Impact of War on Children* notes that during the 1990s, over two million children died due to armed conflicts, often intentionally targeted and murdered. Over three times that number were seriously injured or permanently disabled. Machel argues, modern-day conflicts are particularly lethal for children since little or no practical distinction is made between civilians and combatants.[40] The UN states that the majority of casualties in today's wars are women and children. One chronic legacy of contemporary war is blast injury to children from landmines. Such blasts leave children without lower limbs and feet, with blindness, deafness and genital injuries.[41]

---

[38] David Rosen, *Armies of the Young-Child Soldiers in War and Terrorism.*
[39] Lisa L. Ossian, *The Forgotten Generation.*
[40] Machel, *The Impact of War on Children.*
[41] J. Pearn, 'Children and War', *Journal of Paediatrics and Child Health* 39, no. 3 (2003): 166–172.

Machel Study 10-year Strategic Review: Children and Conflict in a Changing World by the UN states that in many conflicts, children and young people are not just bystanders but targets.

Brutalities routinely committed against children in armed conflict pose a huge challenge to International Law, notwithstanding the fact that the international community has created formidable instruments to protect human rights and to prosecute the perpetrators of genocide. However, these treaties remain only as effective as the willingness of States parties and others to uphold them, and many have disregarded their responsibilities and obligations with impunity.[42]

In August 2018, UNOCHA pointed out that a number of long-running wars have witnessed new spikes in the maiming and killing of children in attacks. Warring parties have indiscriminately or deliberately attacked hospitals, schools and essential water infrastructure; used children as human shields; employed children into armed factions and State forces; killed children with chemical weapons; sexually exploited and raped children; and forced them to become suicide bombers.[43]

GROWING UP DURING CONFLICT

Wars may leave lasting scars within the minds of children, and with schools, health services and basic infrastructure destroyed; children are deprived of leading a healthy and normal life. Wars destroy the social fabric often leading to

---

[42] United Nations, *Machel Study 10-year Strategic Review: Children and Conflict in a Changing World.* (New York, NY: UNICEF, 2009).
[43] https://www.unocha.org/story/5-ways-better-protect-civilians-conflict-zones

separation of children from their families and community. Key areas of concern as regards children in conflict include physical safety, disruption of education, militarization of young minds and the psychosocial impact of the conflict.

The disruption of basic services, especially education, and militarization of everyday life may in turn lead to militarization of children and youth. This may manifest in their active involvement in conflict as combatants or the militarization of young minds even though they are not active combatants.

PHYSICAL SAFETY

Armed conflicts have left a large number of people vulnerable to horrendous forms of violence, including systematic rape, sexual exploitation, abduction, amputation, mutilation, forced displacement and genocide. It has been widely observed that the wide availability of inexpensive, light small arms has contributed to the use of children as combatants. The collapse of social protection makes girls vulnerable to unwanted pregnancy and threatens children with orphaning, separation from their families, increased risk of sexually transmitted infections, disability and severe, long-term psychosocial consequences.[44] UNICEF in its campaign 'Children Under Attack' observed:

> The number of countries with violent conflicts is the highest it has been in the last 30 years. One in four children live in countries affected by conflict or disaster. As of early 2018, nearly 31 million children have been forcibly displaced by violence and conflict,

---

[44] https://www.unicef.org/chinese/protection/files/Armed_Conflict.pdf

including 13 million child refugees and more than 17 million inside their own countries. Attacks on children continue unabated. From Afghanistan and the Central African Republic to South Sudan and Syria, warring parties are flouting one of the most basic rules of war: the protection of children.[45]

According to a UN report, 2018 was documented as the worst year for children caught up in armed conflict. The year witnessed the highest numbers maimed or killed since the UN began to monitor the violation. 'In the 20 conflict situations monitored in the 2018 edition of the Annual Report of the Secretary-General on Children and Armed Conflict', over 12,000 children were killed or maimed that year. Children continued to be used in combat in 2018, particularly in Somalia, Syria and Nigeria: approximately 7,000 have been drawn into frontline combat roles around the globe. They also continue to be kidnapped, to be used in hostilities or for sexual violence: over half of the 2,500 reported cases took place in Somalia. Some 933 cases of sexual violence against girls and boys were reported, however, this is considered as an under-estimate, due to stigma, lack of access and fear of reprisals.[46]

During my visit to Afghanistan, Afghanistan–Pakistan border, Kashmir, Lebanon, Lebanon–Syria border, India–Pakistan border along the state of J&K and Sierra Leone, some of the statements I heard frequently by those who grew up during conflict or continue to live amid conflict were: 'We are always worried for our children when they leave for school'; 'Due to

---

[45] UNICEF, *Children under Attack* (n.d.), https://www.unicef.org/children-under-attack
[46] UN, 'New UN Report Shows Record Number of Children Killed and Maimed in Conflict' (2019), https://news.un.org/en/story/2019/07/1043441

the conflict, my mother calls me a number of times in a day till I return home'; and 'Once we leave home we don't know if we will return safely.'

In Kashmir, a number of bystanders including children have been injured in the pellet firing by the security forces to control the protests, which have often turned violent. In 2016, during the protests, which ensued after the killing of Burhan Wani, the Hizbul Mujahideen commander, I visited the SMHS hospital in Srinagar. Yusuf Lone, a 14-year-old from Pattan Palhalan was among eight pellet victims I interviewed at the hospital. In an impassive voice he said, 'I was sitting in an orchard when pellets struck me in one eye.'

He continued, 'The incident took place on 18 August when the security forces opened fire on the crowd in Pattan Palhalan, two other people were also injured.' 'The locals took me to a hospital in Palhalan from where I was shifted to SMHS,' he explained. 'Although I have undergone three surgeries within 10 days, yet I am not able to see anything. I feel there is no improvement. I don't know if I will ever be able to read again?' lamented the 9th standard student.

In 2019, during a discussion on the turmoil in Kashmir at Baramulla College, Aisha, a student of political science anxiously told me, 'Whenever I come to college, my daddy calls me two three times and asks where have I reached—*matlab kucch hua mat* (meaning if everything is alright).'[47] The same year during my visit to Lebanon, Sabrina who grew up during the war in her country, movingly spoke about not just her physical safety during the war, but how anxious she

---

[47] Name changed.

would get as a child when her father was away from home.[48] Reminiscing about her childhood, she said, 'I remember each day I would have to listen to the radio to make sure there was no sniper fire in our area because my dad would come walking from work. Every day I would worry if my dad will arrive safely or not.'

'When I was a child once or twice we had this small rocket coming towards our house but it did not explode,' she paused and then continued, 'But we have heard stories. One of my colleague's grandmother died when a shell landed in their house. So you listen to the stories of young boys and women.' 'My cousin, for example, was held by a militia and couple of other boys I knew, were also kidnapped by other militias. I don't know what happened to them.' I asked her if she experienced constant fear as a child. She quickly responded, 'Yes there was constant fear, but we had parents who feared the most about us. We were children. We did not realize what it really meant. We would just listen to these scary stories.'

EDUCATION HAMPERED

War or conflict often has a huge negative impact on education, which is among the most formative processes in an individual's life. Conflict frequently displaces people, leaving children and youth out of schools and colleges, not merely hindering their cognitive skills and social development, but also affecting their prospects of finding a job in future. In some cases, frequent curfews and shutdowns (like in Kashmir) disrupt regular and formal education.

---

[48] Name changed.

Indiscriminate bombings and attacks may lead to destruction of educational institutions. Besides, parties to an armed conflict have often launched deliberate attacks on schools. A 2019 UN report stated, while attacks on schools and hospitals have declined overall, they have intensified in some conflict situations, such as Afghanistan and Syria. Mali offers the most grim example of children being deprived of access to education as well as the military use of schools: '827 schools in Mali closed at the end of December 2018, denying some 24,400 children access to education.'[49]

Referring to Ukraine, UNICEF noted, students in conflict-hit eastern Ukraine experienced a four-fold increase in attacks on schools during the first four months of the year 2019, compared to the same period in 2018, traumatizing school children and putting them at risk of injury or death. In 2019, between January and April, there were 12 attacks on schools, compared to three incidents during the same period of the previous year.

Henrietta Fore, UNICEF Executive Director observed, 'School children are bearing long-lasting mental and physical scars of eastern Ukraine's conflict.' Fore continued, 'Daily life at school is disrupted by shelling and shootings, forcing children to take cover in school basements and underground bomb shelters. In many cases, children have become too terrified to learn.'[50]

[49] UN, 'New UN Report Shows Record Number of Children Killed and Maimed in Conflict'.
[50] https://www.unicef.org/press-releases/attacks-schools-quadruple-conflict-hit-eastern-ukraine-unicef

KASHMIR: 'STUDENTS ARE THE WORST SUFFERERS'

It was the time of elections and the security situation in South Kashmir, Shopian and Pulwama districts in particular, was quite tense. On 23 May 2019, just when the election results were announced, the Indian army said that Zakir Musa, described as 'India's most wanted' militant, was shot dead after they trapped him in a house in Tral, South Kashmir.[51] Musa was the chief of Ansar Ghazwat-ul-Hind and a close aide of Burhan Wani. In May 2017, Musa split from Hizbul Mujahideen and pledged allegiance to Al Qaeda after he threatened 'to decapitate and hang Hurriyat leaders' and warned against 'calling Kashmir a political dispute but an Islamic one'.[52]

After Zakir Musa's killing, anticipating protests and deterioration of the security situation, the state administration suspended mobile Internet services and imposed a curfew in the region. During that time, I was residing in a hotel in the civil lines area of Srinagar. The day after his killing, during my conversation with the hotel owner, I mentioned to her, 'Last night I woke up to the sound of some people protesting outside and chanting slogans which referred to Zakir Musa.' 'Is the situation tense?' I asked.

'Quite possible, but in this part of the city, it's still alright. In such cases, the situation in the downtown area gets even more tense,' she responded.

'The turmoil in Kashmir terribly affects common people like us. But no one gets as affected as students, they are the worst

---

[51] BBC, 'Zakir Musa: Thousands at Kashmir Militant's Funeral', BBC (2019).
[52] https://www.thehindu.com/news/national/other-states/belying-police-claims-islamic-state-shadow-lengthens-over-kashmir-valley/article24956847.ece

sufferers. Those who are into business can still recover the losses somehow. For college students anywhere else in India, it takes three years to complete graduation, however, here it takes four years due to curfews, shutdowns and erratic security situation,' she explained.

Over one week after Musa's killing, I travelled to Baramulla and Sopore in North Kashmir. During an interaction with the students of Baramulla College on the conflict's impact on education, Hasan, a student at the History Department said, 'Every morning we get late to college since the army stops the movement of public transport to allow its convoy to move first. This is happening on a routine basis. Every day we miss our 10 AM class.'[53]

Sameera, another student at the Medical Science Department added, 'Conflict does not just affect education but it hampers other areas of life as well. For instance, when Burhan Wani was martyred, *yahan par bahut zyada sakhti thi* (there were harsh restrictions here). I was in 12th standard during that time.'

'My family members used to be worried how will I study for my board exams? As another student mentioned earlier, we are not able to make it in time to college due to the army convoy. We leave quite early for our classes, yet due to the convoy we usually miss our first class,' she reiterated.[54]

Saima, another Medical Science student poignantly said, 'To be honest I still cannot understand why there is conflict in Kashmir? Whenever my younger sister asks me—why we cannot go to school today, why was that person killed—I

---

[53] Name changed.
[54] Name changed.

cannot answer those questions. I do not know what to tell her. I cannot understand it myself. That is all I can say.'[55]

Due to the prolonged conflict and consequent curfews and shutdowns in the valley, students have always suffered. The abrogation of Article 370 and the ensuing strict restrictions, which included closure of educational institutions, followed by protests had a huge negative impact on education.

The abrogation took place at a time when the students had their exams in the upcoming months, which were postponed. Most students I met were extremely disappointed by the government's decision to close the educational institutions since they were compelled to sit at home and unable to complete their course for the exams. Although, after a while the Government announced the opening of educational institutions, parents were not willing to send their children to schools due to the communication blockade and tense security situation.

When I met Aisha, a student from Makhdoom Sahib, in February 2020, over six months after the abrogation, she dejectedly said, 'Since the abrogation of 370, we have seen such harsh restrictions. The Internet was snapped for a long time. Now the 2G is working, even that the government keeps snapping.' 'The Internet is very important for our education. I would often study online before the Internet was snapped. Students could not even fill their online forms this time,' she wearily explained.[56] Around the same time, Razia, who works with an NGO in Srinagar, said, 'The younger generation is tired of the curfews and shutdowns which hamper education and prospects for job in the valley.'[57]

---

[55] Name changed.
[56] Name changed.
[57] Name changed.

MILITARIZING YOUNG MINDS

KASHMIR

Security forces in large number lined the closed shops and houses; a group of men, young and old, sat talking outside a closed shop; a sweet vendor seemed to wait endlessly for customers, a few flies were his only visitors. After responding to the question— 'Where am I headed?' —by some security personnel, I made my way through the concertina and came across a park saturated by security personnel. A little girl, possibly 5–6 years of age, who was accompanied by more children, almost all older than her, requested a security person to let them in. He asked her to enter from the other side. When I asked the same security person if the children can enter the park, he said its closed and they would have to walk all the way and get in from the second gate. I bent towards the little girl and asked if I could help her getting inside through the other gate. She looked at me with anxious eyes and said, '*Mujhko inse dar lagta hai* (I am scared of them).' That small group of children soon left and so did I.

It was 14 August 2019. Article 370 had recently been scrapped by the Indian State, and the entire Kashmir Valley was in a state of lockdown. Strict restrictions were in place, downtown area in particular, where I had just met the little girl who was understandably scared of the security personnel clad in heavy uniforms and weapons.

Over two or three weeks after this incident, I visited an area called Khwaja Bazar in the downtown area to meet Humaira.[58] The door was open. As I entered, a young boy,

---

58 Name changed.

Ajaz, Humaira's son, greeted me with a warm smile.[59] I sat on the carpet beside him and asked, 'How is the situation today? Any protests or stone pelting incidents?'

He looked at me with pensive eyes and said, '*Kanjung thode din se kam hai* (Since few days stone pelting incidents have reduced). *Kafi ladkon ko arrest kiya hai* (A lot of young boys have been detained).' His grandfather offered me some tea and cake. As I sipped the tea, Ajaz continued to watch some videos of the slain militants (or Shahid as many Kashmiris call them). After a while, he handed me his phone to show me a video of the Islamic State.

The moment I saw a member of the ISIS slitting the throat of a 'Kafir', I almost jumped and immediately flung the phone on to the floor. In an anxious tone, I said, 'Please do not show me these videos, I would not be able to sleep.'

'You are a coward, aren't you?' Ajaz said in Urdu with a faint grin on his face. 'This is nothing, we have grown up seeing violence, blood and killings. Ask my grandfather.' His grandfather, possibly in his 70s, said something in Kashmiri, which I could partially decipher. Ajaz translated, 'He is saying that all their lives they (Kashmiris) have seen killings, firing, encounters and corpses. In fact, pools of blood spattered on the streets of Kashmir have always been a common sight.'

'We are now immune to all this,' Ajaz exclaimed as he browsed through his phone for some more videos. After a while, his younger brother Ayaan, age 13 years, entered the room and sat next to him.[60] Ajaz pointed towards his younger brother and said, 'You should speak to Ayaan about the conflict in

---

[59] Name changed.
[60] Name changed.

155

Kashmir; *yahaan bacha bacha India se Azaadi chahta hai* (Here every child seeks freedom from the Indian State).' Our conversation revolved around the conflict, Taliban and the Islamic State.

'Why do you have Welcome Taliban and ISIS written on the walls, particularly in the downtown area of Kashmir; what do you know about them?' I asked. Ajaz, still looking at his phone, responded, 'Honestly, I do not know much about them. *Magar jisse Hindustan ko problem hai hum wahi kareinge* (Whatever India has a problem with we will do precisely that) *Hindustan ne yahan jagah jagah fauj rakhe hain* (India has deployed a large number of security forces in the valley).'

I had heard similar statements before from a number of Kashmiri youth. In 2014, when I was teaching at the Kashmir University, some students at the university as well as other youth outside of it, did not seem to have much idea about the Taliban or the ISIS. Some of them had even mentioned that both the outfits are fighting for the rights of Muslims. They did not seem to be aware of the long history of brutalities by both the Taliban and the Islamic State. However, a number of Kashmiri youth I interacted with in different parts of the valley, including the volatile downtown areas of Srinagar, spoke against the brutalities committed by both armed outfits.

After the abrogation of Article 370, I happened to meet Mufeed, a young boy at Gojwara in the downtown area of Srinagar.[61] As we talked about the Taliban and the Islamic State, he mentioned to me about a protest he was part of, few

---

[61] Name changed.

months prior to the abrogation of Article 370. 'There were teenagers who were part of the protest against the Indian State and were raising ISIS flags. We (older boys) asked them not to do it. But they refused to listen to us.' 'They possibly did not even know much about the ISIS,' he explained.

Coming back to Ajaz and Ayaan, Ajaz pointing towards his younger brother said, 'You should speak to him about *Azaadi* (freedom) and the Taliban.' I looked at Ayaan innocuously staring at me.

'Ayaan, do you know who the Taliban are?' I asked. 'They are from Pakistan,' he responded in Urdu. 'What are their objectives?' I further probed. 'They want to establish Islamic *hukumat* (governance) in Kashmir.'

I looked at him curiously and asked, 'Is it a good thing?' 'Yes. It is. *Woh Islami Taalim denge aur Shariat Nafis karenge. Quran ka Nizam banega* (They will impart Islamic education and establish Shariat),' Ayaan responded enthusiastically.

'From where have you learnt about the Taliban?' I queried. 'Our seniors in school'.

Just when Ayaan finished talking about the Taliban, Ajaz handed him the phone, which displayed a violent video of the Islamic State. Ayaan looked at me and insisted, 'You should also watch it.'

'No I will not,' I said adamantly. 'You are a coward, aren't you?' he quipped as he continued to watch the video and simultaneously nibble on the chips.

Although, I have met many young people across the Kashmir Valley, particularly in the downtown area of Srinagar and

South Kashmir, who reflected militarized mindsets, yet it would not be a fair assessment to say that in a situation of armed conflict or war, all the young people will speak the same language of violence or internalize militarized attitudes. Armed violence or militarization of everyday may make young people immune to violence or prone to militarization of the mind. Some may be more prone to it than the others. Even in the volatile downtown area of Srinagar, known for stone pelting by young people against the security forces, children and youth reflected a range of emotions and diverse reactions towards everyday militarization in Kashmir.

LEBANON: 'AS CHILDREN, WE WERE TRYING TO BE INSIDE THE WAR NOT OUTSIDE THE WAR'

At a quiet cafe in Beirut, Zico and I seated ourselves by the window. As he lit a cigarette, I curiously asked, 'Can you describe your first impressions of the war as a child?'

Zico, an architect and a former combatant, quickly responded, 'I was barely 10 years old when the Lebanese war began in 1975. We were always hearing the sound of the fighting. We were hearing the fighting from abroad, *yaane* (meaning), 200 or 300 metres away, not so close to us but we would hear a lot of noise.'

Did this make you feel scared or anxious all the time? I asked. His voice grew strong and confident as he responded, 'No, I was not scared; I never felt scared from the beginning. In fact, I wanted to participate in the war.' Amused, I enquired, 'You wanted to participate in the war?'

He said, 'Yes of course. I grew up in Beirut in Sanayeh. We saw the beginning of war from our balcony. When the war started we stopped going to school. We would play with *kartoosh* (empty bullets), not just me but other kids as well. War intensified after 1982. We were hearing the sound of the fighting.'

He paused briefly and carried on, 'We wanted to participate in the fighting because it was like play. I was not scared at all. We would collect the bullets. I even asked my father to make a pistol for me.'

'You know fighters—they are very cool people, they play with you, they tell you good things because you are their neighbour and they are not criminals. They were fighting for a cause, you understand? We played war all the time. We would try to have weapons. I remember, all the time we were trying to be inside the war, not outside the war. But we were kids during that time. I was barely 10,' he explained donning a faint smile.

'How would you define war?' I asked

Zico responded, 'War is freedom because there is no authority and you are responsible for yourself. Whenever a fighter entered a house, any house, they stole furniture, paintings and other things. We would see this from our balcony. People seemed to be stealing because there was no authority, there was only religious authority, *yaane*, it was up to you to steal or not steal.'

'Do you mean your own conscience?' I queried. 'Yes. That's right. And also there is a reason for everything, for instance, to not go to school,' he said with an impish smile.

'Are you saying that war gave you a reason or an excuse to not go to school?' I asked. 'Yes that's right. Till now we have used war as an excuse for everything,' Zico said. 'I used war as an excuse all the time. During war a lot of people have the opportunity to lead another life because it is very easy to be in a party and sometimes they give you food, *khalas* (that's it).'

'If you don't have your family, you can be part of another family (militia). You can make this choice early during war.' Referring to participation in the militias during war, Zico pointed out, 'Everybody needs you to join them because they need one more, that is why there is a lot of opportunity in working, in being somebody, in having friends; it's very easy, *yaane*, you make friends very easily.'

'Do you remember the longest period when you did not go to school?' I enquired. 'Two to three months,' he responded. As he lit a cigarette and ordered for another cup of coffee, further probed, 'During the war did you leave Lebanon at all?' 'In 1975–1976, we were in Beirut and then left for Syria for some time. My father said he would have to send the kids to study there. We enrolled ourselves in a school in Syria. After sometime we returned to Lebanon,' Zico explained.

'Was there a time when you lost all hope?' I asked. 'No. Because I was a kid and kids don't lose hope.' 'But when you were growing up,' I looked at him curiously. 'No I didn't. All the time I was active during the war. I was fighting in the war,' he said as his eyes sparkled with confidence.

'When did you first fight in the war?' I queried. 'In 1982, when Israel attacked Lebanon. I was carrying weapons, everybody with me would carry weapons. I had weapons to protect myself,' he explained and carried on, 'In 1982, when

I was just 17, along with 12 people, I decided to go to the front. There was a big guy who took all of us there.'

As the cafe began to get noisy and the music grew louder, Zico said, 'We could perhaps meet the next day and continue the conversation.'

While I was unable to meet Zico again, some other locals who grew up during the war in Lebanon also told me when they saw the gun fighting they wanted to participate. Maher, a carpet trader in Beirut shared his stories of war when I met him at Hamra street. With a sense of amusement in his voice, he said, 'I remember during my school days, when one day I saw a fighter standing with his gun on the first floor of the school building, it was scary but also amusing.' 'As we were growing up, we got used to it,' Maher continued.

'You got used to violence?' I hesitantly asked. 'No. Not violence. We got used to the sound of bombs.' Interestingly, a number of people who have lived through the war in Lebanon told me that as children, war sometimes seemed like a game. However, they also shared the frightening side of war. For instance, although Maher talked about his fascination for the gun, he also mentioned that his first impressions of war were death and fear.

YOUNG PEOPLE AS SOLDIERS

In conflict zones, children and youth are vulnerable to abuse, exploitation and recruitment in armed groups or are at risk of getting trapped into a culture of guns and drugs. While young people may voluntary take up arms for various reasons, they are often coerced or even lured by the armed groups and forces into joining them.

Once recruited they spend their early life with armed groups often devoid of education. When the war ceases or these young soldiers disarm, due to stigma families and communities may be reluctant to accept them. As far as girl soldiers are concerned, they are vulnerable to sexual abuse more than boys. It is often challenging for them to reintegrate into civilian life. Sometimes families and communities do not accept them because of their association with armed groups and the stigma of sexual abuse since most are exploited by the commanders or/and other combatants in the group.

SIERRA LEONE: 'I WAS SIX WHEN I WAS ABDUCTED BY A REBEL COMMANDER CALLED RAMBO'

Militarization of young children has been a key feature of almost all armed conflicts and Sierra Leone has been cited as one of the worst examples of this practice. As mentioned previously, a large number of children and youth participated in the conflict in Sierra Leone. RUF, AFRC and the pro-government CDF which included the Kamajors were responsible for recruiting children in their ranks. Zack-Williams states, according to conservative estimates the number of child soldiers who participated on each side of the conflict in Sierra Leone is between 5,000 to 7,000.[62] However, another estimate suggests that the number of child combatants between 1998 and 2002 was 48,000 (Save the Children 2004).[63]

[62] A. B. Zack-Williams, 'Child Soldiers in the Civil War in Sierra Leone', *Review of African Political Economy* 87 (2001): 73–82.
[63] Save the Children, 'Sierra Leone: Country Brief 2004', *Save the Children* (London: Save the Children UK, 2004).

The war in Sierra Leone began in March 1991 and continued in varying intensity throughout the 1990s, and peace was formally declared on 18 January 2002. 'The war has been described as one of the most brutal in the late twentieth century, its level of brutality compared to that of Rwanda or even Cambodia in the 1970s.'[64]

In 2011, during my visit to Sierra Leone, most of over 70 former soldiers (who were particularly former child soldiers) I interviewed in the country (Freetown, Bombali district, Moyamba district and Kono district) said that they were abducted or forcibly recruited. Some children were captured when they were as young as five or six. Rugged, a former girl soldier, wearing a solemn look, described the life during Sierra Leone war.

She spoke of the brutalities committed by the armed groups, the RUF in particular. She explained how gratuitous killings, rapes and amputations defaced and bloodied her mesmeric country, her home; leaving its landscape funereal and turning its turquoise seas and lush forests blood red.

She explained, 'When I was just six, I was captured in the Tonkolili district by a rebel commander from the RUF called RAMBO (he was one of the leading commanders trained by Foday Sankoh).[65] I was frequently gang raped and was made to engage in cleaning and cooking. At the age of seven, I was given a gun and received orders to shoot but I could not pull the trigger.'

Child soldiers in Sierra Leone were used in both combat and non-combat roles. They were used as combatants, cooks,

---

[64] Chris Coulter, *Bush Wives and Girl Soldiers: Women's Lives through War and Peace in Sierra Leone* (Ithaca, NY: Cornell University Press, 2015).
[65] Foday Sankoh was the founder of the rebel group RUF.

servants, porters and spies. During my visit to Makeni (Bombali district), where I interacted with 20 former child soldiers, PLK, an ex-child soldier told me, 'In 2000, I was abducted by the RUF in Makeni. I was just seven. I was forced to carry heavy load from one village to another on foot. I worked as a servant. I did cooking, laundry and cleaning.' In Makeni, another former child soldier named Aminho poignantly said, 'In 1996, the RUF captured me in Makeni. I was just seven. They treated me like a slave. When I was nine they gave me a gun. However, I never killed anyone.'

Some former child soldiers told me that they were forced to kill or amputate their 'enemies'. Alusain Kabia said, 'When I was seventeen I was captured by the RUF in Kono. RUF forced me to kill and amputate people.'

INVISIBLE SCARS OF THE CONFLICT

The exposure to armed conflict or war with its multiple adversities is a significant interference with the development of the child. Yet the plasticity, cognitive immaturity and adaptive capacities of the child have frequently veiled the impact of war in a certain obscurity. There is a controversial and conflicting literature 'debating the existence, frequency and configuration of psychiatric morbidity in children exposed to war'.[66]

The first studies regarding children's attitudes towards war and peace appeared in the 1930s with the development of a Pacifism–Militarism Scale by Droba (1931). He was followed

---

[66] J. A. Shaw and J. J. Harris, 'Children of War and Children at War: Child Victims of Terrorism in Mozambique' (2003), https://www.researchgate.net/profile/Robert_Ursano/publication/233583753_Individual_and_Community_Responses_to_Trauma_and_Disaster_The_Structure_of_Human_Chaos/links/02e7e530e1762077e1000000.pdf

by researchers who analysed this issue during the Second World War[67] and during the Vietnam War.[68]

However, not until the past decades, particularly since the 1992–1995 conflict in Bosnia Herzegovina and the 1994 genocide in Rwanda, there was an upsurge in psychosocial interventions for children in conflict-affected areas. Increasingly, the base assumption was developing that children who experience fighting, killings and turmoil have to suffer from some form of psychological anguish and therefore require, not merely physical rehabilitation (such as food, medical aid, construction of houses and schools), but also mental healthcare and psychosocial support.[69]

Euwema, Graaff, Jager and Kalksma-Van Lith note that in general, two approaches to psychosocial interventions regarding children in war-affected areas have emerged—the curative and the preventative approach.[70] On the one hand, there are interventions from a curative perspective, aiming at psychosocial and psychological treatment of conflict-affected children. The approach is strongly trauma-oriented, aiding children deal with the stressful experiences they may have undergone. On the other hand, the other approach is rather preventative in nature. Instead of focusing on past experiences, preventative interventions address the impact of conflict and its present challenges. They aim towards helping

---

[67] Bender and Frosch (1942); Eliot (1942); Preston (1942).
[68] Cornell (1971); Tolley (1973); https://www.researchgate.net/profile/Gordana_Kuterovac_Jagodic2/publication/235734429_Is_war_a_good_or_a_bad_thing_The_attitudes_of_Croatian_Israeli_and_Palestinian_children_toward_war/links/0912f512f7666deb10000000.pdf
[69] Mathijs Euwema, Donatien de Graaff, Ans de Jager And, Brechtje Kalksma-Van Lith, 'Research with Children in War-affected Areas', in *Research with Children: Perspectives and Practices*, eds. Pia Christensen and Allison James (Abingdon: Taylor and Francis, 2008).
[70] Ibid.

children develop healthily within their social context in order to protect them from future social and mental disorders. Euwema, Graaff, Jager and Kalksma-Van Lith further argue that although 'most programmes are not archetypes but moderate versions, to be found somewhere along a continuum. Many programmes combine elements of both approaches'.[71]

While there are several scientific and systematic studies based on qualitative or quantitative research on psychosocial impact of war on children and youth, this book is primarily based on narrative enquiry and highlights my experiences with the children and youth living in conflict zones. As mentioned previously, it argues not all children or young people will react or respond to conflict similarly. During war, young people may suffer from acute and chronic traumatic stress.

The impact of war on the mental health of children is determined by various psychological, social and environmental factors. These include a child's psychobiological make up or disposition, death and separation or other losses, family and community breakdown, the intensity and duration of the experience, and the child's immediate environment. To heal or recover from the trauma of war, children require family and community support, education, security and a healthy environment.

CONFLICT AND SPECIAL CHILDREN IN KASHMIR: NOTES FROM THE FIELD

Aaqib, a tall, medium-built boy, who stood next to the window, began chanting 'Musa Zakir Musa'.[72] As he continued

---

[71] Ibid.
[72] Name changed.

to raise his one hand and chant the slogans of Azaadi, another boy, Farooq, joined him. While the sound of the slogans grew louder in the brightly lit room, other children (between 5 and 17 years of age) continued to be engaged in their own activities, displaying a range of emotions.[73] One of them placed his hands on his ears as if to curb the sound of slogans. Two children talked to themselves and the one with over-sized spectacles kept flapping his one hand and moving in circles. While another seemed to be immersed in his own thoughts, the one in the corner of the room tirelessly gazed at the ceiling. The one who sat next to the window continued to murmur, another broke into laughter and the one next to her began to weep.

While I looked at Aaqib and Farooq in amazement as they frantically shouted slogans, Hina, one of the counsellors quickly said, 'This is adaptive behaviour,' as she asked the boys to be quiet and maintain discipline in the class.[74]

It was my first day as a volunteer at the Centre for special children in Srinagar, Kashmir. Hina had taken me on a round of the Centre, which had three separate classes termed as mild, moderate and severe. The disorders among the children who were enrolled at the Centre ranged from autism, downs syndrome, Angelman syndrome to mental retardation and cerebral palsy.

Aaqib, 17 years, was diagnosed with severe mental retardation and ADHD. Hina mentioned that he came to the Centre 10 years ago. 'His father who was a daily wage labourer, was killed under unknown circumstances, before he enrolled

---

[73] Name changed.
[74] Name changed.

at the Centre,' she said. I asked if his father's death was related to the conflict in the valley. 'I don't know,' she quickly responded.

'Aaqib comes from economically humble background and was abandoned by his mother after his father's death. He does not have any siblings and stays with his grandmother in Habba Kadal.' She continued, 'He is illiterate and indulges in excessive talking. His behaviour is in fact, quite aggressive and abusive. He is also hyperactive and restless.'

'What about Farooq?' I asked. 'He is 10 years of age and resides with his family in Nowhatta. He was diagnosed with cerebral palsy,' she said. 'He too hails from an economically humble background. That is all the information I have,' she added.

During my interaction with the doctor at the Centre, I asked her if she could explain how the turmoil in Kashmir affects the mental health of these children at the Centre. She noted that while all of these disorders are genetic, the effects of the turmoil can be divided into indirect and direct consequences.

She explained, 'The first is the pre-natal impact. The trouble may begin with the conception. If the mother witnesses a traumatic event or develops trauma due to the conflict, this may negatively affect the foetus and could even lead to mental and physical disability in the child.

Another pre-natal factor is inaccessibility to adequate healthcare experts, medical treatment and shortage or unavailability of medicines during pregnancy due to curfews, shutdowns or hartals.'

'What about the factors which may lead to the deterioration of the child's health, I mean after the birth of the child?' I asked.

The doctor responded, 'Diagnosis can be very late or there could be lack of early intervention. In the urban areas, the situation is still better, but in rural areas due to lack of awareness on mental health and inaccessibility to mental healthcare, it could even be as late as 8–11 years of age. Late intervention may affect the progress or development of the child.'

'Moreover, there are few centres in Kashmir which provide services to such children and very few child neurologists,' she explained.

She also mentioned, how most children at the Centre come from the thickly populated downtown area of Srinagar with narrow lanes, where houses are adjacent to one another. 'During shutdowns and curfews, children are mostly confined to their homes. This may negatively affect their mental health or deteriorate it further,' she added.

I shared with her how Aaqib and Farooq were shouting slogans in the class and asked if the staff at the Centre has witnessed any transformation in their behaviour during the time of protests or when there are shutdowns and curfews for long periods, even months. She immediately said, 'Yes of course, when they return to the Centre after long shut downs, some of them, especially from the severe class, get extremely violent. They begin to throw things and even cause self-harm.' This is something other staff members also shared with me later. One day when Hina was discussing the case histories of children at the Centre, she mentioned that the health of some of them often deteriorates when they return after long shutdowns. She said, 'Whatever progress some of them had made would get negatively affected.'

Hina also mentioned how some children would display adaptive behaviour. She shared the case of Ayaan, 5 years of age, from Rainawari who was diagnosed with downs syndrome.[75] 'Whenever there are protests, he chants Azaadi slogans in the class, but in the bus he chants even more loudly. Perhaps he feels there is no one to check him there,' she smiled. Hina and the doctor had both mentioned how hyperactivity among these children, those with autism and ADHD in particular, usually increases during turmoil in the valley. Both noted that those with autism and ADHD get more hyperactive compared with those with downs syndrome.

While the physical or tangible impact of the armed conflict on children includes death, injury, orphaning, separation from families, destruction of schools or lack of access to education and recruitment in armed militias, the psychological impact may be rather impalpable. Besides, as mentioned previously, not each child or youth, even during a similar situation and under similar circumstances, will react and respond to the conflict in the same manner. Some may be able to adapt or cope better than the others.

Statements I have heard too often by those who grew up in conflict zones are: 'We were children we did not realize what was happening' and 'We were children, and children often adapt easily.' Laila, a freelancer from Beirut who grew up during the war in Lebanon, told me, 'We got used to the war. Also we were little, perhaps that is why we got used to it. We saw it as a game. You get adjusted, you adapt. It's easy for children to adapt I think. It's very easy.' Visiting Syrian refugee

---

[75] Name changed.

Image 5.2

Syrian Boys at a Refugee Settlement, Masna, near Lebanon-Syria Border

camps along the Lebanon–Syria border and Rohingya camps along the Bangladesh–Myanmar border; spending time with children in the downtown area of Srinagar, Kashmir during the peak of turmoil or visiting orphanages in Kabul and Jalalabad, Afghanistan; I found, no matter how dire their situation, most children just wanted to sing and play.

However, spending time with children and youth in different conflict zones, I have seen some children or young people adapting to the conflict situation more easily than the others. I have also come across cases where beneath the veneer of adaptability or indifference to the conflict, lurk anxiety, fear and insecurity due to the prolonged armed violence.

A number of factors may alleviate the negative impact of war on children and young people. These include family and community support; education that is detached from the military interference or influence of the armed groups; various kinds of therapies; access to mental healthcare; community healing mechanisms; finding hope through various means including faith or religion; and coping through humour, art, poetry, music and sports.

As Sabrina[76] who had a strong support system during the war in Lebanon told me, 'My parents decided that we had to leave the country because the schools were closed and the situation was turning quite bad. We fled to France. I feel we were very lucky because we heard ugly stories from our neighbours. We had the chance of going out of the country for two years and returning when it was relatively peaceful.'

Responding to my query on finding hope during the war, Sabrina asserted, 'I am a believer so my only hope is god. I pray a lot. As a child, I learnt to pray because of war. I used to pray every day. I prayed for my parents to be ok, for my country to be ok. I do not trust anyone, the system, our leaders, no one at all. The only entity I trust is my god. I believe that he is holding this country from collapsing and that has always been my belief.'

---

[76] Name changed.

CHAPTER 6

GENDERED VIOLENCE

Nasima spoke hastily in Dari, her words rambled and her face glimmered with a half grin, soon turning melancholic.[1] 'I am afraid of war. I am also afraid of cats and boys. I am not able to get sleep,' she looked away and continued, 'When I was 5 years old, Taliban killed a lot of people in my village. Then I moved to Pakistan with my family. Since then I am afraid of war. Now I am always so worried about the Daesh (Islamic State).' 'Whenever I watch suicide bombings, killings, Taliban and Daesh on television, I am very scared and not able to get sleep at night,' she said fretfully.

Nasima, 22, from Parwan province in Afghanistan, is among the many patients I met at a government mental health hospital in Kabul (100-bed facility, of which 25 beds were for females). It was rather intriguing how I was introduced to Nasima. When I entered the hospital ward with Aisha,[2] one of the staff members, and Ahmad, a local, Nasima, donning a pleasant smile stood talking to other patients in Dari. She turned her gaze towards me and gave a warm smile, which soon faded as she looked at Ahmad.

---

[1] Name changed.
[2] Name changed.

In Dari, she asked Ahmad something, which I could not comprehend clearly. I saw Ahmad visibly baffled and queried, 'Are you alright? What did she just say?' 'She is asking if I am Talib (member of Taliban) or from *Daesh* (Islamic State)?' Ahmad responded. Aisha, one of the staff members who had accompanied us, introduced me to Nasima and said, 'She came here three days ago. She is very talkative but also cries a lot. She gets angry very quickly.' Nasima, seeming extremely jovial, said something in Dari to me. Aisha translated, 'She is asking where are you from?' 'I am from India,' I said and asked Aisha more about Nasima. 'She has completed class 12 and wanted to pursue her studies in psychology but failed her exam. She gets scared easily, especially when she sees boys.'

The next woman I spoke to was Farzana from Ghazni province who had lost her father. It was not clear if her father died in war-induced violence.[3] Dressed in an ash-grey hijab, Farzana glanced at me and then looked away, visibly quite coy. Aisha said, 'She came here just four days back. She has been diagnosed with depression and cannot sleep during the night.' I asked Aisha if she knows more about Farzana's family and her life in Ghazni. 'Not yet,' Aisha replied.

Next, Aisha introduced me to Firoza from Kunduz province who had been diagnosed with schizophrenia.[4] Her face appeared deadpan and her eyes vacant, as she sat quietly in a corner. 'She does not want to talk,' Aisha explained and continued, 'Firoza came to this hospital 13 days back. According to her medical file, she was merely 15 when she was diagnosed with schizophrenia. She developed this mental condition 20 years ago after her father disappeared. She has three

---

[3] Name changed.
[4] Name changed.

brothers and three sisters.' I asked Aisha if Firoza or her family has had any personal experience with the Taliban. She spoke to Firoza for a few minutes in Dari and said, 'In 2017, Taliban attacked her village in Iman Sahib district, Kunduz. However, neither she nor her family had any personal experience with the Taliban.' 'But since this attack, she is extremely scared of the Taliban and constantly worried about the suicide bombings,' Aisha explained.

Like Nasima and Firoza, many women in Afghanistan said they are persistently worried about possible suicide bombings and violence in their country, maybe not with the similar intensity that Nasima did. Nonetheless, they also mentioned that they are 'used to the situation'. In other conflict situations and even in countries, which have experienced protracted conflicts such as Lebanon and are no longer at war, some women told me they fear that their country might relapse into conflict. They mentioned that this was because of Lebanon's strategic location as it is surrounded by volatile neighbours.

In Kashmir, when I spoke to hundreds of girls and women across the valley in 2019 prior to the abrogation of Article 370, at the time when it was abrogated and few months after its abrogation in 2020, their emotions ranged from frustration, anger, fear and anxiety. In all my interactions with girls and women across different conflict and 'post-conflict' zones including Kashmir, there has of course never been any uniform response. Some of them have expressed fear and anxiety towards frequent violence and killings and unstable security situation, while others said they no longer fear living in the midst of conflict or they are used to it. Many in Kashmir expressed anger towards militarization of the valley and policies of the Indian State, and some in places like Aanchar, Soura in Kashmir said they will continue to protest against the policies of the Indian government and support boys and men in stone pelting against the Indian security forces.

Besides, interestingly during my conversations with same females in different situations or circumstances, each one on different occasions has reacted differently—at times expressing fear or anxiety and at other times expressing anger and even indifference towards the unpredictable security situation.

KASHMIR: POST ABROGATION OF ARTICLE 370

It was February 10, over six months after the abrogation of Article 370. The presence of security forces in Srinagar was considerably lower than in the first few months of revocation of Kashmir's autonomy. Vehicles were plying on the road and people were moving about the streets. After walking through the narrow lanes in the downtown area, I reached Khwaja Bazar. I entered Humaira's house who was visibly shocked and happy to see me after four months.[5] She was alone in the house waiting for Zeenat, her daughter to return from tuition classes.[6] She mentioned that Zeenat's cousin sister would also be visiting soon. She spoke about the current situation in the valley, which she explained was relatively better than the past few months when Article 370 had just been abrogated. Mobile services had been resumed and low-speed Internet was available.

'But there is still a lot of anger among the people due to abrogation of Article 370 which most Kashmiris felt was a chord that connected Kashmir with India,' she said in Urdu

---

[5] Name changed.
[6] Name changed.

and added, 'Kashmiri people suffered a lot during these six months after the abrogation, and ordinary people like us have been crippled financially. My daughter's education has also suffered tremendously.'

'Due to the turmoil and the heavy deployment of security forces, I feel,' she paused and soon continued, 'I feel trapped and helpless.' 'I also want to go out and protest, like the boys, to vent out my frustration,' Humaira said hastily, her voice heavy with anger.

'We have lived through such harsh restrictions in these past few months. Mobile and Internet services were snapped. All this happened around *Bada* Eid, our major festival and during the tourist season, the time when we earn so that we can relax during the harsh winters,' her eyes blazed with rage. Now the situation seems to be improving a little. She said as her facial expression somewhat eased, 'My husband is a daily wage labourer. He makes copper utensils. He was not able to earn a single penny when India imposed curfew after revoking Kashmir's special status. After the government lifted curfew, people protested by keeping their shops closed.'

As she was speaking, Ajaz, her son entered.[7] He looked at me and said, 'Where have you been for over four months?' 'I was away for work,' I explained. We briefly spoke about the situation. 'Now there are not much protests happening. A lot of boys have been detained,' he said. 'Are protests not taking place due to the fear of being detained?' I asked. He looked at me, his eyes glaring with conviction and responded, 'We are not scared of anything now. We will continue our struggle against the Indian State.' He stood up and sat next to Humaira.

---

[7] Name changed.

'Although the situation appears to be improving, but now we are exhausted. We feel caged. As a woman, I feel extremely helpless,' Humaira said dejectedly. After a brief silence, I probed, 'While the conflict or turmoil does touch the lives all individuals, yet it affects different groups or people differently—women, children and elderly. In that sense, how do you think turmoil in the valley affect women differently?'

She immediately said, 'I feel due to the heavy presence of security forces, women and girls, more than men, are not able to move about freely.'

'Just few days back, at around 6:30 in the morning, I had gone out to feed the pigeons at the shrine; when I saw a vehicle of the security forces, I got extremely scared. I anxiously turned to return home and sprained my foot. When I step out of home, I always carry the fear of the security forces. What if they detain us or take us for interrogation. These are the fears I have, so I assume all the women and girls must be experiencing similar fears and anxieties.'

When I asked Humaira how she copes with the stress arising out of conflict or turmoil, Ajaz interrupted, 'From the beginning or their early childhood, females are taught to pray and to stay at home. They slowly learn to adapt to the situation.' 'And whoever offers Namaz or prayers is unlikely to be stressed or depressed,' he said. Humaira interjected, 'only those who engage in wrongdoing or do not offer *Namaz* to Allah are likely to be depressed.'

Like Humaira who spoke about her anger against the policies of the Indian State and inability to do anything or protest on the streets to vent her frustration, Aisha, from Makhdoom Sahib also shared how helpless she feels. Aisha, who is a

12th standard student at Khanyar Higher Secondary School, referring to most females in Kashmir said, 'If we are angry with the Indian State, we cannot go out and protest, at least I cannot. Because girls do not go out and protest from my house. In Islam, girls should be in Purdah.'[8]

When I mentioned about girls in different parts of Kashmir, particularly in the downtown area of Aanchar Soura, protesting frequently against India, although not in very large numbers like the boys, Aisha responded, 'Of course there are girls who participate in protests here, but a lot of it depends on your own thinking and atmosphere in the house, but everyone has a right to express himself or herself.' 'Even when I am angry, I am not able to express myself, I cannot protest,' she reiterated as her face grimaced.

Aisha also shared her discomfort with the presence of security forces. 'When I go for tuitions to Hawal, on the way I have to cross Islamia College, where the forces are usually deployed in large numbers. It makes me extremely uneasy.' Similarly, Nargis, a student of Cluster University in Srinagar, who belongs to Handwara in Kupwara district told me, 'Whenever there is heavy deployment of security forces, I feel insecure going out. Boys can still manage but girls feel more vulnerable, at least it makes me very uncomfortable.'[9]

Interestingly not all women or girls living in Kashmir spoke of the discomfort with the presence of security forces. Sarabjit, who has been living in Kashmir since her wedding 40 years ago, said, 'The presence of security forces does not make me feel uncomfortable. In fact during festivals, I often offer

---

[8] Name changed.
[9] Name changed.

sweets to them.' 'But barring the time of abrogation of 370, the security forces are usually not deployed in large numbers in my area,' she continued.[10]

Sarabjit, who has lived through the worst phase of militancy in the valley, said she was not against the abrogation of Article 370. 'In fact after the abrogation we, from the Punjabi community in Kashmir, feel more confident. Otherwise, there was always this anxiety and fear of belonging to a minority community in the valley,' she explained.

In contrast to Sarabjit, Ranjeeta, a counsellor at an NGO in Srinagar, who belongs to the Sikh community, said, 'Although I am from a minority community in the valley, I do not feel threatened at all. I am a Kashmiri. I was born here. We have been living with the people of different communities in harmony.'[11] Ranjeeta who is originally from Baramulla district added, 'I am against the abrogation of 370. We had our own identity as Kashmiris.'

When I asked that from her perspective, how does conflict or turmoil in the valley affect women, she explained, 'Females, I feel, are more affected by conflict than are males. Firstly, women and girls, more than boys and men are constantly worried about their families. In case of unrest, curfews and shutdowns, male members of the family can still step out, females mostly have to stay confined to their homes.'

'Almost for six months after the abrogation, I rarely stepped out. Occasionally I would just go out in the neighbourhood, and a few times, I went to the office for night duty. But on those few occasions, when I travelled to the office, I would

---

[10] Name changed.
[11] Name changed.

be engulfed with fear emanating due to communication shutdown and not being able to contact my family.' Ranjeeta also mentioned that she feels insecure due to the heavy presence of security forces. 'Although I have never had any bad experience with them, I have heard of unpleasant experiences from people around me', she explained.

Ariba, from Lal Bazaar who works at the same NGO as Ranjeeta, said, 'I do feel insecure whenever there is a heavy presence of security forces in the vicinity of our homes or in public places. Yet to a certain extent, forces are required to control militancy.'[12] Ariba, who is an arts and crafts teacher and has a diploma in electronics and communication anxiously said, 'I feel very restless at home. I like to go out and work. But, in my view, if militancy increases in the valley, girls and women would just have to sit at home. Whatever progress they have made so far will be negatively affected.' During my visit to Aanchar in Srinagar, a place where both males and females participate in protests and stone pelting against the security forces, I interacted with many females—children, adolescents, young girls and elderly—on the turmoil in the valley and the heavy presence of security forces. Most children and young girls said that the presence of security forces makes them uneasy while also mentioning if their brothers sustain injuries due to pellet firing and shelling, they are more than willing to join the struggle against the Indian State.

Asra, a BA student from Aanchar said, 'I feel very scared of the military. The kids also feel very scared.'[13] Maliha, a 10-year-old interjected, 'Yes I am very scared of the forces but

---

[12] Name changed.
[13] Name changed.

once I also pelted stones along with others. The forces were quite far away. If they continue shelling, firing and injuring our brothers, we will not remain silent.'[14] Asra reiterated what Maliha had just said.

After interacting with these young girls, I came across a middle-aged lady at the Mosque who passionately remarked, 'We (females in Aanchar) are no longer scared of these security forces. We die just once and if it has to be through the bullets, we are ready for it. We will protest against the Indian State and the forces if they continue to blind or injure our people through pellets.'

While women and girls as a group or category experience war or conflict differently from men by virtue of them being female, yet females belonging to a certain ethnic and religious community may experience conflict in a different manner than those from the other community. Besides, each one of them from the same community may have experiences that are different from other girls and women within their own community.

They may also not respond or react to the conflict in the same manner. Some are more prone to anxiety and fear than the others. Besides, the reaction of each female to the conflict situation depends on her immediate environment, circumstances and psychobiological makeup. Some may be able to effectively cope with even the harshest experiences while others may get enmeshed in real or perceived fears arising from frequent violence, bombings and attacks which are hallmark of armed conflict or war.

---

[14] Name changed.

Before delving into the gender roles and impact of conflict on women and girls, let's first briefly understand the term gender.

INTERPRETING GENDER

Traditionally, the term 'gender' has been used to designate psychological as well as sociocultural aspects of femaleness and maleness. On the other hand, the term 'sex' mostly designates the biological components of femaleness and maleness. Considering this perspective, there are two sexes, male and female, and, respectively, two genders, masculine and feminine.[15]

Gender is believed to be 'directly related to, and map onto, sex—men are masculine and women are feminine'. Feminists, however, have questioned this perspective. They have argued that gender is social characteristics only assumed to be 'related to perceived membership in the biological categories of male and female.' Some of the traits traditionally associated with masculinity include strength, aggression, leadership, domination, protection, rationality and public life. On the contrary, those traditionally associated with femininity include weakness, vulnerability, submission, emotion, passivity, care and privacy.[16]

Although gender is frequently divided into masculinities and femininities (described as behavioural norms, stereotypes, expectations, and rules allocated to men and women), it does not imply that 'gender-based expectations for human

[15] Suzanne J. Kessler and Wendy McKenna, *Gender: An Ethnomethodological Approach* (Chicago, IL: University of Chicago Press, 1985).
[16] Laura Sjoberg and Sandra Via, eds., *Gender, War and Militarism* (Westport, CT: Praeger, 2010).

behaviour are constant across time and place'. In fact, the content of gender categories experiences change over time, place, religion, culture and various other factors. Laura Sjoberg and Sandra Via argue, genders are 'sets of discourses that shape, construct, and give meaning to social and political life'.[17]

HISTORICAL PERSPECTIVE ON GENDER AND WAR

In the context of war, women have mostly been portrayed as victims—dying, suffering and mourning for their loved ones. It is true that since ancient times, they have been indirect or direct victim of war, and a large number of casualties in today's wars are women and girls. Besides, sexual abuse or exploitation of women is rampant during conflict and is often used as a deliberate strategy of war. Women and girls are frequently displaced, separated from their families or left to mourn for their deceased family members in conflict situations. Young girls have been forcibly recruited in armed groups and armed forces. Yet, women and girls have also voluntarily participated in combat.

Historically, women have participated in war not merely as camp followers and caregivers but also as active combatants. Joshua S. Goldstein notes, the two documented historical cases of significant organized female participation in warfare by state armies are the Dahomey Kingdom in West Africa during the 18th and 19th centuries and the Soviet Union in the Second World War. Goldstein argues, only in the Dahomey

---

[17] Ibid.; Laura Sjoberg and Sandra Via, eds., *Gender, War and Militarism* (Westport, CT: Praeger, 2010).

Kingdom significant female combatant participation lasted for longer than a short crisis phase. Females made up one wing of the standing army, known as 'Amazon corps', and sometimes constituted a third of all combatants.... In the case of Soviet Union, during the completely desperate times of the Second World War, Goldstein argues, females were mobilized into combat units, however, on a shorter term and smaller basis than for Dahomey. At the peak of this period, reportedly, around 8 per cent of the total Soviet forces were female. Most were medical workers and a few thousand were soldiers.

Goldstein observes, an issue with this case is determining how many of these accounts were war propaganda. In general, the evidence suggests that the females fought about as well as the males—both were to some extent merely 'cannon fodder', argues Goldstein. Nonetheless, he continues, as soon as circumstances allowed, the female units were 'disbanded and the Red Army returned to all-male combat units'.[18]

Haleh Afshar notes, the recorded participation of females in combat preceded Islam and became fundamental to Islamic politics at the time of the Prophet about 14 centuries ago; and both the Sunni Muslims and the Shias have historical memories of women warriors.[19] Referring to Muslim women, she notes, they have continued to participate in armed conflicts and struggles across the centuries. For instance, in Iran there has been both a long history of female participation in revolutions, protests and rebellion, and often a

---

[18] Joshua S. Goldstein, *War and Gender: How Gender Shapes the War System and Vice Versa* (Cambridge: Cambridge University Press, 2003).
[19] Haleh Afshar, 'Women and Wars: Some Trajectories towards a Feminist Peace', in *Development, Women, and War Feminist Perspectives*, eds. Haleh Afshar and Deborah Eade (Nairobi: Oxfam, 2004).

close link 'between their actions and those of the religious establishment'.[20]

April Carter notes that women's primary roles in war are as mothers, wives and girlfriends 'waiting for their soldiers to return and caring for the wounded'. Carter goes on to argue, however, women's emancipation during the last century and the demands on manpower in the First and Second World Wars have led many females to participate directly in war, such as serving in munitions factories and in the armed forces.[21]

Besides serving in the armed forces, women have also participated in struggles and revolutions for centuries across the globe in both combatant and non-combatant roles. They have also been involved as freedom fighters in a number of countries across different continents. Yet, mostly they have been a minority in both male-dominated state armed forces or armed militias in different parts of the world. They have also been perpetrators of violence as combatants or commanders in armed groups in various armed conflicts.

War has often contributed to the transformation of gender roles due to displacement, destitution and deaths of male family members. During war, owing to the deaths of their husbands, women may end up heading the households.

In certain cases, circumstances surrounding war may lead to an increase in decision-making power of females to some degree. Women and girls may have to take up a job to fend for themselves and their families in otherwise orthodox family structures. Their political participation may increase

[20] Ibid.
[21] April Carter, 'Should Women Be Soldiers or Pacifists', in *The Women and War Reader*, eds. Ann Lois Lorentzen and Jennifer Turpin (New York, NY: New York University Press, 1998).

as well. Yet, mostly the traditional notions of gender relations where women are considered subordinate to men persist or are even reinforced during war or armed conflict. Many feminist thinkers have highlighted the presence of gender subordination in times of war and how women—combatants, camp followers and civilians—have mostly been assigned gender-based roles since the ancient wars to the contemporary ones.

POST-COLD WAR ERA

As the nature of wars has changed, particularly in the post-Cold War period, gender roles have also undergone transformation. For instance, while females have always played some (mostly unrecognized) role in combat, but their representation in state armed forces, guerrilla organizations, as well as terrorist organizations has increased substantially in the recent times.[22] However, females are still a minority in these male-dominated organizations. In many instances, women in these organizations follow gender-defined roles and are often prohibited from directly participating in combat or assuming significant or leadership roles.

Yet the presence of women in today's wars or in the post-Cold War era, whether as direct or indirect combatants, has been substantially higher than any time in history. While girls and women lose their lives and are injured as combatants in struggles, revolutions and armed conflicts across the globe, majority of them still die as civilians in armed conflicts. The UN has frequently pointed out that the majority of casualties in today's wars are women and children.

---

[22] Sjoberg and Via, *Gender, War and Militarism.*

There has been increasing attention to the plight of women in war at the International level and in the policy-making circles across the globe. For instance, United Nations Security Council Resolution 1325 calls on 'all parties to conflict to take special measures to protect women and girls from gender-based violence, particularly rape and other forms of sexual abuse, in situations of armed conflict'.

The resolution reaffirms the significant role of women in the 'prevention and resolution of conflicts, peace negotiations, peace-building, peacekeeping, humanitarian response and in post-conflict reconstruction'.[23] There are several other initiatives internationally to address the issues confronting women in conflict. While these efforts seem to be steps in the right direction in dealing with the critical issue of gender-based violence and atrocities during armed conflict, yet women and girls continue to be grossly affected during today's wars.

WOMEN IN CONTEMPORARY WARS

In wars, women and girls suffer just like everyone else but also by virtue of them being female. UN has pointed out that a large number of casualties in today's wars such as Syria, Yemen and Afghanistan are women. They are also vulnerable to sexual abuse and torture. Across the globe, females have been forcibly recruited in armed groups and forces. Women and girls in large numbers have had to flee their homes in Syria and other war-torn countries. Majority of refugees in today's wars happen to be women and children. Besides, one of the areas which war or conflict often negatively affects is education. Physical repercussions of armed conflict are likely to negatively affect the mental health of women and girls.

---

[23] Ibid https://www.un.org/womenwatch/osagi/wps/.

UNICEF in its report *War Hits Home When It Hits Women and Girls* notes, 'Women and girls in particular experience conflict and displacement in different ways from men because of the gender division of roles and responsibilities.' It further argues, 'The targeting of women and girls by armed forces further exacerbates the situation.' According to WHO, 'Gender-based inequity is usually exacerbated during situations of extreme violence such as armed conflict.'[24]

PHYSICAL SAFETY

Besides being casualties in war, one of the most gruesome crimes which women and girls experience during war is rape or sexual abuse. Amnesty International notes, 'Rape and sexual abuse are not just a by-product of war but are used as a deliberate military strategy.'[25] A report by MSF states, it first came across rape as a weapon during the 1990s. 'In Bosnia, systematic rape was used as a part of the strategy of ethnic cleansing,' the report notes, 'Women were raped so they could give birth to a Serbian baby.'[26] While it is true that a large number of rape or sexual abuse victims during armed conflict are women and young girls, men and young boys too experience sexual violence. A 2018 report by the UN states,

> For the past six and a half years, parties to the Syrian conflict have subjected thousands of women, girls, men and boys to sexual and gender-based violence..... Such acts have been used as a tool to instil fear, humiliate

[24] UNICEF, 'War Hits Home When It Hits Women and Girls' (n.d.), https://www.unicef.org/graca/women.htm
[25] http://news.bbc.co.uk/2/hi/4078677.stm
[26] Ibid.

GENDERED VIOLENCE

and punish or, in the case of terrorist groups, to enforce draconian social order.[27]

This UN report titled *I Lost My Dignity: Sexual and Gender-based Violence in the Syrian Arab Republic'* is based on 454 interviews with survivors, relatives of survivors, healthcare practitioners, lawyers, defectors and members of affected communities. It examines 'the perpetration of sexual and gender-based violence by parties since the uprising in March 2011 through December 2017'.[28]

Myanmar is another recent case where the UN reported that rape and sexual violence were systematically used by the Myanmar forces against the Rohingya girls and women. The UN report stated that there was 'systematic selection of women and girls of reproductive ages for rape'.[29] The UN further noted, girls and women were beaten up, raped and held as sexual slaves on military bases. The report also documents cases of rape and sexual torture of men and boys.[30]

In 2019, I met a number of females at both Hindu and Muslim Rohingya camps at Kutupalong in Ukhia, Cox's Bazar. However, I felt certain discomfort talking to them about the reports of sexual abuse experienced by females in the Rakhine state by the Myanmar security forces. During my interaction with Rohingya boys and men, some mentioned how Rohingya girls and women were systematically raped by the Myanmar forces. In the case of Kashmir, since the early 1990s, human rights groups have frequently reported cases of sexual abuse, rape and other rights violations by the security forces against the civilian population. During my interaction

27 https://www.ohchr.org/EN/HRBodies/HRC/Pages/NewsDetail.aspx?NewsID=22833&LangID=E
28 Ibid.
29 United Nations, 'UN Fact-finding Mission'.
30 Ibid.

with the locals in the Valley, particularly in the rural areas, many have spoken about sexual exploitation of women and girls by the forces.

In 1992, during the early stage of militancy, representatives from Asia Watch and Physicians for Human Rights (PHR) documented rape and other human rights abuses and violations of the laws of war by Indian security forces in Kashmir. They also reported incidents of abuse by militant outfits.[31]

Further, during my visit to Sierra Leone in 2011, all the ex-girl soldiers I interacted with across different provinces spoke about sexual abuse and exploitation they had experienced during the conflict. Maria, from Koidu province, said, 'I was abducted by the RUF when I was just 7 years old. I was made to do household chores at the camp. I was also frequently gang raped,' she said poignantly. In Sierra Leone, sexual violence and rape was largely carried out by the RUF and the AFRC. These groups frequently used girls and women as sex slaves. Males also experienced sexual abuse at the hands of these groups but to a lesser degree than females.

Besides being a victim of rape or sexual abuse, women and girls are frequently displaced or rendered homeless during conflict. While being displaced from their homes, females are extremely vulnerable to sexual abuse. In November 2018, the UN estimated that 80 per cent of the people stranded at Rukban in Syria were women and children. The aid groups further noted, 'pregnant women at the camp have given birth without basic medical care.' These people began arriving in Rukban in late 2015 after fleeing areas of Syria previously controlled by the Islamic State.[32]

[31] https://www.hrw.org/sites/default/files/reports/INDIA935.PDF
[32] https://www.bbc.com/news/world-middle-east-46084546

GENDERED VIOLENCE

A Syrian Woman with a Child at a Refugee Settlement, Masna,
near Lebanon-Syria Border

In Lebanon, during my visit to the Masna border crossing
between Lebanon and Syria, and the Syrian refugee settlements in Tripoli, I met many such women and girls who fled
the war in Syria, some of whom lost their family members
and friends during the war. I also came across many Syrian
women in Beirut who were left to fend for themselves and
their children. There were others, who under extremely harsh
circumstances, equally shouldered the responsibility of raising
their children along with their husbands without losing hope.

TRIPOLI: JANUARY 2019

It was around one-hour drive from Beirut to Tripoli. I drove
along the seaside promenade in Beirut, past swish hotels and

cafes, and into the outskirts of the city. After covering over 15 miles along the Mediterranean Sea, I reached Jounieh, a coastal city girded by captivating mountains. Navigating through the cobbled streets of the city flanked by swanky cafes and pubs, the taxi whizzed along the sea towards Tripoli. Souks, streetside markets and meandering alleys marked the landscape of this ancient city. After a quick meal of shawarma and hummus in the downtown area of Tripoli, I headed towards the UNHCR office for a meeting with Omar on the Syrian refugee crisis in Lebanon. Omar connected me with Amjid, a local, who then accompanied me to the Syrian refugee settlements.[33]

It was dusk when we reached there. The sun turned auburn making the distant buildings appear gilded against the dreary landscape. On entering the settlement, I noticed many children wheeling around a sandy field, laughing, screaming and punching each other playfully. After crossing the field, Amjid, Khaled, the taxi driver and I walked through the narrow lanes which led us to a shelter of a Syrian refugee family. As we reached their shelter, Amjid went in to check if anyone from the family was home. A woman, possibly in her 30s, came out along with Amjid and asked us to enter her shelter. Amjid introduced us to her as Zainab, a Syrian refugee, who came to Lebanon along with her family in 2011.

As we seated ourselves on the floor, Zainab said something in Arabic, which I could partially comprehend. 'She is from Homs in Syria. Is that what she is saying? She also mentioned something about her children right?' I asked. Khaled responded, 'Yes she is from Homs. She also says she has six children.'

I asked her a few questions, which Khaled translated into Arabic, 'What exactly made her flee Syria? Was it easy to cross the border or they had to show some papers?'

---

[33] Names changed.

Donning a vacant expression, she said, '*Al-harb* (War)' and added something else in Arabic. Khaled translated, 'She along with her family came to Tripoli in 2011. She also says that time, it was easy to cross the border. Now it is difficult.'

'What about her husband? Does he work?' I asked. 'In Tripoli, he works as a daily wage labourer. He does whatever work he can get. He was a driver back home,' Khaled translated.

Just when Zainab was saying something in Arabic, a middle-aged man of medium height entered the shelter whom Zainab introduced as Junaid, her husband. Junaid sat beside her and joined the conversation. 'He is just coming from work,' Khaled said and continued, 'Junaid says it is very difficult to get work here. In the entire month, I work for only 8 days. During winters, especially when it's raining, I do not work.'

'What about other basic necessities like food and medicines?' I asked? Khaled said, 'Junaid says either they borrow money or the families living in this camp help each other. They have to buy medicines themselves.'

Referring to Zainab I queried, 'What about her life in the camp?' 'She says initially they had received some assistance from the UNHCR. But now they have to manage everything on their own,' Khaled translated and added, 'They don't have the money to rent a house. It is very expensive. She says there are 75 families in these two camps, which are adjacent to each other. All of them jointly rented this land and built the camp themselves. On an average each family pays around 100 dollars per month for rent but it also depends on their paying capacity. If some family is unable to pay that much amount, then others pay more. Some families pay 50 dollars each month.'

'What about her children. Are all of them here?' I probed. 'She has five girls and one boy. All of them are here in Tripoli,' Khaled said.

'Do they go to school?' I queried. 'None goes to school and three of them are married,' Khaled said. Just then two young boys entered and stood near the door.

Zainab pointed towards them, 'They are my children; one is 13, and the other is 14,' she said in Arabic. Both were visibly shy, the older one kept turning his head towards the door and soon stepped out of the shelter.

'Were you studying in Syria?' I asked the younger one. 'He says he studied till Class 1,' Khaled translated. I looked at Zainab and through gestures and in broken Arabic queried, 'Does he *dirasa* (study) at home?' '*Ana aelamuh* (I teach him),' she explained. While Zainab has studied up till Class 9, her husband studied till 6th.

'What are the major problems you are confronted with in the camp?' I asked. 'The main problem at the camp is that they never have enough money to buy food nor medicines. And the winter time it is extremely difficult since they do not have any heating system,' Khaled responded.

'Would they like to go back to Homs since a lot of Syrian refugees are returning to Syria?' I queried. 'Zainab says their house was destroyed during the war after they left for Tripoli. They got to know through their relatives back home,' Khaled explained. Zainab turned her gaze towards her husband and raising her hands began to speak frantically in Arabic.

'So they would not want to go back now?' I asked.

'*La* (no)! She says the state forces will recruit her husband in the army in a combatant role. But they miss their country too much and can return only if the war ceases,' Khaled translated. 'Do they feel safe here?' I asked looking at Zainab and Junaid. '*Al hamdulillah*,' Junaid responded with a faint smile, as Khaled translated what I had just said. Zainab said something in Arabic, her voice turning gloomy and her face pale.

Khaled explained, 'Zainab loves her country and longs to go back. However, they can only return if the situation in Syria gets better. Until then they do not have another way. No solution. They have to accept their life the way it is.'

EDUCATION

Due to instability and insecurity during war or armed conflict, females may be prevented from going to schools, colleges and universities. Besides, gender relations or orthodox gender roles may be reinforced or strengthened during conflict, which may prevent girls from continuing with their education. For instance, during the Taliban regime in Afghanistan, females were not allowed to pursue their education.

Across different conflict zones, reportedly girls are more likely to stay out of schools. According to the ONE Campaign's 2017 report detailing the top 10 toughest places for girls to have access to good quality education, South Sudan ranked first followed by Central African Republic, Niger and Afghanistan and some other African countries. The index measured rate of attendance, amount of expenditure on education, and the number of teachers trained, along with other factors.[34] Some of these places have been experiencing prolonged or protracted armed conflicts. In October 2017, Human Rights Watch noted

---

[34] https://www.bbc.com/news/business-41558486

that an estimated two-thirds of Afghan girls do not attend school. It further stated that as security in Afghanistan has deteriorated, 'the progress that had been made toward the goal of getting all girls into school may be heading in reverse—a decline in girls' education in Afghanistan'.[35]

During an armed conflict, a large number of people including children may get uprooted from their homes, and may also be compelled to flee their countries. In January 2019, during my visit to Tripoli, Masna border crossing and Beirut in Lebanon, I met many Syrian refugees who had to flee their country due to war. Many Syrian children I met in these places, majority

Image 6.2

Syrian Girls at a Refugee Settlement, Masna, near Lebanon-Syria Border

---

[35] https://www.hrw.org/report/2017/10/17/i-wont-be-doctor-and-one-day-youll-be-sick/girls-access-education-afghanistan

of whom were girls, did not have an access to schools. Many were not even able to pursue informal education.

In Bangladesh, which has seen a huge influx of Rohingya refugees, a senior police official told me that the Rohingya children are restricted from enrolling in schools. Towards the end of 2019, during my trip to the Kutupalong camp for Rohingya refugees in Ukhia, Cox's Bazar, Arif, a Rohingya who is from Buthidaung in the Rakhine state, mentioned, 'Rohingyas are prohibited from enrolling in schools in Bangladesh. However, some international organizations and local NGOs are providing informal education to children.' In Rohingya Hindu camp in Kutupalong, while I was interacting with the people who had fled the Rakhine state following reported attacks on them by ARSA, I saw children,

Image 6.3

A Rohingya Girl at Kutupalong Camp, Ukhia, Cox's Bazaar, Bangladesh

many of whom were girls, gathering with their notebooks in a dusty field.

As the children seated themselves on the mats, a female teacher arrived with a stick in her hand and asked them to open their notebooks. The children began to loudly read in a chorus, moving their torsos back and forth. One of the Rohingya's pointing towards the children said, 'Since the children don't have access to schools outside the camp, they have classes inside the camp. We send both boys and girls for the lessons. But this is merely informal education where they don't learn much.'

The education in Kashmir has suffered a huge setback due to shutdowns (*bandhs*), curfews and unrest in the valley. In early August 2019, when the Government of India curtailed the Amarnath pilgrimage in Kashmir, asked all tourists to leave the valley citing a terrorist threat and revoked the autonomy of Kashmir, it also announced the closure of schools, colleges and offices. Additional troops were deployed and strict restrictions imposed in parts of J&K, Kashmir in particular. Phone lines and Internet services were snapped.

When I met Sheema, a resident of Nowpora in Srinagar, on 14 August 2019 amid strict restrictions, she told me, 'On the day of *Bada* Eid, Sameera (her five-year-old daughter) woke up at 6 AM and said, "*Mai chu school gasun* (I want to go to school)."' 'Due to strict restrictions and closure of schools since 5 August, she did not realize it was Eid on the 12th of this month,' Sheema explained despondently.[36]

As we sat talking on a bench overlooking the CRPF camp, Sheema said, 'Everyday she wakes up and says she wants to

---

[36] Name changed.

go to school. She gets extremely bored at home and misses her friends.'

Even when the government announced the resumption of schools, parents were mostly reluctant to send their children due to insecurity and communication shutdown. Few months after the abrogation, most girls in Kashmir told me that during curfews and shutdowns boys can at least step out sometimes but females are mostly confined to their homes.

During unrest or turmoil, girls may not feel safe stepping out of their homes due to unstable security situation, or in certain cases, due to heavy deployment of armed personnel on the streets.[37] Their parents may also be uncomfortable in sending their daughters to schools and colleges. Nargis, a student of Cluster University in Srinagar, pointed out, 'After the abrogation, when the college resumed in November, I could not join it. My brother would get the study material for me,' she added.

'Why were you unable to join college?' I asked. 'This was due to heavy deployment of the security forces around that area. It made me feel very insecure. I joined college on December 25 when the presence of the military (security forces) reduced.' 'We have exams in March now for which we have not been able to prepare due to communication shutdown. Colleges were shut and we could not even use the Internet to study,' she said dejectedly.

MILITARIZATION OF WOMEN

While majority of those who have participated or continue to participate in combat have been boys and men, girls and

---

[37] Many boys in Kashmir also mentioned that they feel insecure stepping out of their homes due to the presence of the security forces. Yet during unrest, girls, more than boys, are confined to their homes.

women have also been involved in war, freedom struggles and revolutions. Even though females have always contributed to war effort and have been involved in armed forces and guerrilla organizations, their roles and position, as mentioned previously, have largely been defined by orthodox gender relations.

Besides voluntary participation of both males and females in combat, armed forces and militias have frequently recruited them forcibly during conflict situation. Females in different conflicts across the globe have been abducted and forcibly used in armed militias. Some have been used as combatants but most have been used in non-combatant roles or as sex slaves. Further, even if women and girls do not participate in direct combat, growing up in a conflict zone may also contribute to militarization of their mind.

AANCHAR, KASHMIR: MILITARIZATION OF MIND[38]

Two little girls, Saima, age 10 years and Saeeda, age 11 years, both clad in hijab, pulled my hand and took me to a park adjacent to a Mosque. They pointed towards two young boys who were seated on the branches of a barren Chinar tree and playfully said in half Urdu and half Kashmiri, 'They are asking you to click a picture.' As I lifted my camera to take their picture, another girl named Asra joined us.

Asra, a BA student at Nawa Kadal, said in Urdu with a smattering of Kashmiri, 'Let's go up. There is an empty hall next to the prayer room. We can sit and talk there.' As Saima, Saeeda, Asra and I entered the hall and seated ourselves on

---

[38] All names have been changed.

the floor, some children, mostly girls, came in and sat next to us.

Asra began to talk about the turmoil in the valley. It had been almost six months since the revocation of Kashmir's autonomy. She indignantly said, 'I was very angry when the Article 370 was abrogated. For months we have lived through such harsh restrictions. Our brothers have suffered pellet injuries. So many of them have lost their lives in the struggle for *Azaadi*. There are security forces and bunkers everywhere.'

Wasifa, 11-year-old who sat next to her 6-year-old sister, interjected, 'We have grown up seeing the military (security forces), shelling, firing, frequent curfews and shutdowns.' Saima, 10, looked at me and nervously said, 'My cousin suffered injury in both his eyes. I was standing near the crowd and a pellet hit my shoulder.' 'I feel very scared of the forces but due to anger I have also pelted stones from a distance,' she continued. 'The mark of the pellet injury is still there on her shoulder,' Wasifa added.

I looked at Asra, who was intently listening to Wasifa and Saima, and asked, 'Have you had any personal encounter with the security forces?' 'Yes. I was in school at that time.' She responded and added, 'In 2010, when I was in the 5th standard, CRPF and the military entered my home and broke things. They also beat up some of my family members and detained my brother and my cousin accusing them of stone pelting. I was standing quietly and shivering with fear. I began to weep uncontrollably. Everyone else, all the women and girls, began to cry as well. My grandmother was hospitalized immediately after this incident. It also left a deep scar in my father's psyche.'

'My brother and cousin were set free after two months. But it was a very difficult time for us,' she explained.

'Now we are exhausted. We neither want to be with India nor Pakistan, and will continue our struggle for Azaadi along with our brothers.' Farhana, a 10-year-old interjected, 'If our brothers are tortured, we will also go out and protest.'

Wasifa, a 6th-standard student, who had mentioned previously that they have grown up amid militarized spaces, shelling and firing, frequent shutdowns timorously said, 'We feel extremely scared of the military (security forces and the army). We literally shiver when we see them with weapons, but it makes us angry when they use pellet guns and shells against our brothers.' 'There have been times when we have supported our brothers by filling buckets with stones,' Wasifa said. During my previous visits to Aanchar, when the people were protesting against the abrogation of Article 370, some boys had also mentioned how their mothers and girls in the colony break stones and hand them over to the boys for pelting against the forces.

As two young boys entered and began to scamper across the hall and a little girl standing near the edge of the staircase shrieked in excitement, Wasifa looked at me and nervously said, 'But the presence of security forces makes us very uneasy.' Riya, a student of 8th standard, at Government Middle school, Tiploo Mohalla zealously added, 'Despite all our fears, when our brothers are injured by the forces, we join our brothers in the struggle for *Azaadi*.'

WOUNDS OF WAR

War or armed conflict is likely to affect the mental health of all individuals including women and girls. Yet some may be more prone to anxiety and depression than the others. War's impact can be determined by psychological, social, economic and environmental factors such as death of family members or relatives, family and community breakdown, destruction of home and loss of livelihood, and collapse of social system. The direct impact of the conflict or exposure to violence is likely to make an individual more prone to war stress. For instance, witnessing the death of a family member in war-induced violence such as armed attacks or suicide bombings, being compelled to flee due to destruction of home or a threat to one's life, or even being exposed to killings and attacks.

As Nasima from Nowhatta in Srinagar, Kashmir mentioned, 'Life goes on as normal, at least for me, unless I witness an incident of violence during the turmoil. When I am exposed to killings and violence, it tends to have a huge impact on my psyche.'[39]

Further, in a case narrated earlier, Asra, a BA student from Aanchar in Srinagar, Kashmir, had mentioned how her grand-mother was hospitalized immediately after the security forces entered her home in 2010 and allegedly beat up her family members, detained her brother and cousin, and vandal-ized their belongings. She also said, 'Ever since I have been instilled with the fear of the security forces.'

Besides exposure to conflict-induced violence or direct impact of conflict, perceived threats or fears are also instrumental in adversely affecting the mental well-being of a female even if she has not experienced or witnessed any war-induced violence. This may depend on the female's psychobiological makeup or her disposition, social support, immediate environment

---

[39] Name changed.

and accomplishments in terms of education and profession. In some cases, the exposure to violence may leave a deep scar within the psyche of a female, which refuses to grow faint, leaving her enmeshed in a web of perceived threats and fears. Congenial environment, empowerment through education and job opportunities, and family and community support can play a huge role in ameliorating the negative effects of war-induced violence.

KASHMIR: SPECIAL CHILDREN AND EXPOSURE TO CONFLICT-INDUCED VIOLENCE[40]

It had been over seven months since I volunteered at the Centre for special children in Srinagar, Kashmir and six months since the abrogation of Article 370. When I reached the Centre, some children were seated in the bus, some were standing outside the Centre's office, and others were inside their classes. Asif, from Nowhatta, who had possibly recognized me, waved his hand. As I entered the class for severe category, I saw Abid from Habba Kadal crooning and playfully sauntering across the room. Muzzamil from Saida Kadal started to sing along with him. Both Abid and Muzzamil began yelling and wheeling around in circles.

I sat next to Seerat from Nawa Kadal, who gave me a warm smile and affectionately pulled my hand. Saeeda, arts and crafts teacher for the severe class, who was asking all the children to quietly sit down, greeted me and said in Urdu, 'It's been a long time.' I asked in half Kashmiri, *Theek peth? Asal peth?* (How are you?) How are the children doing?'

---

[40] All names have been changed.

'They are fine. Due to the situation post abrogation of Article 370, children were home for a few months. But now most are back at the centre,' Saeeda said flashing a wide smile. 'But the centre was providing them home-based teaching during the curfew and bandh (shutdown),' she continued.

'Does their behaviour change when they return from prolonged unrest accompanied by violence and killings?' I asked.

'Mostly the behaviour of children changes during the unrest, some become more aggressive than the others and they mostly stop following commands. We have to start from scratch,' Saeeda responded 'The behaviour of children, both boys and girls, during the unrest transforms more from the downtown area in Srinagar which is more affected than the other areas.'

She spoke about Seerat's case whose behaviour changed when she returned after spending a couple of months confined to her home during the 2016 protests ensuing Burhani Wani's (the Hizbul commander) killing. Seerat, 15, from the downtown area of Nawa Kadal has been at the NGO or home for special children for over 9 to 10 years. Seerat, who comes from an economically humble background, has been diagnosed with severe mental retardation. Saeeda said, 'Normally, she is very lazy but very calm. Earlier, a couple of years ago, she would hit her grandmother. Now she no longer does that. But she can be quite moody.' 'During the unrest of 2016, her behaviour transformed,' she pointed out.

When I asked if she could describe what changes she saw in her behaviour and if she became aggressive, Saeeda responded, 'I don't remember exactly. But we had to work a lot with her when she returned. She had forgotten whatever was taught here. Although, she did not turn aggressive, she stopped following commands and became inattentive. But there are some children from the downtown area who become quite aggressive when they return after prolonged unrest.'

She mentioned there are more girls in the mild class, which is supervised by Arshee, and I could possibly speak to her about their cases. After the children left for their homes, I spent few hours with Arshee discussing about the impact of turmoil on girls in her class.

First, she spoke about Ayesha, 14, who has been diagnosed with intellectual disability (mild category):

'She has been here for at least 10 years. She resides in Gawkadal with her parents. Her father owns a shop in that area.'

'Her temperament is quite calm, she follows commands and is committed towards academics and other tasks. However, she is very lazy and takes time in comprehending what is taught in the class. Yet she does well in academics due to her commitment.'

'Her behaviour does not change whenever there is unrest. One of the reasons could be that she is mostly confined to her house and is not exposed to protests and violence during the turmoil.'

'However, recently when she returned to the Centre after few months, whatever progress she had made has been adversely affected.'

'Girls are usually confined to their homes, boys still go out and may be exposed to stone pelting and firing during protests. Some boys become more aggressive after they return from protests,' she added. Arshee cited another case of Sanaf, 14, who has been diagnosed with downs syndrome (mild category). A resident of Khanyar in the downtown area, Sanaf belongs to a middle-class family whose father has a small business. 'She has a speech problem. She is lazy and forgets easily but follows commands. Her commitment towards academics and other tasks is average. Her temperament is similar to Ayesha's,' Arshee said and continued, 'She was confined to her home for past few months after the abrogation of Article 370. Her house is away from the main street, therefore, she was possibly not exposed to the violence during protests. This could be one of the reasons why her behaviour did not change. However, she has forgotten whatever was taught in the class. She says no one teaches her at home.' 'There is another girl in my class, Aiman, 10, from Natipora who has been diagnosed with ADHD (mild category). She returned to the Centre after over eight to nine months. She is very caring but indulges in self-harm and gets aggressive too. She turned more aggressive when she returned.'

Few months back, the doctor at the Centre had mentioned that most children come from the densely populated downtown area of Srinagar, where houses are contiguous to one another. 'During unrest children, females in particular, are mostly confined to their homes. This may have a huge impact on their mental health and immensely deteriorate their progress,' she added.

While environmental factors such as exposure to violence or being confined to stifling spaces, and restriction of movement may adversely affect the mental well-being of individuals including females, other cumulative factors such as family support and one's personality or disposition may play a huge role in influencing an individual's mental health. For instance, as stated by Arshee, the behaviour of Ayesha and Sanaf, both of whom have a calm temperament, does not undergo change during the unrest. On the other hand, Aiman who has been diagnosed with ADHD and is intrinsically aggressive by nature, turned even more aggressive when she returned to the Centre after spending a couple of months at home. However, there are also cases when even individuals with calm temperament may turn aggressive or experience negative changes in their behaviour due to prolonged conflict.

As Arshee sat in a corner of the room, immersed in her thoughts, I asked, 'What about you? As a woman, how do you think conflict or the instability in Kashmir affect you? What was it like to live amid the communication shutdown, and perhaps the harshest restrictions in the valley ever?'

Arshee, who has a diploma in electronics and communication, looked up hesitantly and said, 'This time it was very difficult. The restrictions were extremely strict. For months, I just stayed at home. Inside the four walls. During curfews and shutdowns, women and girls mostly stay at home. Male folk of the house still step out of their homes. I believe it affects us psychologically. At least, I get very stressed. All these months, while at home, I used to get very irritable and fight with my parents. My behaviour turned quite aggressive.'

She added, 'We have been closed from the social media, from the outside world. I had my exams for electrical engineering in December which were postponed. Now we have our exams in either June or July.'

'I don't like sitting at one place. Those initial months after the abrogation were extremely depressing and stressful for me. At that time, like some other girls from the NGO, I did not even go to the office for night duty.'

'Why was that?' I asked. 'To reach the office, I would have to cross the downtown area which was affected by protests,' she responded.

It was already 6 in the evening, and I had to reach my hotel before it got dark, which was a couple of kilometres away from the Centre. Just when I thought of leaving the Centre, Arshee said, 'Soon it will turn dark. It may be difficult for you to find a vehicle. *Haalat theek nahi hai* (The situation is not stable here).'

When I got up to pick up my bag, Arshee wearing a serene smile said, 'Since October when the office resumed, I feel relatively relaxed.'

There may be scores of women and girls like Arshee who are forced to sit at home due to instability and insecurity arising due to armed conflict or orthodox gender roles that are reinforced and strengthened in conflict situations. Women and girls have always been either directly or indirectly affected by conflict, majority of casualties in contemporary wars have been reported to be women and children. Females have been subjected to sexual abuse and rape more than males. They have suffered not just physical consequences of the conflict but psychological as well.

Yet, there is burgeoning literature on silences surrounding status of women during armed conflict. Patriarchal structures and conformist or orthodox attitudes buttressed during conflict situations frequently prevent the voices of women from being heard.

In Kashmir, while some men introduced me to the female folk in their family for understanding their perspective on the conflict, in two cases, the reaction of the males to my query reflected certain patriarchal assumptions. When I asked these men if there is a possibility of interacting with some females in their family to understand how the conflict affects them as women, I was told: 'Women and girls are mostly confined to their homes, therefore, they may not be able to speak much about the conflict,' and 'Since they mostly stay at home, they will all tell you the same things.'

These patriarchal assumptions deny women and girls agency, rendering them invisible as individuals who may have any opinions and thoughts on the conflict or turmoil, which in fact affects them enormously. Despite all the challenges thrown up by war or armed conflict, women and girls have often shown extraordinary resilience and courage in different roles and identities—as mothers, wives, sisters, caregivers, combatants and even freedom fighters.

CHAPTER 7

RESILIENCE, COPING AND HOPE

As Noorina[1] took me through her paintings, mostly sombre in shades and tone, she stopped to describe one of her works depicting a marketplace in Herat city, north-western Afghanistan. Streams of faded crimson, amber and leaden-blue appeared to flow through the skies into the evening market, lending certain heaviness to the entire landscape. Pointing towards the silhouettes of people outside the cafes and shops, she explained in Urdu, which she said she had learnt from Indian films, 'Mein logon ka milna julna, unki dosti, unki zindagi jo bazaar mein hai, is tasveer mein laana chahti thi (I wanted to portray the meeting and friendship of people, and their everyday life in the marketplace through this painting).

Noorina was studying at the Faculty of Fine Arts, Herat University, when I met her in Herat in December 2017. At that time, approximately 65 per cent students of this department were female. This was certainly heartening to know in a country which is often rated as among the worst places in the world for girls' education. According to Ministry of Higher Education (2010), the universities with higher enrolment of females are in Herat (34%), Kabul (27%), Balkh (25%),

---

[1] Name changed.

Samangan (24%), Faryab (23%) and Badakhshan (21%). Even today, Herat continues to have one of the highest female enrolments in universities in Afghanistan.

While there has been some progress in enrolment of Afghan women in universities in certain cities of Afghanistan, yet due to several constraints including unstable security situation and rigid patriarchal structures, significant hurdles remain before a large number of Afghan women. Despite the hurdles, many girls including Noorina I met in Herat and other places in Afghanistan expressed determination to continue with their education.

As I stood glancing at Noorina's painting of the magnificent blue-domed mosque adorned with intricate art work, she remarked, 'This is the famous mosque of Herat. The city has an extremely rich history of art and culture.' 'Yes. That's right. I have read that Herat has long been known as a centre for art and learning in Afghanistan. In fact, I believe, contemporary higher education in the country has deep roots in this province,' I said.

Just half an hour back, prior to my visit to the hall where Noorina's and other female students' paintings were displayed, Professor Habibullah, one of the lecturers at the Centre spoke to me about Herat being an important cultural and trade hub connecting Afghanistan with Iran and Central Asia.[2]

'The great share of the cultural renaissance in the region, particularly in the beginning of the 15th century is credited to the Timurid Queen Gawhar Shad, wife of Shahrukh, the youngest son of Tamerlane,' he pointed out.

---

[2] Name changed.

Gawhar Shad is said to have been instrumental in the construction of schools, colleges, libraries, mosques and hospitals. Under her patronage, Persian art and culture flourished. She broke the age-old tradition that prevented women from patronizing mosques by building two Mosques in Herat and Mashaad (a city in Iran that shares a border with Herat in Afghanistan).[3] It was the Mosque built under the patronage of Gawhar Shad in Herat, which Noorina had captured beautifully in her painting.

Mahira, another student at the Faculty of Fine Arts entered the hall and stood next to Noorina who was speaking to me about her work.[4] After a while, both of them accompanied me to the other side of the hall where some more paintings were displayed. My eyes fell on a painting of two Afghan women clad in blue flowing hijab, which covered their faces entirely.

'Who's made this painting?' I asked.

'This is Mahira's work,' Noorina said. 'It is reminiscent of the Taliban regime, even though I have seen some women covered entirely in blue hijab in some parts of Afghanistan,' I said. Noorina, Mahira and I got into a conversation about the life of women in Afghanistan after the Taliban regime.

'Women in Afghanistan, particularly in Herat and Kabul, have come a long way since the collapse of the Taliban regime,' Mahira pointed out in broken urdu.

'Professor Habibullah had mentioned that in the early 90s, prior to the Taliban period, due to its history, Herat had a

---

[3] Nushin Arbabzadah, 'Women and Religious Patronage in the Timurid Empire', in 'Afghanistan's Islam: From Conversion to the Taliban', ed. Nile Green, (2017, University of California Press)
[4] Name changed.

high concentration of educated people, which included a large number of women,' I said. 'Yes, Herat has always been a place for art and learning,' Mahira responded.

After the collapse of the Taliban regime in 2001, women once again began to enrol in schools, colleges and universities. However, it was reported that females in many parts of Afghanistan—including Herat, which was ruled by provincial governor (2001–2004) and warlord Ismail Khan—continued to face repression. Since then Herat has come a long way in terms of women's education.

'While violence against women, gender inequality are rampant in Afghanistan, today women in Herat enjoy relatively more freedom than many other provinces of Afghanistan,' Mahira said. 'Despite the challenges and insecurity thrown up by the ongoing conflict, many attend schools and universities and continue to work,' Noorina added.

After spending few hours at the hall where the paintings were displayed, and interacting with some Fine Arts students, both boys and girls, in the adjacent room, Noorina and I left for the hall close to the Faculty office. Paintings of all sizes and shades adorned the walls. While some students continued to paint in their respective places, Noorina and I seated ourselves in a brightly lit corner close to a window.

She spoke to me about the security situation in Afghanistan and her interest in art and culture. 'Despite the dismal situation of women in Afghanistan, my parents have always encouraged me. My family is extremely supportive,' she said flashing a bright smile. 'I have grown up in the midst of violence since suicide bombings and armed attacks are normal or commonplace in Afghanistan. Yet I never lost hope and despite all the obstacles and challenges, I would like to continue with my education,' Noorina asserted as her voice grew strong with conviction.

Her eyes sparkled as she talked about close cultural and historical ties between India and Afghanistan, and her love for India and Indian films. 'I would like to pursue MA in Fine Arts in India'. 'Herat is known for its art and culture and so is India, I would like to fuse the art forms in Herat and India to create something new,' she explained.

'I love to paint about everyday life in Herat. There is a world beyond violence and suicide bombings in Afghanistan. Like in other places or countries, people in Afghanistan too attend schools and universities, spend time in cafes and market-places,' Noorina said. 'It really upsets me when people associate Afghanistan only with violence and suicide bombings,' she continued, 'Afghanistan has such rich history and culture. Herat, for instance, has so much to offer in terms of art and music. Besides, its architecture and landscape are breathtaking. However, violence, terror and suicide bombings are mostly what you see in the media about Afghanistan. I would like to change that image of my country.'

'Despite frequent violence, common people here continue with their everyday life,' she said. In fact, in different conflict zones across the globe, I have observed that regardless of unstable security situation, common people may exhibit extraordinary resilience, construct hope and find ingenious ways of coping.

'What is it that keeps you going despite all the challenges and hurdles?' I asked. 'Painting. I find hope in art. I am able to express myself through my paintings and that's how I am able to cope with unstable security situation in Afghanistan,' she explained.

While Afghanistan seems to evoke images of violence, terror and despair in the minds of outsiders, seemingly, little is known about the spectacular art, culture and architecture of places such as Herat to the outside world. Noorina and some other female Fine Arts students I met at the Herat University are determined to change this by displaying their paintings of Herat's rich history and culture in different parts of the world.

All of Noorina's paintings—the vibrant marketplace in Herat, the magnificent blue-domed mosque, haunting portrait of a Herati girl, and two young boys innocuously playing in the snow, seemingly oblivious of the bombings and terror that frequently afflict their country—epitomize Herat's art, culture and everyday life. Certainly, there is a world beyond terror and bombings in Afghanistan, which is often reflected in Noorina's paintings.

THE SCIENCE BEHIND RESILIENCE

A. S. Masten notes that resilience can be broadly defined as the capacity of a dynamic system to adapt effectively 'to disturbances that threaten system function, viability or development.' The concept can be applied to systems of several kinds at many interacting levels, living as well as non-living, 'such as a microorganism, a child, a family, a security system, an economy, a forest, or the global climate.'[5] However, there are a number of other definitions of the term resilience. In the resilience literature, many have raised concern regarding the proliferation of different meanings of this concept

---

[5] A. S. Masten, 'Global Perspectives on Resilience in Children and Youth', *Child Development* 85, no. 1 (January/February 2014): 6–20.

across different fields of study, and have called for a common definition of resilience.[6] However, as Ken Menkhaus rightly notes, 'This is simply not possible.'

Historically, the concept of resilience entered the health sciences from applied physics and engineering, where it implies 'the ability of materials to "bounce back" from stress and resume their original shape or condition'. For instance, a rubber ball. The term was apparently first used in medicine to illustrate the recovery of patients from physical traumas such as accidents and surgery. Sometime later, it was adopted into psychology, initially for the study of children of mentally unstable mothers. It is now understood to indicate a person's capacity to recuperate from, adapt, and remain strong during adversity.[7]

How can personal resilience be distinguished from community resilience? Community resilience is not just a collection of personally resilient individuals. The distinction between the two, which is enormous and frequently missed, maybe understood, partly, by recognizing that the whole is more than the sum of its parts. Therefore, a community comprising personally resilient individuals is not necessarily resilient.[8] Community resilience emerges from collective activity wherein individuals come together in efforts that foster response and recovery for the whole. Besides, in resilient

---

[6] Ken Menkhaus, 'Making Sense of Resilience in Peacebuilding Contexts: Approaches, Applications, Implications', Paper No. 6 (Geneva: Geneva Peacebuilding Platform, 2013).

[7] Jo Boyden and Gillian Mann, 'Children's Risk, Resilience, and Coping in Extreme Situations' (2005), https://www.researchgate.net/publication/239782304_Children's_Risk_Resilience_and_Coping_in_Extreme_Situations.

[8] R. L. Pfefferbaum and R. W. Klomp. 'Community Resilience, Disasters, and the Public's Health', in *Community Engagement, Organization, and Development for Public Health Practice*, ed. F. G. Murphy (New York, NY: Springer), 275–298, 2013.

communities, individual and collective actions are strengthened by physical and social conditions and structures that allow resilience to manifest itself in the face of adversity.[9] Further, families and communities can contribute to resilience among individuals in distress.

Froma Walsh in her article 'Traumatic Loss and Major Disasters: Strengthening Family and Community Resilience' argues, resilience involves 'mastering the possible', being able to accept what has been lost and cannot be altered, 'while directing efforts to what can be done and seizing opportunities for something good' to emerge out of the tragedy. In the wake of overwhelming trauma, we can help families regain hope in their future possibilities.[10] Similarly, families can help their family member in distress regain hope.

Shaul Kimhi and Michal Shamai who have conducted field research on community resilience and adult response to Israel's withdrawal from Lebanon, note that according to their findings, the level of threat has an important impact on community resilience, which implies, 'that living in situations with a high level of threat over a long period of time results in a lower level of community resilience'. Furthermore, 'community resilience serves as a partial mediator between the level of threat and the effect of stress and life satisfaction'. The findings highlight the significance of 'perceived community resilience as an individual resource for coping with the threat created by war and terror, thereby connecting between micro-and macro-levels in events related to political violence'.[11]

---

[9] Ibid.
[10] Walsh, 'Traumatic Loss and Major Disasters'.
[11] Shaul Kimhi and Michal Shamai, 'Community Resilience and the Impact of Stress: Adult Response to Israel's Withdrawal from Lebanon', *Journal of Community Psychology* 32, no. 4 (2004): 439–451.

Both individual and community resilience are dependent on a number of common factors such as the level and time period of threat, a sense of belongingness in the community, and shared beliefs and values that buttress a sense of collective hope. However, individual or personal resilience may also be contingent on the individual's circumstances, his or her sense of achievement, family and community support, and the individual's disposition.

HOW COPING AND HOPE PLAY THEIR INSTRUMENTAL ROLES

> By coping we refer to the things that people do to avoid being harmed by life— strains. At the very heart of this concept is the fundamental assumption that people are actively responsive to forces that impinge upon them. Since many of these impinging forces are social in their origins, the understanding of coping is a prerequisite for understanding the impact that societies come to exert on their members.[12]

In a formal sense, hope 'is defined as a cognitive set that is based on a reciprocally derived sense of successful (a) agency (goal-directed determination) and (b) pathways (planning of ways to meet goals)'.[13] I. N. Corner notes that hope is a fundamentally positive phenomenon essential for healthy coping, its main purpose being the avoidance of desolation, with the secondary function of allowing the individual

[12] Leonard I. Pearlin and Carmi Schooler, 'The Structure of Coping', *Journal of Health and Social Behavior* 19, no. 1 (March 1978): 2–21.
[13] C. R. Snyder, C. Harris, J. R. Anderson, S. A. Holleran, L. M. Irving, S. T. Sigmon, L. Yoshinobu, J. Gibb, C. Langelle, and P. Harney, 'The Will and the Ways: Development and Validation of an Individual-Differences Measure of Hope', *Journal of Personality and Social Psychology* 60, no. 4 (1991): 570–585.

RESILIENCE, COPING AND HOPE

psychologically to circumvent continuing unpleasant or traumatic situations.[14]

Hope may play an instrumental role in resilience and coping among individuals and communities. Through hope, people and communities may be able to heal faster and cope more effectively. While individuals living in conflict zones or under extremely difficult circumstances may adopt negative or positive mechanisms to cope with their situation, hope may enable them to adopt healthy coping mechanisms. Negative coping mechanisms may involve getting into a habit of drugs or alcoholism every time an individual is going through tough times or is unable to deal with his/her situation through positive healing.

Susan Folkman notes that hope is essential for individuals 'who are coping with serious and prolonged psychological stress', and 'hope is not a perpetually self-renewing resource; it has peaks and valleys and is at times absent altogether'.[15] This somewhat resonates with the reactions I saw among the people living in conflict zones. There were times when despite the continuing conflict or challenging circumstances, many did not lose hope for a better life, at other times hope for them was at a lowest ebb or was altogether elusive.

Hope and psychological stress share several formal characteristics. Folkman argues,

> Hope, like stress, is appraisal-based, it waxes and wanes, is contextual, and is complex. Hope has a cognitive base that contains information and goals; it

---

[14] I. N. Korner, 'Hope as a Method of Coping'. *Journal of Consulting and Clinical Psychology* 34, no. 2 (1970): 134–139.
[15] Susan Folkman, 'Stress, Coping, and Hope', *Psycho-Oncology* 19 (2010): 901–908.

generates an energy, often described as 'will', that has a motivational quality; it has both negative and positive emotional tones due to the possibility that what is hoped for might not come to pass; and for many people hope has a basis in religion or spirituality whereby it is equivalent to faith.[16]

Daniel Bar-Tal distinguishes between fear and hope. He argues,

> Fear has a physiological basis, whereas hope does not; fear can be processed unconsciously, whereas hope always requires conscious cognitive activity; fear is basically activated automatically, whereas hope is always based on thinking and requires various cognitive skills such as creativity and flexibility. Fear is grounded in the perceived threatening present, often based on the remembered threats in the past; hope is based on a positive imagination of the future. Fear often leads to aggressive-protective behaviors used in the past; hope requires conceiving of new behaviors to achieve the desired, positively valued goal.[17]

While 'hope has both negative and positive emotional tones due to the possibility that what is hoped for might not come to pass', as Folkman argues, yet hope, even under most extreme or difficult circumstances, may encourage an individual to effectively deal with his/her stress and fears due to its 'motivational quality'.

In the middle of war or conflict, individuals and communities may make an effort to find or build islands of peace and

---

[16] Ibid.
[17] Daniel Bar-Tal, 'Why Does Fear Override Hope in Societies Engulfed by Intractable Conflict, as It Does in the Israeli Society?' *Political Psychology* 22, no. 3 (2003): 601–627.

RESILIENCE, COPING AND HOPE

hope. They may literally attempt to create 'safe' spaces or construct isles of 'normalcy' to deal with the stress and brutality of the conflict. Some may find solace in religion, god or faith while others may find creative ways of coping such as poetry, writing, music, humour and sports to deal with the anomaly of war. Social life, if and whenever possible, amid the uncertainty of conflict or spending time with family and friends can be a great source of coping for most during wartime. Some people may even move to safe spaces either within their own country or outside of it to cope with the violence of war.

Some individuals who have lived through the war in Lebanon told me whenever there was intense fighting in their area, they would find safe places to move to. When I asked Sabrina, a local who has lived through the war in Lebanon, about the coping mechanisms she and her family would adopt to deal with the conflict situation, she responded: I remember my parents trying to find safe places when things get really bad. My father used to plan a weekend in the mountains. For us it was vacation but for him he was thinking of safety and security. During firing we had to go to the basement. I always think even now where to go when things get bad and plan an exit. I don't have other nationality like many other Lebanese. For instance, many Lebanese like to give birth outside the country in the US or in Canada and others go to France, Germany, or the UK. They spend time there so that they can get the nationality of that particular country and then return to Lebanon. If anything happens or there is a crisis in Lebanon, they can then move to that country.[18]

---

[18] Name changed.

Leila a freelancer, who grew up during the war in Lebanon similarly noted, 'Coping was basically—just move from place to place. When fighting is intense in one place we move to another place. This is a kind of coping.'

In Kashmir, a senior police officer told me, 'Here people try to stay away, as much as they can, from the conflict and make an attempt to lead normal lives.' 'Many even move out of Kashmir to cope with the conflict,' he explained.

FINDING SOLACE IN RELIGION OR GOD

Pargament argues that students of religion have attempted to get to 'the heart of religion, that which sets it apart from other human experiences'. Two kinds of response have been provided. Consistent with one perspective, it is the sacred that makes religion distinctive. Religion is fundamentally concerned with God, supernatural beings, deities, transcendent or divine forces, and all that is associated with these higher powers. According to the other perspective, religion is distinguished by 'its special function in life rather than by a divine entity'. Mostly, religion is said to be particularly concerned with how individuals 'come to terms with ultimate issues in life'.[19]

While focusing on certain moral and spiritual values and beliefs, religion often stipulates certain guidelines or rituals for people to follow in their everyday life. For many individuals, religion may provide solace and hope in their most difficult times.

---

[19] Kenneth I. Pargament, *The Psychology of Religion and Coping: Theory, Research, Practice* (New York, NY: Guilford Press, 1997).

To offer an interesting example, during the war in Sudan, Magne Raundalen and Atle Dyregrov asked 124 school children between the ages of 15 and 20 to write essays on 'Myself in the Year 2000'. Their essays reflected an impression of a 'lost generation'. Despite difficult times, many of these students continued to have hope for the future. The students were keen to pursue their education. Besides, in these essays, God was portrayed as their strongest friend. Majority of the children placed their hope in the 'will of God'. They all strove to be good Muslims or good Christians and, therefore, to be a model for their own future children.[20]

Similarly, during my interaction with the people of Kashmir, most mentioned hope or faith in God as a way of coping with the turmoil or unstable security situation in the valley. When Article 370 was revoked and strict restrictions were in place in the valley, Humaira from the downtown area of Srinagar, Kashmir, told me she has placed all her hope in God.

As mentioned previously, when I asked her what keeps her going regardless of the turmoil, Ajaz, her son interjected, 'From the beginning or their early childhood, females are taught to pray and to stay at home. They slowly learn to adapt to the situation.' *'Jo Namaz karega, Allah mein ummeed rakhega, usko depression ho hi nahi sakta* (Whoever offers Namaz or prayers is unlikely to be stressed or depressed).' 'There is always a new dawn after a dark night,' Ajaz said, his eyes glowing with conviction.

'Is it because you have hope that the situation in the valley will improve?' I asked. 'Yes, but not just in anyone, I have

---

[20] Cole P. Dodge and Magne Raundalen, *Reaching Children in War: Sudan, Uganda and Mozambique* (Uppsala: Nordic Africa Institute, 1991); Magne Raundalen and Atle Dyregrov (1991).

hope only in Allah,' he explained. 'Only those who go astray and do not offer prayers to Allah are likely to be depressed,' Humaira added.

In another instance, during the summer of 2019, around the time of revocation of Kashmir's autonomy, as I stood near a shop of Kashmiri bread at Makhdoom Sahib Shrine in Srinagar, an elderly lady at the shop looked at me with distressed eyes and said, '*Haalat theek nahi* (the situation is not good). *Bahut zulm* (extreme torture),' she exclaimed.

When I asked what keeps her going in these difficult times, throwing her hands up in the air in a gesture of prayer, 'Allah', she said, her eyes glimmering with hope.

AN ENCOUNTER WITH A LEBANESE CARPET TRADER ON THE STREETS OF HAMRA

It was a pleasant afternoon and the streets of Hamra were abuzz with people and vehicles. As I walked on the pavement lined with shops, my eyes fell on exquisite carpets portraying everyday life woven in minute details. I entered the shop and a middle-aged man sporting a salt and pepper beard greeted me warmly. Just above the chair where he was seated, a portrait of Lenin hung on the wall. I glanced across the shop in amazement and then shifting my gaze towards the man smiled. '*Jamila* (beautiful), the carpets are just amazing.' In his broken English interspersed with Arabic, he said, 'Wait. Let me call my daughter, she speaks English.' 'Sure,' I responded and in broken Arabic asked, '*min ayn hadhih carpets?* (where are these carpets from?).' '*Tabrez, Iran*,' he responded.

227

Min ayibalad ant? (where are you from?) he asked. 'India,' I replied. Just when I was about to ask him to show me more carpets, I heard the sound of footsteps and looked at the staircase inside the shop. A girl with deep blue eyes, fair complexion and long flowing tresses walked down the staircase. 'My daughter. She is in school right now,' he smiled. She introduced herself as Mahira.[21] As she showed me the carpets, I happened to notice some paintings on the wall near the staircase. Mahira immediately said, 'These are made by my brother. He is an artist.' 'They are just amazing,' I exclaimed. In his broken English, Mahira's father who introduced himself as Maher, said that he would be coming to the shop soon and I must meet him.

Mahira asked me what brings me to Lebanon. I told her about my research on the lives of people who have either lived through the war or are living in conflict zones. She immediately said that her father grew up during the war in Lebanon.

Just when I was about to ask Maher about his life during the war, a lanky young boy entered the shop. 'That's my brother Ibrahim,' Mahira smiled. 'I just saw your paintings, they are beautiful,' I said. Ibrahim asked me the purpose of my visit to Lebanon.[22] Which I explained to him. He quickly said, 'My father and mother have lived through the war.' 'Yes, I just got to know that,' I responded and then asked Maher, 'What was it like growing up in a war zone?'

'My father says that they were used to the war since they grew up amid it. They would see dead bodies on the streets and

---

[21] Name changed.
[22] Name changed.

on television, they were used to them,' Ibrahim translated and carried on, 'My father was just seven years old when the war began. His father, meaning my grandfather, was not afraid and he inherited this trait from him. When he was in school, once he saw a fighter with a gun on one of the floors of the school building. He was scared but also fascinated.'

Just when I was about to ask another question, a middle-aged man of medium built, sporting a cap and a jacket, entered the shop. Maher rose from his chair and enthusiastically said, '*Marhaba* (Hello), *Kifek* (How are you?).' 'My friend, he is professor,' Maher exclaimed in excitement and said something in Arabic. Pointing towards Maher's friend, Ibrahim translated, 'My father is saying that you should interview his friend, Dr Abdel, who is a professor at a university in Beirut.'[23] Dr Abdel intervened, 'I was not here during the war. I went to the UK to study.' 'My friend is the right man to talk about the war, he was here during that time.'

Looking at Maher I asked, 'Can you describe your first impressions of the war in your country?'

Mahira translated it in Arabic and Maher immediately said, '*Khauf, maut* (death and fear).' 'My father says his first impressions were death of innocent people and of course fear,' Ibrahim explained.

'Can you describe your experience of the war?' I asked.

Mahira translated his father's response for me. 'My father says that people became vengeful during the war. There were cases when someone from a Muslim family was killed, the

---

[23] Name changed.

family members would kill anyone from any Christian family or vice versa. Innocent people died for revenge.'

Dr Abdel added, 'People did not know if they would return once they left their homes. Lebanese have a lot of depression due to war. Lot of people have neurological disorders. To conclude, we lived the war and we became real men, we endured the hardship and the agony of the war.'

I jumped in, 'What about women?'

'Women mostly stayed at home. They have endured the hardships like men. Men would go out on the streets, but women would essentially take care of their husbands and their families. However, there were some women who fought in the war, especially the Christian women.' 'And the Palestinian women,' Ibrahim interjected. Maher also said something, which his son translated, 'My father says each man in the war revealed his true character.'

Dr Abdel remarked, 'Maher also says that people were like animals, they took revenge. The one who was carrying the gun thought that he was ruling the streets, but, in the end we all love each other.' He looked up and began to gaze at a painting on the wall, which portrayed a man embracing a donkey, and humorously said, 'Man even loves a donkey, this picture symbolizes friendship and love and, in fact, you trust the donkey more than human beings.'

'Living amid the war did you ever lose hope?' I asked Maher.

Ibrahim translated my question in Arabic. As Maher began to speak, I could just understand a few words such as *maut*, *al harb* and *Amrika*. Dr Abdel explained, 'My friend says that he was sorry for the deaths of innocent people. However, he was in high morale. I was trying to bring him to America to take him out of the war. Since he is a strong man, he endured the hardship and the agony of war.'

I looked at Maher curiously and asked, 'You did not want to go outside the country?'

Ibrahim responded, 'My father says he wanted to leave the country but it was very difficult for him to stay away from home. He went to Roma, Italia (Rome, Italy) for a week but felt homesick and came back. At that time he was barely 20 years old.' 'Belief in Allah,' Maher suddenly exclaimed. 'My father says he did not lose hope due to his belief in Allah, the belief in god,' Ibrahim explained. Dr Abdel interjected, 'We Lebanese, whether Muslim or Christian, it's irrelevant. We are all Lebanese. We are Arabs. Even if he were Christian, he will still be my friend. We all have faith in God. That is what keeps us going.'

While Dr Abdel was speaking, a middle-aged woman entered the shop. 'My wife Nasima,' Maher exclaimed.[24] Ibrahim introduced me to her and added, 'My mother also grew up during the war. You could speak to her about her experiences.' Nasima seated herself beside Maher and in fluent English said, 'War was very frightening. We closely experienced the fighting and gun firing. We had to sit in the basement shelter for two-three days continuously.'

'Did you ever despair?' I queried.

'No. Not at all. We were kids and kids do not lose hope,' Nasima responded with a faint smile.

---

[24] Name changed.

LEBANON–SYRIA BORDER: 2019

It was a freezing day in the border town of Lebanon in the Bekka Valley, which was located just a few kilometres from the Syrian border (near Masna Border Crossing). Imran, the taxi driver stopped the car near a settlement of Syrian refugees.[25] Few men were standing in the dusty field outside the shelters covered with tarpaulin. Little children, mostly girls, possibly in the age group of 5 to 13 years, who were ambling across the ochre field speckled with stones, came running towards the vehicle. While some raised their hands to wave at me, radiating exuberant smiles, others chuckled playfully covering their faces with their palms.

Some children began to speak in Arabic and chuckled again. 'This is Anjar settlement of the Syrian refugees,' Imran pointed out. While I attempted to interact with the children in broken Arabic, Imran spoke to the men outside the shelters, who then asked me to come in.

Many people, both men and women, came out of their shelters and gathered near a large bench. One middle-aged man, who introduced himself as Mohammad, pulled out a chair for me and asked me to be seated.[26]

'When was this settlement set-up?' I asked. Imran translated it to Mohammad in Arabic. After speaking to Mohammad briefly about the camp, Imran explained, 'This settlement was set-up in 2012. Most of the Syrian refugees here are from Aleppo and some are from Hama. It was in 2012 that the rebels took control of Aleppo's eastern half. Around that time, these people had to flee Aleppo.'

---

[25] Name changed.
[26] Name changed.

Imran added, 'Mohammad who is from Aleppo says it was very dangerous to continue living in Syria when the war began. Although he never witnessed any fighting, due to fear he decided to flee along with his family. He is not in touch with anyone in Aleppo.'

While Imran was translating what Aisha, Mohammad's wife, had just said about the war in Syria, many children began to crowd near the bench.[27] One of them curiously looked at me and smiled. As the chatter of the children grew louder, Imran said vociferously, 'Aisha says it was very dangerous to live in Aleppo, they had no choice but to leave their home.'

'Who has set-up this settlement?' I queried.

Imran briefly spoke to Mohammad and other people at the camp who were either standing or seated on the bench and said, 'They are saying there are no formal refugee camps in Lebanon in response to the inflow of Syrian refugees. There are only spontaneously set-up tented settlements in the country. Most of these settlements have been built by the refugees themselves.'

Just then, a woman named Hayat came forward and began to speak in Arabic.[28] She stretched her hand and pointed towards the shelters, and then looked at her robe, lightly pulling one of the sleeves. 'She says the condition at the settlement is miserable. The settlement lacks basic amenities. They do not even have proper clothes to wear,' Imran translated. Other people also shared the problems they face at the camp. Salman

---

[27] Name changed.
[28] Name changed.

233

who stood near Hayat agitatedly began to speak in Arabic.[29] 'Salman says there is no provision of clean drinking water,' Imran translated and added, 'According to Mohammad, each person receives merely $27 per month from the UN, which is not adequate. He says they have to manage everything including food within that amount.'

'Mohammad says he wants to go back to Syria, to his home, along with his family. They can return only when the war ceases or the situation in Syria improves. Until then they have to continue living here at this settlement,' Imran pointed out.

'Despite their ordeals back home when the war began, their arduous journey to Lebanon, and a miserable life at the settlement, what is it that keeps them going?' I asked.

Imran translated what I had just said. Most of the people stretching their arms upwards as if to offer prayers seemed to speak in a chorus—'Allah'.

A little girl who was standing near the bench whispered in Arabic. 'She says that she will show you the settlement,' Imran translated. As she pulled my hand, other girls also joined in. As we moved towards the field, I noticed many children cackling and running, innocuously teasing each other, seemingly oblivious of the suffering that war brings.

While some must have been extremely young, barely one or two years old, when they came to Lebanon along with their families, and others were born here, yet despite the wretched condition at the settlement as pointed out by their parents, most children radiated optimism.

---

[29] Name changed.

A Syrian Girl at a Refugee Settlement, Masna, near Lebanon-Syria Border

This is reminiscent of what many people in Lebanon who had lived through the prolonged war told me: 'Children never lose hope.'

When the little girls and I began to walk towards one of the shelters, an elderly man said something in Arabic. Soon the little girls began to giggle. A young man who had accompanied the elderly translated in broken English, 'Sing beautiful'.

While some of the girls began to sing enthusiastically, others hesitantly joined in. The chorus grew louder, soon fluctuating—ebbing and rising—as the girls kept joining in and leaving it. The faces of the little girls glowed with optimism as they sang the song that, Imran later mentioned, was emblematic of peace and hope.

COPING THROUGH CREATIVE EXPRESSION

Individuals and communities may use different creative mechanisms to deal with death, loss, everyday violence, stress and uncertainty in conflict zones. Arts, music, sports, poetry and even humour are some of the important means through which people may be able to cope even during their toughest times.

Amid the destruction, absurdity or senselessness of war, creativity may offer a meaning to one's life. Through creativity, an individual who has either lost loved ones or has witnessed a violent encounter that has negatively affected his/her perspective of life may be able to find resilience and hope to go on.

Creative expression through arts, music and poetry may also act as a catharsis relieving a person of the trauma or stress he/she may have accumulated over a period of time. In fact, those who are unable to verbalize their trauma for various reasons may find it easier to express themselves through drawings, sketches and even writing which would not just relieve their stress but also enable a counsellor or a psychologist to provide them appropriate therapy. Psychologists or therapists have frequently used this approach in different conflict zones with children who have been immensely affected by conflict or have experienced war-induced violence.

People living in conflict zones may also use humour to ease their stress, pain or suffering. Humour or laughter may lighten the mood and at least momentarily alleviate stress. For instance, during my visit to Kabul, Afghanistan, some people at the gurdwara (Sikh place of worship) likened the suicide bombings to firecrackers which seems to at least outwardly reduce the intensity of the act and the gravity of their situation.

Creative coping mechanisms may even prevent negative thoughts or divert an individual's mind from fears and anxieties or even the trauma he/she may be carrying. This does not imply mere escape from undesirable thoughts but an ability to channelize one's energy towards an optimistic thinking that may offer a sense of empowerment.

Sports too can be an extremely beneficial way of dealing with pain and stress. They have this motivational quality and may also engender a healthy competitive spirit among individuals and work well with those who have lost interest in life due to trauma or everyday stress. Sports such as football and cricket, besides reliving pain and kindling a competitive spirit, are also good for building a team spirit and encouraging social life, favourable for those who may have isolated themselves due to depression. Many reconciliation and DDR programmes in 'post-conflict' states have used sports as a therapy with conflict affected individuals and communities. In Sierra Leone, I met many players from Amputee Football, which was started in the country around two decades ago by the Single Leg Amputee Sports Association. The team had represented Sierra Leone in several countries. The individuals I met had lost their limbs due to war-induced violence. Some of them had been amputated by the RUF during the conflict, others lost their limbs because of landmines.

Despite the suffering and despair the brutal and prolonged war brought into their lives, they spoke of football as a way of coping with the trauma of war. Abdul Sesay gushingly pointed out, 'Being part of the amputee football team has given me a new life. It gave me hope to carry on.'[30]

---

[30] Name changed.

While Noorina and Mahira from Herat, Afghanistan chose arts or painting to express themselves and to cope with the stress of armed violence in their country, Abdul from Sierra Leone and as described in the following pages, Saeeda from Kandahar, Afghanistan and Farooq Wani from Srinagar, Kashmir, turned to sports to cope with conflict-induced stress and/or severe psychological trauma.

KABUL: 'FOOTBALL MOTIVATES ME TO GET AHEAD IN LIFE'[31]

A couple of years ago, I happened to meet Saeeda, a bright young girl, barely 18 years of age at an orphanage at Darulssalam Road in Kabul. I got introduced to her by the staff at the orphanage who had called her to translate our conversation from Dari to English and vice versa. After my conversation with the staff, Saeeda accompanied me till the main gate. On the way Saeeda briefly spoke about her siblings, her life at the orphanage, her love for sports and her determination to pursue higher education. I happen to remember only snippets of our conversation, however, what was unforgettable was her extraordinary resilience and determination to pursue her aspirations despite her challenging circumstances.

Saeeda, who is originally from Kandahar, had mentioned that she is the oldest sibling and it was her responsibility to take care of her siblings who were all at the orphanage at that time. Therefore, soon she will have to find a job. Donning a congenial smile, she said, 'When I came to Kabul few years back, I knew only Pashto. Now I can speak Dari and as well as English. I love learning new languages.'

---

31 Name changed.

When I asked her what she would like to pursue higher education in, she said, 'I would like to be in the medical profession.'

'What about your other interests?' I queried.

'I love sports, football in particular. I have also represented Afghanistan in other countries,' she explained as her eyes seemed to glisten with joy. 'I am extremely passionate about football and want to continue representing Afghanistan in different countries.'

What is it that helps you cope with the volatile and unstable security situation in your country?' I asked.

'Its football. It helps me release all the stress and also motivates me to get ahead in life,' Saeeda explained.

GAWKADAL, KASHMIR: 1990

'I used to be quite daring. I was a sportsman, an athlete and extremely passionate about football and swimming,' Farooq Ahmad Wani said with a hint of conviction in his voice. Pausing briefly, he continued as his face turned sombre, 'Now I get scared easily. I am not that courageous anymore. However, despite the brutal experience, I never lost hope in life. It has been three decades and the symptoms have almost faded.'

What was it that changed Farooq Ahmad Wani's life 30 years ago? In fact, not merely his life, but his personality and the thought process as well.

'It was the deadly Gawkadal Massacre of 1990 that changed my entire life,' explained Farooq Wani, the retired chief engineer at the J&K Public Works Department and the lone survivor of the Gawkadal Killings. The incident took place on the Gawkadal bridge in Srinagar, Kashmir where the CRPF opened fire on a group of pro-freedom protesters. Just two days before the incident, on 19 January the Government of India appointed Jagmohan as the Governor for a second time. Subsequently security forces carried out extensive house-to-house searches in the Srinagar city, in search of militants and illegal weapons. In response to the crackdown and alleged abuses by the forces, a large number of Kashmiris took to the streets. Consequently, Jagmohan put the city under curfew.

'It was 21 January, 10 in the morning. I was on my way to the DM's office ahead of Jehangir Chowk to fetch the curfew passes for myself and the staff. At that time, I was field engineer at the Water Supply Department, Kashmir,' Farooq explained and continued, 'At Jehangir Chowk, I was stopped by the CRPF and then pushed back. On retreating to Lal Chowk, I thought of taking a Shikara home but the CRPF around that area did not allow. Then I considered going to my uncle's place across Gawkadal in Mandir Bagh. To get there I had to cross the Gawkadal bridge.'

He paused for a while and carried on, 'As I tried to get to the bridge, a procession shouting Azaadi slogans reached Budshah chowk. I decided to merge in the procession, which was going towards the downtown area.'

Soon I heard a barrage of gunshots that were fired on the procession. It was a horrifying sight. I heard the cries of the ladies behind me. Because of the chaos, there was a possibility of stampede. To save myself from any forthcoming shots, I tried to jump in the lake.'[32]

'Did you jump?' I asked curiously.

Farooq said, 'No. I could not. A fellow pushed me and instead he jumped in the lake. I fell in the middle of the bridge. The firing continued, so I decided to lay prostrate on the bridge to escape any imminent shots. After a while, the firing stopped. There was silence. I wanted to run away.'

'Soon I saw a CRPF officer towards the edge of the bridge which led towards Mandir Bagh. He was holding SLR a (Self loading rifle). Fearing he may fire, I continued to lie down. When the officer began to walk on the bridge, after noticing I was alive, he pointed his gun towards me. I rose up and said I am an officer on duty', Farooq paused, his eyes seeming moist.

Soon he noted with a faint grin, 'The officer said, "*Sala Pakistan maangta hai* '(You want to be with Pakistan),' and shot multiple bullets at me. My body was burning. As I collapsed, that officer went a little ahead. After a while, another CRPF officer came and aimed his gun on my forehead. The officer who had fired bullets at me yelled from a distance, "*Goli zaya mat karo* (Don't waste the bullets)."'

---

[32] According to the J&K police, a huge crowd raising anti-India slogans was heading towards Lal Chowk and the security forces tried to stop the protesters near Gawkadal. The police record stated, instead of dispersing, the protesters started pelting stones at government buildings and security force personnel. Some activists argue that there has been no credible government investigation into the case. http://archive.indianexpress.com/oldStory/69437/

'I remember all the while I was weeping, thinking of my daughters and my wife. I thought it's all over,' his eyes turned pale as if he were re-experiencing the pain.

'I continued lying down for 5–10 minutes. Then CRPF troopers came to pull the dead bodies into the truck. I asked one of the troopers to carry me into the truck that was covered with tarpaulin. He agreed. After a while, the truck stopped at the Police Control Room. The police asked the troopers what is inside the truck. The troopers responded-dead bodies', Farooq explained with a wry expression and continued, 'When they removed the tarpaulin, my head was hanging. Someone called a doctor from the PCR who then shifted me to the SMHS hospital. I regained consciousness at 5 or 6 in the evening.'

'What were your first thoughts when you regained conscious-ness?' I asked.

'I could not believe it. It seemed like a different world. I thought about my family. There was also a feeling of humiliation. The CRPF officer fired at me even though I had mentioned that I am an officer on duty, What upsets me the most is that there has been no credible government investigation into the case.' Farooq explained.

'When did your family learn about this incident?'

'I noticed a young boy at the ward who seemed to have been weeping for a while looking at my condition. I gave him my phone number and asked him to inform my family that I was slightly unwell, therefore, decided to visit SMHS hospital,' Farooq remarked, 'But the boy informed my family about my actual condition, and my wife and others immediately rushed to the hospital. My wife, in particular, was horrified to see me in that condition,' he said ruefully as if he were reliving those moments.

'How long were you at the hospital?'

'I was at the SMHS for three days. Thereafter, I was shifted to the bone and joints hospital at Barzalla where I stayed for 20 days,' he explained.

'Prior to the Gawkadal Massacre, did you experience any personal violent encounter?' I probed.

He immediately responded, 'I did not really have any such experience,' his face turned reflective as he continued after a few minutes, 'Once in 1989, around Jehangir Chowk, I happened to get caught in the cross-firing between the CRPF and the militants. But I managed to get out of it. I remember once there was a colleague of mine who, due to the cross-firing between the CRPF and the militants, lost his one eye. But I had not experienced anything like that.'

'How did you react when you got caught in the cross-firing in 1989?' I queried.

'Of course at that time, I was a little scared on the spot. My heart sank. However, later I had no recurring thoughts,' he explained.

'But the Gawkadal incident just changed my life. I was no longer the person I used be-daring, sociable or outgoing. I am scared now. If someone from the army or the forces stops me, I get jittery. Besides, to some extent, I became reluctant to socialize as well. After the incident, I began to get recurring thoughts before going to sleep, even nightmares. During daytime, I would mostly be engrossed in work.'

'What kind of thoughts would you mostly get?' I asked hesitantly.

'Voices of people crying, gunshots, troopers shouting, the officer's voice who shot at me,' he explained.

'How long did it go on? I mean for how long did you get those recurring thoughts?' I asked.

'It happened for around two to three years. After the incident, I found certain psychological as well as biological changes perhaps due to blood transfusion,' he said.

'I would get frequent headaches and lose my temper quickly. I began to get scared easily, and would would tremble, especially after seeing security forces. Therefore, around three months after the incident, I decided to visit a psychologist who advised that I also consult a neurologist. I was put on medication which continued for around 12 years.'

'Although the nightmares ceased and the recurrent thoughts faded, I have not recovered fully. The scar is still there in my soul.', Farooq explained.

'Despite the trauma that you have been carrying, what is it that kept you going?' I asked.

Farooq's eyes appeared buoyant and his face exuded relative calmness as he said, 'All through, my daughters and wife have been extremely supportive. I felt I should live for them. Playing golf also helped immensely. Two years after the incident, I began to play. I was a beginner then but slowly developed a passion for it.' He said with a smile, 'The sport itself and spending three to four hours at the golf course, interacting with the people there took my mind off the recurrent thoughts of the incident. That was the basic reason why I continued playing golf. Besides I was extremely dedicated to my job which helped me in diverting my mind.'

'It has been three decades since the Gawkadal incident, from that day until now, how do you see yourself in terms of your mental health?' I queried.

'While my mental and physical health considerably improved over a period of time, yet I feel, psychologically and neurologically I am not that fit any more,' Farooq explained, 'That day (Gawkadal incident) was perhaps the beginning or the early stages of turmoil. Today the conflict persists. We continue to live in fear psychosis. Sometimes I feel that I may get caught in an encounter again.'

Farooq's eyes sparkled with optimism as he continued, 'Despite everything I never lost hope. The biggest source of strength for me has been my family—my wife and three daughters.'

The Gawkadal killings took place just two days after 19 January 1990, which is observed by Kashmiri Pandits as the "exodus day" a large number of whom fled the Kashmir Valley due to an atmosphere of fear. It has been reported that they were being targeted by the Jammu and Kashmir Liberation Front and other Islamic insurgent groups. However, there are activists and writers who say that both Muslims and Pandits who were thought to be close to the ruling establishment or the armed forces were being targeted. After 19th January (exodus day), massive search and crackdown operations were carried out in search of the insurgents. On 21st January, reportedly in response to these searches and crackdown, a large number of Kashmiris took to the streets and many were killed by the CRPF in what is known as the Gawkadal Massacre.

There are different narratives on why Pandits left the Valley. From the perspective of Kashmiri Pandits, the fact that the targets were exclusively Hindu implied that the threat was essentially a communal one. On the other hand, according to several separatist leaders it was the Indian state, working through Jagmohan, the governor of Jammu and Kashmir at the time, engineered the exodus of the Pandits so that the government could deal with the Muslim militants with a free hand. According to Mridu Rai, the author of *Hindu Rulers, Muslim Subjects: Islam, Rights and the History of Kashmir*, since this issue is shrouded in a great deal of controversy, 'it is safe to say that there were probably elements of both circumstances at work in explaining the departure of the Pandits from the valley'. (https://www.aljazeera.com/indepth/spotlight/kashmir theforgottenconflict/2011/07/2011724204546645823.html)

In 1992, Asia Watch and Physicians for Human Rights (PHR) reported, in early 1990, militant outfits "threatened, assaulted and murdered Hindus residing in the Kashmir valley—driving many to flee to refugee camps in Jammu and Delhi." They noted, militant outfits have also kidnapped and killed Muslim civilians whom they suspected of being informers or of not supporting their political views. (https://www. hrw.org/sites/default/files/reports/INDIA935.PDF)

While I had spoken to some Kashmiri Pandits who did not leave the Valley, it was significant to talk to those who fled the Valley before the Gawkadal Massacre or soon after. Those who continued to stay told me that a large number of Pandits fled due to fear, however, they remained in the Valley due to various reasons including support by their Muslim neighbours, unwillingness to leave their homeland or vulnerable economic situation. Through contacts of some family friends and 'non-migrant' Pandits, I tried to speak to those who left the Valley in 1990. Most were reluctant to talk for two reasons: First, they did not want to relive their painful memories; second, they felt it was futile to repeatedly speak about their experiences since they saw no hope in being able to return to their homeland. Finally, I managed to have brief conversation with few Pandits who were compelled to flee.

One of them was Kuldeep Bhatt, originally from Srinagar. In early 1990, when he was compelled to leave the Valley, he was working in the private sector. 'It was 19th January 1990. Around 10:30 in the night, I still remember that we were watching television. Suddenly we heard slogans—Hum kya chahte hain Azadi. Azadi ka matlab kya-la illahi Allah, Pakistan se rishta kya- la illahi Allah, Kafiron aur Zaalimon-Kashmir hamara chhor do. Yahan par kya chalega-Nizam-e-Mustafa. We were extremely frightened and felt intimidated'.

'At that time, one of my brothers was already working in West Bengal and another had gone to Delhi for a meeting and finally got a job transfer from Kashmir to Bihar. That dreadful night of 19th January, I was with my parents when a large number of protesters poured on to the streets', he explained. 'On 5th March, I decided to leave with a small suitcase for Jammu by air. It was an open ticket. Fortunately, I got a seat. When I reached Jammu, I stayed with my mother's sister for a month till my company transferred me to Pathankot, Jammu'.

"What about your parents?" I probed. "My father was reluctant to leave, but somehow I got my parents here with me to Pathankot on 2nd May the same year. We finally sold our house in 2005'. 'My father was very healthy in Srinagar. After coming to Jammu, his health deteriorated. He was constantly battling with anxiety and high blood pressure and a couple of years ago he passed away, longing for our home in the Valley'.

After a brief silence, Bhatt added, 'After leaving Kashmir in 1990, I have visited it only once in 2011 along with my wife and children." "Would you want to return to the Valley?' I asked. 'Now Kashmir is alien to us, but somewhere deep inside I still have a desire and an ounce of hope to return home', he said poignantly.

In conflict zones, people may be exposed to violence or experience looming threat of armed attacks or suicide bombings for sustained period, some like Abdul Sesay from Sierra Leone and Farooq Ahmad Wani from Kashmir may have a direct or personal encounter with violence. Those who are exposed to violence are perhaps more likely to get affected psychologically due to the trauma they may be carrying. As Farooq Wani movingly said, 'Although my nightmares ceased and the recurrent thoughts faded, I have not recovered fully. The scar is still there in my soul.' Even among the individuals who suffer direct impact of violence, some may be more prone to psychological stress than the others. This is contingent on a number of factors such as the intensity of violence, the time period of violence, family or social support, the individual's environment as well as his/her personality or disposition.

During conflict, while people may be rendered homeless due to bombardment or destruction of their homes, many even leave their homes, cities or countries in search of 'safer' locations. While those who migrate may be able to find a secure life abroad, for many who continue living amid conflict need to find ways of coping with everyday threat of violence. Even those who migrate to 'safe' locations for various reasons, particularly those who have suffered a direct impact of violence may find it difficult to mentally and emotionally distance themselves from the past or the violent experience. Scars of the past, etched deep in an individual's mind may profoundly affect his/her well-being. Consequently, it becomes imperative for the person to find ways and means to cope with the trauma.

While different coping mechanisms may engender hope among an individual, which may motivate her/him to find meaning in life and achieve the desired goals. The construct of hope has long been debated whether it aids in inspiring an individual to rise up during harsh times or whether it imperils life leading the individual towards illusions. Nonetheless, hope has an inherent motivational quality that enhances an individual's ability to cope with stress. Therefore, coping and hope work reciprocally. Hope and coping are both instrumental in healing, recovery and even building resilience.

While some may adopt ingenious and creative coping mechanisms such as art, poetry, music, humour and sports, others may resort to simple ways such as practicing normalcy, watching television, listening to music, using the Internet, spending time with family and friends to deal with their stress. Family and community support can be huge enablers for coping among individuals in distress. Family support or a strong bond with friend(s) may offer a meaning to one's life and can be a great source of strength, comfort, and security. As Zonun and some other Rohingya refugees I met at Kutupalong camp in Cox's Bazar pointed out that being with friends and family helps them in dealing with stress and unpleasant experiences of the past.

Similarly for Aisha, a student, from the downtown area in Srinagar, Kashmir, coping meant spending time with family or friends. When I met her at Makhdoom Sahib few months after the abrogation of Article 370, she dejectedly said, 'Due to strict restrictions after the revocation of Kashmir's autonomy, we had no choice but to stay at home. It was very stressful and frustrating. To relieve my stress, I would basically spend a lot of time with my family since I could not even meet my friends outside.'

'Before the Internet was snapped, I would watch movies online,' she added.

Mudasir, a student and Aisha's cousin said, 'For me coping meant using the Internet. I would chat with my friends.[33] Unfortunately, the Indian government snapped the Internet after the abrogation which was extremely frustrating.' 'For us (Kashmiri youth), the Internet is more important than even food,' he humorously added.

Praying is another significant coping mechanism that individuals may adopt to cope with life strains. Many people across different conflict zones told me that despite their conflict-induced trauma or frequent threat of violence, they are able to cope due to their faith in God. For Humaira from Khwaja Bazar and the elderly lady at the Makhdoom Sahib Shrine, Kashmir, coping with the stress of living amid turmoil meant offering prayers to Allah. Similarly, for Sabrina, a Communications Manager from Beirut, who grew up during the war in Lebanon coping meant praying. As she ardently remarked, 'I am a believer so my only hope is god. I pray a lot. As a child, I learnt to pray because of war. I used to pray every day.'

Individuals may also use multiple coping mechanisms to deal with their stress or trauma. For instance, in the case of Farooq Wani, from Srinagar, Kashmir, besides a strong family support, playing golf and spending time with friends helped in dealing with his deep trauma.

While feelings of fear, anxiety, and insecurity are certainly common in conflict zones, the ubiquity of violence and death and the realization of life's transiency may prompt some to celebrate life till it lasts. Perhaps that is their way of coping

---

[33] Name changed.

with the uncertainty of life and constant threat of violence. During my interaction with some locals in Afghanistan, one of them remarked, 'People in conflict zones are more alive since the threat of death, attacks or bombings is quite imminent,' while the other quipped 'Suicide bombings are everyday affair in Afghanistan but we wouldn't stop living.' While spending time in conflict zones, I have also observed that same individuals who have expressed feelings of fear, anxiety and insecurity to me, on other occasions, radiated hope and a zest for life, despite the continuity of the conflict.

As the physical body may get used to the pain that persists for a prolonged period, individuals living amid conflict or turmoil may adapt to the sights and sounds of militarized violence, which slowly become normalized. They often improvise or adopt different coping mechanisms, which may help them in adapting to challenging circumstances. While anxieties or fears and deep scars of the past in particular, may be difficult to expunge, yet coping and hope may expand an individual's mind by stimulating feelings of joy and optimism.

Finding hope amid turmoil may well be akin to spotting a fresh leaf on a barren tree or sudden rain in blazing sun. Hope is a compelling feeling that can fill you up with buoyancy and fortitude to rise up even during times of deepest despair.

Individuals in conflict or war zones seem to carry a 'piece' of war—large or small—which may even outlive the hostilities. They may also carry 'pieces' of war depending on the varying intensity of the conflict and direct or indirect experiences of conflict-induced violence. Other than the extreme cases, they mostly do not appear to carry war in its entirety; hence, there remains a space for survival, resilience, coping and even hope.

ABOUT THE AUTHOR

Meha Dixit has a PhD in international politics from Jawaharlal Nehru University. Her thesis is titled *Human Security and Post-conflict Reintegration of Child Soldiers: Disarmament Demobilisation Reintegration (DDR) Programmes in Mozambique and Sierra Leone.*

She has conducted field research in various conflict and 'post-conflict' zones such as Afghanistan including Afghanistan–Pakistan border, Lebanon, Lebanon–Syria border, Sierra Leone, India–Pakistan border, Kashmir, Maoist insurgency regions in India (Odisha, Chhattisgarh, Jharkhand and Andhra Pradesh–Odisha border) and northeastern states in India (Manipur and Assam) and on the Rohingya issue in Cox's Bazar, Bangladesh, and Bangladesh–Myanmar border.

She has worked with Amnesty International and Save the Children. She has also taught at Kashmir University.

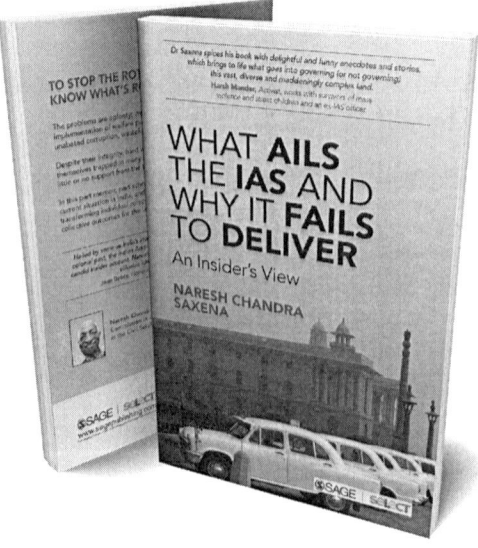